Bolton

Soldiers and Sailors in the American Revolution

Esther K. Whitcomb & Dorothy O. Mayo

Bolton Meeting House and the Liberty Pole

HERITAGE BOOKS, INC.
1985

Published By
HERITAGE BOOKS, INC.
3602 Maureen Lane, Bowie, MD 20715
(301)-464-1159

ISBN 0-917890-56-6

Home of General John Whitcomb in Bolton.
Built by his father ca 1710, and owned
by General Whitcomb, his sons and
grandsons until about 1880. It burned
in 1930.

TO OUR READERS

"I have gon, and rid, and wrote, and sought, and searched with my own and friends' Eyes, to make what Discoveries I could therein.---I stand ready with a <u>pencil</u> in one hand and a <u>Spunge</u> in the other, to add, alter, insert, expunge, enlarge, and dilete, according to better information. And if these my pains shall be found worthy to passe a <u>Second Impression</u>, my faults I will confess with <u>shame</u>, and amend with <u>Thankfulnesse</u>, to such as will contribute clearer Intelligence unto me."

from Fuller's <u>Worthies</u> <u>of</u> <u>England</u>, 1662

The authors heartily subscribe to the sentiments above. Kindly send corrections and further information to:

    Esther K. Whitcom, 48 Hudson Road, Bolton, MA 01740 or,
    Dorothy O. Mayo, 442 Great Road, Bolton, MA 01740

"In writing history, two things are impossible --- absolute accuracy and completeness."

Blynn E. Davis, Historian of Bridgeton, Maine

FOREWORD

This book is the result of a request to the authors from the Daughters of the American Revolution to copy the inscriptions on the gravestones of all the Revolutionary soldiers of Bolton, Massachusetts, including the present town of Berlin which was the South Parish of Bolton until 1784. Looking at this list we realized that only a small percentage of the Bolton men in the war were buried in our cemeteries. Curiosity led us to wonder what had happened to the others.

After years of searching we find that on the waves of the Great Migration our soldiers were scattered from Maine to Michigan and from Ohio to Kentucky. We have found many in far-away places, but some are still "lost."

We have not attempted to detail each man's service as this may usually be found in the seventeen volumes of Massachusetts Soldiers and Sailors in the American Revolution. Henry Stedman Nourse's copious and accurate book, Military Annals of Lancaster, Massachusetts, has constantly been called on for the service of our men. However, the most valuable asset that we possess we have called "Bolton Revolutionary Records" (BRR). These are scraps of paper which contain receipts for bounties paid by the Town of Bolton; lists of Bolton soldiers and where and by what officer they were mustered; and, most interesting of all, the action taken in regard to those few who preferred not to go into the service of their country. These records are in the possession of the Town of Berlin Archives. They were apparently among the papers saved from the Berlin Town Dump in the early 1930's by Clara L. S. Eager. They were returned to the Town Archives by her son and daughter-in-law, Vincent and Doris Eager.

At the time of the Centennial in 1876 Rev. Richard Edes, for many years Town Clerk of Bolton, inserted in any space he could find in the Town Record Books, copies of Captain David Nurse's Records (DNR), to which Rev. Edes apparently had access at that time, although they have since disappeared.

The BRRs and DNRs are extremely valuable primary sources which have not been used in previous publications. Names have been found which do not appear elsewhere and we thus gained several, mostly older men, who enlisted in Captain Nurse's Company in the darkest moments of the war.

Due to the fact that the biographical skeches have been arranged in alphabetical order, a complete name index did not seem necessary. However, a cross-index has been compiled which covers all names which do not appear in the correct alphabetical order, including the maiden names of mothers, wives, etc. Names are spelled as found, although often incorrect by modern usage. Dates are sometimes obviously incorrect, as in a case where two children of a soldier were born in a six-month period. This is how they were found and any descendant who wishes may unravel the mystery. We do not claim this book to be a finished work, but rather a reference for researchers.

Our thanks go to many people who have given us information, suggestions or corrections. It is impossible to name each one, but we want to mention some who deserve the particular thanks of the authors: Elvira L. Scorgie of Harvard; Barry Eager of Berlin; Noel Hanson of Bolton; Frances Pratt Tapley of Sterling, now deceased; Joann H. Nichols of Brattleboro, VT, President of the Genealogical Society of VT; Lydia Wilson Ross of Crown Point, NY; Grace Pittman of Bloomington, IL; Betty Robinson of Bradford, PA; Leon and Eleanor Stiles of Penn Yan, NY; Eliot Allison of Dublin, NH; David Holman of Clinton, MA; the Librarian and Staff of Lancaster, MA Public Library; Audrey Gardner of Southborough, MA who has made sketches for the book; and Maudean Neill of Montpelier, VT.

There was one whom it is a great pleasure to mention: Blynn E. Davis, historian of Bridgeton, ME, now deceased, who gave us constant encouragement, always expressing his confidence in the value of our project.

SOURCE KEYS AND ABBREVIATIONS

The following references have been cited so extensively that they have been given special short titles or keys. Numerous other sources have been cited in the text. The published vital records (VR) of the various Massachusetts towns, other than those listed below, being a prime example. Geographic locations should be assumed to be in Massachusetts unless specified otherwise.

Published Sources and Contemporary Records

S&S	Massachusetts Soldiers and Sailors of the Revolution
MilAnn	Lancaster Military Annals, Henry S. Nourse, 1889
DARPI	Daughters of the American Revolution Patriot Index
BRR	Revolutionary Records of the Town of Bolton
DNR	Capt. David Nurse's Records

Published Vital Records and Local Histories

BHist	Bolton History, 1938
BVR	Bolton Vital Records
BerlHist	Berlin History, Rev. W. A. Houghton, 1895
BerlVR	Berlin Vital Records
HHist	History of Harvard, Massachusetts, H. S. Nourse, 1894
HVR	Harvard Vital Records
LHist	History of Lancaster, Massachusetts, Rev. Abijah Marvin, 1879
LVR	Lancaster B. M. & D.
MHist	History of Marlborough, Massachusetts, Hon. Charles Hudson, 1862
MVR	Marlborough Vital Records
SVR	Stow Vital Records

Gravestone Records

GS1	Gravestone, Old Soth Burial Ground, Bolton
GS2	Gravestone, Pan Burial Ground, Bolton
GS3	Gravestone, West Burial Ground, Bolton
GSB	Gravestone, Old Burial Ground, Berlin Center

Abbreviations

b	born
bpt	baptized
d	died
d/o	daughter of
int	intentions of marriage
Jr	junior--meaning "younger," not necessarily "son of"
m	married
s/o	son of
w	wife
wid	widow

ALLEN, Amos

SERVICE: S&S Vol 1 p 136; BRR May 1776 8 mos bounty Ł100; BRR Cont Army 8 mos 1778 Ł25.
BORN: 1 Aug 1753 Lancaster s/o Ebenezer Jr & Tabitha.
MARRIED: 12 Jul 1781 Rebeckah Thurston (1762-1827) both of Lancaster.
DIED: 1851 Fort Ann NY.
CHILDREN (b Lancaster):
    Lewis - bpt 11 Aug 1782
    Amos - bpt 2 May 1784 d 1854 m Mary Fletcher
    Thomas - b 7 Jun 1787 d 1793
NOTE: Transferred from Lancaster Church to Church at Luzerne NY 6 Oct 1816.
REF: History of Clinton, Andrew E Ford 1896; LVR; DARPI; DAR Lineage Book 105 p 89.

AMSDEN, Joseph

SERVICE: S&S Vol 1 p 229; BHistory, Lex Alarm; BRR 5 mos Dorchester Jul 1776.
BORN: 20 Apr 1749 Marlborough s/o Uriah & Abigail (Lull).
MARRIED: 1) 2 Apr 1771 Bolton, Mary Edwards (d c1781 Henniker NH); 2) Anna Steele (d 1830 ae 77 Lebanon NH).
DIED: 30 Aug 1826 ae 77 Lebanon NH.
CHILDREN (by Mary):
    Joseph - b 9 Sep 1772 Bolton d Lebanon NH
    Joel - b 22 May 1778 Henniker NH m Sally Hustin
    Mary - b 20 Aug 1780 Henniker NH d Lebanon
    Abigail - b 24 Jul 1781 m Dr James Dill
        (by Anna):
    Downing - d unm Norwich VT
    Manly - m Sally (Hustin) Amsden
    Uriah - b Jun 1788 d Chelsea MA
    Amon - b 16 Sep 1792 m Abigail Dutton
    Anna - m John Woodbury
REF: BVR; MVR; Isaac Amdsen and Some of His Descendants, Murry Brown.

ATHERTON, Adjt Eliakim

SERVICE: S&S Vol 1 p 325; MilAnn Adjt of Lanc Militia; MilAnn Lex Alarm; Mil Ann Dep Commissary of Province 1775.
BORN: 15 Dec 1743 Harvard s/o John & Phebe (Wright).
MARRIED: 13 May 1767 Elizabeth Sawyer (m2 Capt Thaddeus Pollard).
DIED: 24 Dec 1786 in 44th yr Bolton GS1.
CHILDREN (b Bolton):
    Elizabeth - b 6 Mar 1768 m Silas Holman
    Phebe - b 8 Aug 1770 d young
    Achsah - b 21 Jul 1773 d young

ATHERTON, Adjt Eliakim (Cont)

    Phebe - 10 Nov 1775 m Amory Pollard 1795
    Achsah - b 15 Aug 1778 m Thaddeus Pollard Jr 1797
    Eliakim - bpt 1 Apr 1787 "Son of Widow Elizabeth"
REF: HVR; BVR.

ATHERTON, Jonathan

SERVICE: S&S Vol 1 p 327; MilAnn Lex Alarm; MilAnn Exped to Quebec.
BORN: 14 Jun 1729 Lancaster s/o Capt Benjamin & Eunice (Priest).
MARRIED: 1) c1750 Ruth _____; 2) 16 Jun 1784 Harvard, Wid Mary Welch (d 1814).
DIED: 1793 Bolton (Probate Records).
CHILDREN:
    Sarah - b 1751 m John Whitney 1771
    Jonathan - b 19 Oct 1752 m Phebe Nurse d/o Sam'l
    Ruth - b 1754 m1 Jacob Davis 2 Thomas Keys
    James - b 1756 m Phebe Nurse
    Abigail - b 1758 twin d young
    Bethia - b 1758 twin d young
    Mathew - b 1 Oct 1760
    Molly - b 1762 m Benj Sampson, Waterford ME
    Benjamin - b 1770 m Lucretia Hudson
REF: LVR; BVR; HVR; Worc Co Probate Records; Atherton Genealogy, F L Weis.

ATHERTON, Mathew

SERVICE: S&S Vol 1 p 328; BRR Service in Boston 1778 Ł18-6-8; BRR Guard troops at Rutland 1778; BRR Convent troops 6 mos 1778 Ł8-4-8; BRR Jul 1778 6 mos Ł18-6-7; BHist 6 mos men 1780; BHist West Point Exped 1781.
BORN: 1 Oct 1760 Bolton s/o Jonathan & Ruth _____.
MARRIED: 1) Elizabeth Adams; 2) Jemima Pelton.
DIED: 3 Feb 1846 Royalton VT GS N Royalton Cemetery.
CHILDREN:
    William - b 7 Dec 1789
    James - b 11 Jan 1791
    Hannah - b 9 Oct 1793
    Betsy - b 23 Apr 1796
    Pamelia - b 16 Jun 1798
    Sally - b 23 Jan 1801
    Ruth - b 25 May 1803
    Phebe - b 3 Sep 1806
    Mary - b 30 Jun 1808
    Patience - b 19 Mar 1810
    Prudence - b 25 Jun 1812
    Abigail - b 21 Oct 1814
NOTE: Descriptive List 1780 - Mathew Atherton 19 years 5'6".

ATHERTON, Mathew (Cont)

REF: BVR; Royalton VT History; DARPI; Pension Records 1832.

ATHERTON, Oliver

SERVICE: S&S Vol 1 p 329; MilAnn Bennington 1777; DARPI Patriotic Serv.
BORN: 1 Aug 1721 Lancaster s/o Ens Joseph & Mary.
MARRIED: 24 Nov 1748 Harvard, Rachel Goodfrey (d 18 Aug 1813).
DIED: 22 May 1813 ae 92 Harvard.
CHILDREN (b Harvard):
  Joseph – b 5 Aug 1750
  Mary – b 28 Jan 1753
  Oliver – b 24 Aug 1755 ml Mary Willard
      m2 Mary Phinney m3 Julia Atherton
  Rachel – b 12 Apr 1761
  Esther – b 13 Jan 1764
  Philemon – 15 Jun 1771
REF: HVR; Atherton Genealogy, F L Weis; DARPI.

ATHERTON, Thomas

SERVICE: S&S Vol 1 p 330; BHist Lex Alarm; Drummer in Capt Hastings Co; BRR to Canada 1776 bounty Ł18.
BORN: 10 Apr 1753 Harvard s/o John & Phebe (Wright).
MARRIED: 15 Dec 1774 Harvard, Betty Whitney of Harvard (b 1756 d/o Moses & Betty).
DIED: was in Wendell 1790 census.
CHILDREN: unk.
REF: HVR; Atherton Genealogy, F L Weis.

BABCOCK, William, also Badcock

Service: S&S Vol 1 p 396 & 432; BRR 5 mos Capt Nurse's Co 1775 Ł3.
BORN: 1741 Northborough s/o William.
MARRIED: 1) Sibbel Green of Northborough (d 1790); 2) 4 May 1793 Hepsibah (Bush) Fife (d 1826).
DIED: 31 Dec 1820 ae 79 Berlin GBS.
CHILDREN:
  Azuba – b 15 Oct 1764 Northborough m Thos Brigham
  Abraham – b 9 Jun 1770 Mason, NH
  Ephriam – b 22 Mar 1772 Northborough
  Wheeler – b 4 Apr 1774 Bolton d 1778
  Sibbel – b 13 Sep 1776 Bolton m John Howe
  William – b 29 Apr 1780 Bolton m Hannah Moores
  Peter – b 9 Sep 1782 Bolton m Betsy Wilder
  Lucy – b 29 Jun 1785 Bolton m Ephraim Fairbank
REF: Northborough VR; BVR; Berlin

BABCOCK, William (Cont)

History, Rev W A Houghton 1895; Babcock Genealogy, Stephen Babcock 1903.

BAILEY, Amherst

SERVICE: S&S Vol 1 p 447; BRR Boston 1776 3 mos; BRR Service Boston 1778; BRR Cont Army 1779 3 mos bounty Ł2-9-3; BRR 2 mos at Claverack Ł32 per mo.
BORN: 27 Jan 1761 Bolton s/o Col Silas & Lucy (Brigham).
MARRIED: 28 Mar 1785 Lydia Barnes (d 1844 d/o Fortunatus).
DIED: 9 Nov 1830 ae 70 GSB
CHILDREN (b Berlin):
  Lucy – b 18 Feb 1787 m Peter Larkin
  William – b 15 Aug 1789 unm
  Persis – b 1793 m Leonard Carter
  Silas – b 28 Feb 1796 d 1797
  Sarah – b 23 Dec 1799
  Calvin – b 1801 unm
  Hannah – 7 Jan 1804 m Simeon Bowman
  Zilpah – b 6 Nov 1806 m Arad Newton
  Lucinda – b 25 Aug 1810 m Geo Stratton
REF: BVR; Berlin History, Rev W A Houghton 1895.

BAILEY, Barnabas

SERVICE: Not in S&S; BRR money raised 3 yrs Capt Nurse's Co Ł5; BRR 5 mos men L 3-1-4.
BORN: 1 May 1715 Marlborough s/o Benj & Deborah (Howe).
MARRIED: 21 Jul 1748 Marlborough, Elizabeth Stephens (d/o Samuel of Marlborough).
DIED: 23 May 1790 Berlin GSB.
CHILDREN (b Bolton):
  Elizabeth – b 2 Apr 1749 m Jacob Moore
  Mary – b 13 Feb 1751 m ___ Richardson
  Phebe – b 13 Jun 1754 m Peter Richardson
  Asenath – b 12 Aug 1760 m Samuel Brigham
REF: MVR; BVR; Berl VR; Berlin History, Rev W A Houghton 1895.

BAILEY, Benjamin, Jr, also Baily, Baley

SERVICE: S&S Vol 1 p 448, 463 & 525; BHist Lex Alarm; BHist 13th Reg't; BRR to York 1776 bounty Ł2-12-6; BRR money raised in Capt Nurse's Co Ł6.
BORN: 29 Aug 1747 Bolton s/o Benjamin & Sibella (How).
MARRIED: unm.
DIED: 6 Feb 1802 ae 56 Berlin no stone.
REF: Berlin History, Rev W A Houghton 1895; BVR.

BAILEY, Calvin, also Bayley

SERVICE: S & S Vol 1 p 448 & 828; BRR Guard at Rutland 6 mos; BRR Guard Conv Troops Jun 1778 6 mos ₤8-4-8.
BORN: 2 Jan 1763 Bolton s/o Col Silas & Lucy (Brigham).
MARRIED: unk.
DIED: No record found; not mentioned in father's will 1793 Worc Co Probate #A2564.
REF: BVR; Berlin History, Rev W A Houghton 1895; Worc Co Probate Records.

BAILEY, Ebenezer, also Baily, Baley & Bayley

SERVICE: S&S Vol 1 p 449, 463, 526, 829; BRR Fishkill 9 mos 1778.
BORN: 1 Jul 1749 Bolton s/o Benjamin & Isabella (Sibella) (Howe).
MARRIED: unm.
DIED: will proved 1790 Worc Co.
NOTE: Mass Archives 1778 Descriptive List - "In Col. Whitney's Reg't, Cap't Houghton's and Cap't Nurse's Co., Ebenezer Bailey, about 27, 6 feet high, sandy complexion, light hair."
REF: BVR; Berlin History, Rev W A Houghton 1895; Worc Co Probate Records.

BAILEY, Col Silas, Sr, also Baley

SERVICE: S&S Vol 1 p 460 & 531; BHist Lex Alarm; BRR Cont Service 1/4 turn pd by James Townsend; BRR to York 5 mos 1778; BRR 6 mos 1778 to Guard Conv Troops at ₤6-6-8 per mo.
BORN: 1723 Lancaster s/o Benjamin & Elizabeth (Howe).
MARRIED: 1) 9 May 1749 Lucy Brigham (d 1778); 2) 13 May 1779 Mrs Elizabeth Rice Brigham (d 1783 ae 56); 3) 26 Aug 1790 Catherine Howe (d 1811).
DIED: 30 Oct 1793 Berlin ae 71 GSB.
CHILDREN (b Bolton):
    Timothy - b 9 Feb 1749-50 killed in war
    Bethia - b 4 Oct 1752
    Silas - b 22 Jul 1756
    Lucy - b 6 Jan 1759 m Jabez Fairbank
    Amhas - b 27 Jan 1761
    Calvin - 2 Jan 1763 d before 1793
NOTE: BRR "Silas Bailey, Major, to David Nurse, Cap't: Order rec'd from Col. Whitney to order you to cause 1 half the Train Band with Alarm List to march to Bennington, immediately with 8 days provision, arms and ammunition as the law directs." Bolton 21 Aug 1777.
REF: LVR; BVR; BerlVR; Berlin History, Rev W A Houghton 1895; Worc Co Probate Records #A2564.

BAILEY, Lt Silas Jr

SERVICE: S&S Vol 1 p 461; BHist Lex Alarm; BRR Resolve 1776 5 mos NY ₤10-5; BRR 3 mos York 1776; BRR 1 yr to York; BRR Bennington Alarm 1777; BRR Guard Stores Jul 1777; BRR Cont Army 1780.
BORN: 22 Jul 1756 Bolton s/o Col Silas & Lucy (Brigham).
MARRIED: 21 May 1779 Levina Bartlett of Northborough (d 1840).
DIED: 3 Oct 1840 Berlin no stone.

CHILDREN (b Berlin also recorded Northborough):
    Timothy - b 2 Aug 1780
    Silas - b 8 Jun1782
    Holloway - b 18 May 1784
    Calvin - b 1786
    Betsy - b 1789 d 1789
    Levina - b 18 Jul 1790 m Martin Houghton
    Lewis - b 2 Jan 1792
NOTES: 5 mos to York 1776 pd by - Joshua Johnson Jr ₤2-12-6; James Townsend ₤2-10; William Pollard ₤2-10; Timothy Bailey ₤2-12-6.
REF: BVR; BerlVR; Berlin History, Rev W A Houghton 1895; Northborough VR; DARPI.

BAILEY, Stephen

SERVICE: S&S Vol 1 p 461; BHist Lex Alarm; BRR 10 mos to York 1776 ₤3-12; BRR 3 mos to Northward; BRR Bennington Sep 1777; BRR Northern Army.
BORN: 29 Sep 1753 Bolton s/o Benj & Sibbil (How).
MARRIED: 8 Feb 1779 Shrewsbury, Sally Crosby d/o Dr Samuel.
DIED: 12 Feb 1815 ae 61 (Dea) GSB.
CHILDREN (b Berlin):
    Clarissa - b 10 Mar 1779
    Algernon - b May 1782 d 1808
    Winthrop - b 7 May 1784
    Eusebia - b 11 Jun 1787 m Jonas Sawyer
    Sally - b 9 Feb 1789 d 1789
    Emma - b 27 Oct 1790 m Asa Sawyer
    Horace - b 23 Apr 1793 m Eliz Whitney
    Myra - b 15 Nov 1795 m John Tyler
    Stephen - b 19 Apr 1798
REF: BVR; Berlin History, Rev W A Houghton 1895; DARPI.

BAILEY, Lt Timothy Also Baly

SERVICE: S&S Vol 1 p 461 & 557; BHist Lex Alarm; BRR 5 mos Capt D Nurse 1775 ₤2-12-6; BRR Resolve 1776 2 mos; BRR Northern Army 30 ds 1777; BRR Northern Army Oct 1777; BRR Cont Army 1780 3 mos ₤19; BRR reinforce Cont Army RI 3 mos Jun 1780; BRR Lt in RI 1781.
BORN: 7 Feb 1749 Bolton s/o Col Silas &

Monument in the Old Burying Ground, Berlin Center

"Commemorative of the name and patriotism of Lt. Timothy Bailey who alone of the soldiers of Berlin died in gaining our Independence, 1777. He was buried in R.I. - A Centennial Memorial by Artemas Barnes, 1876"

BAILEY, Lt Timothy (Cont)

Lucy (Brigham).
MARRIED: 11 Mar 1773 Northborough, Martha Barnard (rec'd pension).
DIED: killed or died in service 1777 GSB see note.
CHILDREN (b Bolton):
  Bethia - b 1775
  Jedidiah - b 1777
  Levi - 1778
NOTE: The death date on the monument in Berlin Old Burial Ground seems to be in error. Lt Bailey was in the Continental Army in 1780, reinforced Cont Army in RI Jun 1780, and was noted as a Lt in RI in 1781. The monument should probably read 1781.
REF: BVR; Berlin History, Rev W A Houghton 1895.

BAKER, Abel

SERVICE: S&S Vol 1 p 467; BRR 3 mos Boston 1776; Mil Ann In the Jerseys 1776-7; BRR 5 mos to York 1776 £5; BRR NY 3 mos 1776 £10; BRR 3 mos RI 1777; BRR 9 mos Cont Army 1778 £37-10; BRR a turn 3 mos 1777 Capt Nurse's Co, 1st pmt £12-10; BRR 9 mos Fishkill 1778; BRR in Capt Nurse's Co 1778 £12-10; BRR 3 mos reinforce Cont Army 1779 £2-9-3; MilAnn 9 mos Claverack 1779.
BORN: 8 Aug 1757 Bolton s/o Sam'l Esq & Susannah (Taintor).
MARRIED: 19 Feb 1784 Bolton, Mary (Polly) Howe.
DIED: after 1789 Concord, NH.
CHILDREN (b Bolton):
  Polly - b 1 Aug 1784
  Betsy - b 31 Oct 1785
  John -
  Marshall - 21 Mar 1788
        (b Concord NH):
  Abel -
  Parna -
  Achsah -
  Susan -
  Samuel -
  Sophia -
  Clarissa -
NOTE: "In consideration of Abel Baker engaging in the service of the State of Mass Bay 2 do 3 months service in Cap't David Nurse's Co., beginning his sd service the 2nd day of April next. I do promise to pay him £12-10 at this date, if not in the service more than 6 weeks not to have any more and if in the service longer, then £10-5 more and if held 2 mos. to have £10-5 in one. But £1-5 the above agreement I promise to fulfil. Witness my hand Bolton March ye 28 1778 David Nurse, Capt." Descriptive

BAKER, Edward (Cont)

List 1778, Mass Archives, Abel Baker about 21 5'9" high, darkish complex, fair hair.
REF: BVR; Berlin History, Rev W A Houghton 1895.

BAKER, Edward

SERVICE: S&S Vol 1 p 474; BRR money raised in Cap't Nurse's Co for 3 years £5.
BORN: 15 Jun 1755 Bolton s/o Sam'l Esq & Susannah (Taintor).
MARRIED: 1) 13 Oct 1778 Bolton, Hepzibah Fairbank; 2) Waterford ME, Polly Fletcher; 3) Waterford ME, Mrs Stevens.
DIED: in Waterford ME GS family lot Baker Hill.
CHILDREN (b Bolton to Hepsibah):
  Sally - b 30 Aug 1781 (1779 per Baker
        Gen) m Josiah Green
  Luke - b 9 Dec 1781 m Eleanor
        Hunnewell
        (b Waterford ME to Hepsibah):
  Kesiah - b 1784 m ___ Daggett
  John - b 1786 m1 Nancy Shurtleff m2
        Martha Stevens
  Edward - b 1788 m Mary Jordan
  Hepsibah - b 1791
  Persis - b 1793 d unm
  Betsey - b 1796 m ___ Gale
  Samuel - b 1799
        (by Polly):
  Nancy - m Artemas Woodman
  Abel - m Clarissa Evans
REF: BVR; Baker Family History, Paul & Blanche Andrews; Hist Waterford ME, Henry & William Warren 1879.

BAKER, Samuel, Esq

SERVICE: Not listed in S&S; BRR 5 mos men 1776 £12; BRR 3 mos 14 ds to Goose.
BORN: 27 Aug 1722 Westborough s/o Edward & Persis (Brigham).
MARRIED: 1) 24 Nov 1747 Westborough, Susannah Taintor (d 1781 ae 62 GSB); 2) 20 Apr 1786 Auburn, Wid Mary Bigelow of Worcester.
DIED: 4 May 1795 ae 73 Berlin GSB.
CHILDREN (b Bolton):
  Susannah - b 1748 m Eli Harrington
  Persis - b 16 Feb 1750-51 m Josiah
        Sawyer Jr
  Samuel - b 3 Jul 1753
  Edward - b 15 Jun 1755
  Abel - b 8 Aug 1757
  Mary - b 5 May 1760 m Jabez Walcott
  Bettey - b 8 Sep 1763 m Jabez Fairbank
NOTE: Judge of Court of Common Pleas; Constitutional Convention; Senator for Worcester Co.

BAKER, Samuel, Esq (Cont)

REF: BVR; Berlin History, Rev W A Houghton 1895.

BAKER, Sgt Samuel Jr

SERVICE: S&S Vol 1 p 496; BHist Lex
Alarm; BRR Siege of Boston 1775; BHist
Resolve Jun 1776 2 mos; BRR 5 mos NY Jul
1776 pd £12 by Sam'l Baker, Esq; BHist
Capt J Sargent's Co 1777; BRR Resolve
Sep 1777 30 ds Northern Army; BRR 2 mos
RI 1777; BRR Nothern Army 1 Oct 1777;
BRR reinforce Northern Army 1778 30 ds;
BRR reinforce Cont Army 1780; BRR Re-
solve 1776 5 mos NY £9.
BORN: 3 Jul 1753 Bolton s/o Sam'l Esq &
Susannah (Taintor).
MARRIED: 25 May 1780 Hannah Bush Jr of
Marlboro (d Templeton 1831).
DIED: 22 Jun 1825 ae 71 Templeton.
CHILDREN (b Bolton):
  Samuel - b 11 Apr 1781
  Susannah - b 19 Sep 1782
  Artemas - b 4 Apr 1784
       (b Templeton):
  Eli - b 19 Mar 1786
  Joseph - b 28 Jan 1788
  Levi - b 15 Feb 1790
  Jonas - b 25 Dec 1791
  Calvin - b 22 Nov 1793
  Luther - b 12 Jan 1797 m Harriet
       Partridge
  Hannah - b 31 Jan 1799 m Avery Turner
  Oliver - bpt 17 Jul 1801
  Otis - b 27 Sep 1803
REF: BVR; BerlVR; Templeton VR; Berlin
History, Rev W A Houghton 1895.

BALL, James

SERVICE: S&S Vol p 538.
BORN: 2 Jul 1729 Westborough s/o James &
Sarah.
MARRIED: 9 Feb 1754 (int) Westborough,
Dinah Fay.
DIED: 15 Sep 1784 Shrewsbury buried
Berlin GSB.
CHILDREN:
  John -
  Hannah - m ___ Johnson
  Patience - m ___ White
  Lydia - m ___ Goddard
NOTE: Also served for Marlborough.
REF: Westborough VR; Berl VR; Worc Co
Probate Records.

BALL, Sgt Jonathan, Jr

SERVICE: S&S Vol 1 p 540; BHist Enlisted
3 yrs 1781.
BORN: 16 Sep 1751 Bolton s/o Jonathan &
Martha (French).

BALL, Sgt Jonathan, Jr (Cont)

MARRIED: 17 Sep 1779 Bolton, Mary Pratt
of Shrewsbury (d 1835).
DIED: 1819 in Bolton no stone.
CHILDREN (b Bolton):
  Becky - b 25 Apr 1778 m Nathan Hosmore
  Elizabeth - b 28 Jun 1783
  Hannah - b 14 Apr 1785 m Ephraim
       Hapgood
  Asenath - b 20 Oct 1788 m Isaac King
  Lucy - b 25 Mar 1789
  Silas - b 18 Nov 1792
  William - b 15 Sep 1796
NOTE: Descriptive List 1781 Mass
Archives - 29 yrs, 5'9", complexion dk,
farmer; pensioned 1813, Sgt, $48, Roll
#15.
REF: LVR; BVR; DARPI.

BALL, Joseph

SERVICE: S&S Vol 1 p 540 & 541.
BORN: 31 Aug 1763 Westborough s/o John &
Lydia.
MARRIED: 1) 10 Feb 1787 (int) West-
borough, Susannah Forbes; 2) 8 Jul 1813
Sutton, Mrs Sarah (Nichols) Nichols.
DIED: 9 Jul 1838 Concord Essex Co VT.
CHILDREN: unk.
NOTE: Pensioned 2 Aug 1832 while living
at Concord VT.
REF: Westborough VR; DARPI 1st Supp;
Sutton VR.

BALL, Nathan

SERVICE: S&S Vol 1 p 542; BHist Lex
Alarm; BHist Col Wade's Reg 1777.
BORN: 16 Jun 1731 Westborough s/o James
& Sarah.
MARRIED: 1) Lucy ___ (d 1768 Northboro);
2) Ruhamah ___ (d 1838 ae 99 Lee).
DIED: 29 Dec 1796 GS Center Cem Lee (now
Fairmont).
CHILDREN (b Bolton to Lucy):
  Luce - b 25 Apr 1754
  Deborah - b 24 Apr 1756
  Abigail - 24 Apr 1759
  Experience - b 3 Apr 1764 m Benj
       Hastings Jr
       (b Stockbridge to Ruhamah):
  Nathan - b 1768
  Lydia - b 1769
  Polly - b 1772
  Sarah - b 1773
  Elizabeth - b 1775
  Martha - b 1776
  John - b 1777
  Anna - b 1778
  James - b 1781
  Isaac - b 1786
  Joseph - b 1787
  Sally - b 1788

BALL, Nathan (Cont)

REF: BVR; Westboro VR; Northboro VR; Lee VR; Family records in poss of a descendant in Cashmere WA.

BARKER, Sgt John

SERVICE: S&S Vol 1 p 612.
BORN: 20 Dec 1742 Acton s/o John & Martha.
MARRIED: 1 Oct 1769 Acton, Prudence Gleason (d Leicester, VT ae 99).
DIED: 11 Jan 1819 GS Brookside Cem Leicester VT.
CHILDREN (b Princeton):
  John - b 20 Jul 1770 d 11 Dec 1771
  John - b 10 Apr 1773 m Sarah Alden
  William - b 22 Mar 1775
  Robert - b 29 Nov 1777 d Leicester VT
  Jonas - d Leicester VT
  Prudence - 3 Mar 1792 m ___ Alden d
      Leicester VT
NOTE: P1 says John Barker b 1748 (error); 7 generations of family in Leicester VT; still living on same land (1976); warned out of Bolton 20 Aug 1765.
REF: Acton VR; Princeton VR; DARPI; Town Records Leicester VT; Soldiers of the Rev Buried in VT, W H Crockett.

BARKER, Joshua

SERVICE: Not in S&S; BRR Resolve of 1776 1 yr Ŀ3.
BORN: 16 Nov 1740 Scituate s/o Barnabus & Mary (Neal).
MARRIED: 28 Oct 1766 Scituate, Martha (Mrs Mary int) Copeland.
DIED: 22 Dec 1804.
CHILDREN: unk.
REF: Scituate VR; Barker Genealogy, Elizabeth F Barker 1927.

BARKER, Nathan

SERVICE: Not in S&S; BRR money raised in Capt Nurse´s Co for 3 yrs Ŀ3; DAR Lineage Book, enl 1781, Capt J Williams´ Co, Col Vose´s Reg.
BORN: 8 June 1761 Pomfret CT s/o Ephraim & Hannah (Grove).
MARRIED: 27 nov 1783 Lydia Baker.
DIED: 7 Oct 1849 Wilbraham; on GS "A Soldier of the Revolution."
CHILDREN:
  James - b 5 Mar 1785 d young
  Elisha - b 13 Dec 1786 d unm
  Calvin - b 24 Jan 1789 m Lucy Woodward
  Dolly - b 3 Dec 1790 d 1812 unm
  Roxanna - b 26 Dec 1792 m Royal Rindge
  Nathan - b 14 Apr 1795 m Eunice Austin
  Sitnah - b 25 Feb 1797 m Alanson Burr

BARKER, Nathan (Cont)

  Gilbert - b 13 Mar 1799 m Persis King
  Cyrus Grove - b 13 May 1801 m Eliza
      King
  Lydia - b 2 May 1803 m Sylvester Hills
  Wm Sedgwick - b 6 Jun 1807 m Hersey
      Knowlton
NOTE: DARPI has wrong wife (Hannah Grove); she was Nathan´s mother.
REF: DARPI; The Barker Genealogy, J C Parshall 1897; DAR Lineage Book 56 p 52; Rev R S Ede´s Rev War records copied in Town Clerk´s book 1876.

BARNARD, John, Sr, also Bernard

SERVICE: S&S Vol 1 p 632 & 986; BHist Lex Alarm; BRR Resolve 1775 6 wks; BRR Resolve 1776 2 mos.
BORN: unk.
MARRIED: 1) 21 may 1751 Waltham, Eunice Priest of Weston; 2) Sarah Fiske (d 1834).
DIED: 13 Sep 1830 Worcester.
CHILDREN (b Bolton):
  Mary - b 8 Feb 1752
  Abigail - b 10 Feb 1754
  John - b 5 may 1760
  Jonathan - b 16 Oct 1763
  Josiah - b 7 Jun 1770
NOTE: Warned out of Bolton 1754 - John Barnard, wife Eunice and children Mary & Abigail.
REF: BVR; Weston VR; Worcester VR.

BARNARD, John Jr

SERVICE: S&S Vol 1 p 632, 633; BHist Lex Alarm; BHist, Cont Army 9 mos 1779 Ŀ37; BHist 6 mos men 1780; BHist 15th Reg 1780; BRR Cont Army 3 mos 1780 Ŀ19; BRR reinforce Cont Army 1780 Ŀ18; BRR 3 yrs Cont Army 1781 Ŀ19 pd by James Goddard; BRR 9 mos service Cont Army 1779 L promised Ŀ7-20 bounty.
BORN: 5 May 1760 Bolton s/o John & Eunice (Priest).
MARRIED: 5 Sep 1785 in Bolton, Betsy Fallass of Bolton d/o Capt William.
DIED: poss Waterford ME.
CHILDREN (b Bolton):
  Betsy - b 26 Sep 1786
  Abby - bpt 14 Oct 1792
  Charity - bpt 14 Oct 1792
  John - bpt 14 Oct 1792
NOTE: Descriptive List 1779 - 17 yrs 5´9"; Treasurer of the Proprietors of Waterford ME starting 1785; bounty set at Indiancorn at 3s per bu & 4s for rye sd John relinquishing all wages to the town.
REF: BVR.

BARNARD, Fifer Jonathan

SERVICE: S&S Vol 2 p 634 & 637; BRR
Guard 3 mos 1779 Ł4-8-8; MilAnn 6 mos
men reinforce Cont Army 1780.
BORN: 16 oct 1763 Bolton s/o John Sr &
Eunice (Priest).
MARRIED: Annis ___.
DIED: 5 Mar 1824 ae 60 Lancaster.
CHILDREN:
   Jonathan - b 1795 d 12 Feb 1799
      Lancaster
   Benaja - b 1798 d 4 Oct 1805 Lancaster
   Julia - b Jan 1804 d 5 Sep 1805
      Lancaster
NOTE: Descriptive List - Capt. Thurs-
ton's Co Col Whitney's Reg age 17 yrs
5'4" complexion light farmer res Lancas-
ter enlisted 28 Mar 1781 for 3 yrs.
REF: BVR; LVR.

BARNARD, Samuel

SERVICE: S&S Vol 1 p 636.
BORN: 18 Jun 1760 Harvard s/o Benjamin &
Mary.
MARRIED: 15 May 1783 Harvard, Hannah
Laughton d/o Jeremiah & Rachel.
DIED: 26 Jan 1831 ae 71 GS Old Cem
Harvard.
CHILDREN (b Harvard):
   Daniel - b 7 Sep 1785 d 1799
   Samuel - b 13 Jan 1789
   John - b 6 Jun 1791 d 1818
   Emery - b 14 Aug 1794 m Susan ___
   Jeremiah - b 2 Dec 1797 m Bilhah
      Merriam
NOTE: Also claimed by Stow.
REF: HVR; Worc Co Probate Records.

BARNES, Fortunatus

SERVICE: S&S Vol 1 p 640; BRR 1775 5 mos
Capt David Nurse Ł4-10-10; BRR Resolve
Sep 1777 30 ds Northern Army; BRR Nor-
thern Army Oct 1777.
BORN: 25 Sep 1738 Marlborough s/o Jona-
than & Rachel.
MARRIED: 18 Oct 1764 Persis Hosmer of
Concord (d 10 Sep 1821 ae 82).
DIED: 7 Nov 1807 ae 70 Berlin GSB.
CHILDREN (b Bolton also recorded Marl-
borough):
   David - b 27 Aug 1765 m Asenath Moore
   Lydia - b 20 Jul 1767 m Amherst Bailey
   Hannah - b 20 Jun 1770 m Ephraim Howe
   William - b 5 Apr 1773 m Hannah
      Goddard
   Persis - b 5 may 1779 ml Silas Priest
      m2 Pelatiah Jones
REF: Berlin History, Rev W A Houghton
1895; MVR; DARPI.

BARRETT, Jonathan

SERVICE: S&S Vol 1 p 675.
BORN: 13 Nov 1757 Shirley s/o Samuel &
Rebecca.
MARRIED: 29 Aug 1781 Bolton, Phebe
Warner of Harvard.
DIED: 5 Nov 1849 Northborough.
CHILDREN (b Harvard):
   Moses - b 6 Nov 1779 d before 1849
      (father's will)
   Elias - b 30 Dec 1782
   Phebe - b 5 Apr 1784
   Lydia - b 10 Mar 1786 d before 1849
   Rebecca - b 18 Feb 1788 d before 1849
   Jonathan - bpt 5 Jul 1790 m Mary
      Hodgman
   Joseph - named in father's will
NOTE: Rev pensioner at $80 per annum.
REF: Shirley VR; BVR; HVR; Northborough
VR; Worc Co Probate Records.

BARRETT, Lemuel

SERVICE: S&S Vol 1 p 682; MilAnn RI
1781.
BORN: 12 Oct 1761 Chelmsford s/o Benj &
Olive.
MARRIED: 1)1 Sep 1784 Lancaster, Rebecca
Knowlton of Lancaster; 2) 1792 Anna
Chase.
DIED: 4 Oct 1842 Lisbon NH.
CHILDREN:
   Clarissa - m Chas Cowen
   Betsy - b 1798 m Russell Dailey
NOTE: Pension 1833 Grafton Co NH,
Lineage Book 43 p 155; widow's pension
1843 Grafton Co NH, Lineage Bk 43 p 155;
pension as pvt in NH Militia, Lineage Bk
53 p 32; substituted for his father,
Lineage Bk; Descriptive List 1780 Mass
Archives - age 17, 5'3", light
complexion.
REF: Chelmsford VR; LVR; DARPI; DAR
Lineage Books.

BARRETT, Sgt Oliver, Jr

SERVICE: S&S Vol 1 p 683; MilAnn Lex
Alarm.
BORN: 23 July 1746 Bolton s/o Lt Oliver
& Hannah (Hunt).
MARRIED: 6 Mar 1775 Sarah Whitcomb (d
1834 d/o Gen John & Becke).
DIED: 11 May 1817 ae 70 GS1
CHILDREN (b Bolton);
   Hannah - b 16 Dec 1775
   John - b 23 Jul 1777 d 1799
   Oliver - b 27 Nov 1780
   Beckee - b 3 Aug 1783
   Asa - b 8 Nov 1787
NOTES: DAR records 2 Oliver Barretts in

BARRETT, Sgt Oliver, Jr (Cont)

war, our research proves only 1, Oliver Jr b 1746.
REF: BVR; DARPI.

BARTLETT, Adam

SERVICE: S&S Vol 1 p 711; BHist Resolve Jun 1776; BRR 5 mos NY Jul 1776 Ⱡ10-10; BRR 5 mos York 1776 pd by Jotham Maynard Ⱡ5-5 & Jacob Moore Ⱡ5-5.
BORN: 27 Jul 1754 Bolton s/o Jonathan & Mary.
MARRIED: 28 May 1792 Northborough, Persis Badcock of Northborough (d 18 Jun 1861).
DIED: 22 Jul 1828 ae 74 Berlin GSB.
CHILDREN (b Berlin):
  Seraph - b 8 Oct 1792 m Rufus Sawyer
  Harriet - b 21 Jan 1794 d 1847 unm
  John - b 4 Mar 1796 m Mary Carter
  Daniel - b 11 Nov 1797 m Zilpah Carter
  Levi - b 1 Aug 1799 m Betsy (Wilder) Babcock
  Persis - b Aug 1801 m Parker Howe
  Miriam - b 26 Nov 1804 m Jotham Holt
  Mary - b 10 Jan 1806 m Lewis H Johnson
  Jonathan - b 7 Aug 1810
  William - b 13 Mar 1813 m Hannah Ball
REF: BVR; Berlin History, Rev W A Houghton 1895; Northborough VR; DARPI.

BARTLETT, Joseph also Bartlit

SERVICE: S&S Vol 1 p 729 & 736.
BORN: 24 Nov 1720 Marlborough s/o Ens Daniel & Martha (How).
MARRIED: 5 Feb 1745 Lydia Coolidge of Westborough.
DIED: unk.
CHILDREN (b Rutland):
  Eunice - b 10 Oct 1747 d young
  Phebe - b 5 Jun 1749 d young
  Josiah - b 26 Apr 1753
  Lucy - b 24 Mar 1758
  Adonijah - b 1761 d 1841 ae 80
  Phebe - b 25 Sep 1766
  Eunice - b 23 Jun 1770 d 1841 ae 71
NOTE: men of this name are found in 1790 census in Hillsborough & Rockingham Cos NH; Portland, Cumberland Co ME; and Salen Town, Washington Co NY.
REF: MVR; Rutland VR; Westborough VR; Worc Co Bibliography Vol 11 p 87.

BATES, Simeon

SERVICE: S&S Vol 1 p 801; no further data.

BAWL, John

SERVICE: S&S Vol 1 p 819.

BAWL, John (Cont)

BORN: 18 Jul 1738 Westborough s/o James and Sarah.
MARRIED: 1) 22 Jan 1761 Lancaster, Abigail Wilder of Lancaster; 2) 5 Nov 1772 Westborough, Mary Baker of Westborough.
DIED: 17 Apr 1801 Northborough.
CHILDREN (b Northborough to Abigail):
  Nahum - b 22 Oct 1761 m Lucy Wyman
  Charlotte - b 6 Jun 1763 m Joel Pratt
  Patty - b 10 Jun 1765 m Levi Bush
  Abigail - b 24 Jul 1767 m John Oaks
  Capt John - 12 Sep 1769 m Eunice Merrifield
      (b Northborough to Mary):
  Polly - b 1 Jun 1773 twin
  Persis - b 1 Jun 1773 twin
  Lydia - b 26 Feb 1775 m James Dawes 1797
  Edward Baker - b 4 July 1778
  James - b 13 Aug 1781 m Sophia Puffer, Berlin
  Susannah - b 12 Jun 1783
  Hannah - b 9 Dec 1785 m Luther Goss 1803
NOTE: DARPI states he was a minute man, but we found no record of it.
REF: LVR; Westborough VR; Northborough VR; DARPI.

BAYLEY, Benjamin Sr

SERVICE: S&S Vol 1 p 828; BHist Dorchester 1775; BRR to Goose 3 mos 14 ds 1777 Ⱡ10; BRR Col Whitney's Reg Ⱡ5.
BORN: 23 Feb 1713 Marlborough s/o Benj & Deborah (How).
MARRIED: 4 Apr 1738 Lancaster, Sibellah How of Westborough (d 1803).
DIED: 14 Feb 1790 a 79 Berlin GSB.
CHILDREN (b Bolton):
  Israel - b 8 Sep 1741 d 11 Sep 1746
  Deborah - b 5 Aug 1743 d 17 Sep 1746
  Joseph - b 8 Sep 1745 d 29 Sep 1746
  Benjamin - b 29 Aug 1747
  Ebenezer - b 1 Jul 1749
  Desiah - b 15 May 1751 m Jonathan Moore Jr
  Steaven - b 29 Sep 1753
  Sibbela - b 19 Jan 1756 m Dr Benj Nurse (1st w)
  Catherine - b 18 Jan 1758 m Dr Benj Nurse (2nd w)
REF: MVR; LVR; Berlin History, Rev W A Houghton 1895; BVR; DARPI.

BIGELOW, William also Biglo, Biglow

SERVICE: S&S Vol 2 p 27, 29 & 35; B Hist Lex Alarm; BHist Siege of Boston; BRR NY 5 mos Jul 1776 Ⱡ12; BRR 6 mos men 1780 bounty 10 bu rye; BRR reinforce Cont Army 1780; BHist enlist 3 yrs 5th Reg

BIGELOW, William (Cont)

1781.
BORN: ca 1744-45.
MARRIED: 1 Jan 1772 Bolton, Hannah Robbins (d 1837 ae 86) d/o Jonathan.
DIED: 6 Oct 1826 ae 81 Bolton GS3.
CHILDREN (b Bolton):
    Jane - b 15 Jul 1774 m Jon´a Houghton Jr 1795
    William - b 3 Oct 1776
    Mary - b 5 Mar 1779
    Jonathan - b 8 Jan 1783
    Ann Bagnall - bpt 9 Oct 1791
NOTE: Descriptive List Jun 1780 - ae 35, 5´6", complexion ruddy; Descriptive List Aug 1780 - ae 36, 5´7", complexion dark, farmer, res Bolton.
REF: BVR.

BLAIR, Timothy

SERVICE: S&S Vol 2 p 121; MilAnn reinforcement 9 mos 1778.
BORN: ca1750.
NOTE: Descriptinve List 1778 - ae 28 6´ complexion light res Bolton.

BLOOD, Corp Joseph Jr

SERVICE: S&S Vol 2 p 206; MilAnn Lex Alarm; MilAnn Coat Rolls Col Longley´s Co 1776.
BORN: 6 May 1747 Harvard s/o Joseph & Rebecca (Warner).
MARRIED: 27 Jun 1770 Bolton, Betty Bruce (d 1816 ae 64 Charlestown).
DIED: 4 Jan 1823 ae 76 "Sat. evening in Charlestown."
CHILDREN:
    Jonathan Knight - b 20 Jun 1771 d 1772
    Betsy - b 14 Feb 1773 m Sam´l Aldrich Westmoreland NH
    Rebeckah - b 8 Mar 1775 m Aretas Pierce Westmoreland NH
    Arathusa - b 20 Jun 1777 m Jos Boynton Westmoreland NH
    Susannah - b 9 Sep 1780
    Mary - b 30 Apr 1783 m Henry Merrick Charlestown NH
    Prudence - b 12 Mar 1786 d Hudson MA 1879
NOTE: In speech by Jos Willard Esq, Lancaster 1826 "Joseph Blood...one of 6 Rev. soldiers still living." DAR: "died after 1826."
REF: BVR; HVR; The Story of the Bloods, Roger Harris 1960; DARPI; Charlestown VR.

BLOOD, Samuel

SERVICE: S&S Vol 2 p 209; BHist Lex Alarm; BHist Jul 1776 bounty Ł10; BRR

BLOOD, Samuel (Cont)

Resolve 5 mos 1776 bounty Ł9-12; BRR Bennington Sep 1777; BRR 3 mos to northward 1777; BRR Northern Army Aug 1777 Ł9-12; BRR reinforce Cont Army 1780.
BORN: 7 Jun 1749 Concord s/o Oliver & Mary (Foster).
MARRIED: 20 Feb 1772 Hudson NH, Lucretia Heywood (d 10 Oct 1827 ae 73).
DIED: 15 Aug 1834 ae 85 GS2.
CHILDREN:
    Lucretia - b 6 Oct 1772 d 1849
    Gen Thomas Heywood - b 3 Feb 1775 m Mary Sawyer
    Lucy - b 15 Mar 1777 m Shobal Allen
    Oliver - b 18 Mar 1779 m1 Mary H Brown m2 Sarah ___
    Samuel - b 11 Apr 1781
    Elizabeth - b 27 Jun 1783 m1 Phineas Cole m2 Joseph Parks
    Joshua - b 24 Sep 1785 m Caroline Seaver
    Mary - b 17 Dec 1787 m1 Joel Harris m2 James Kimball
    Susannah - b 6 Apr 1790 m Stevens Heywood
    James - b 24 Jun 1792
    Harriet - b 14 Sep 1793 m John Walker
    Edmund - b 11 Jun 1798 m Elizabeth Whitman
REF: BVR; Story of the Bloods, Roger Harris, 1960.

BOND, Corp Jonathan

SERVICE: S&S Vol 2 p 258.
BORN: 22 Apr 1736 Waltham s/o Dea Jonathan & Mary H.
MARRIED: 28 Jul 1774 Sarah Crosman of Leicester.
DIED: 26 Jul 1810 Leicester.
CHILDREN (b Leicester):
    Edward - b 7 Aug 1785
    Cynthia - 26 Nov 1787
    Jonathan - 12 Sep 1790 m Mrs Mary Cobb 1818
    Hannah - 22 Apr 1793
REF: Waltham VR; Leicester VR; DARPI.

BOOMAN, JOHN also Bowman

SERVICE: S&S Vol 2 p 272 & 352.
BORN: 3 Jul 1759 Lexington.
MARRIED: 1) ___ 2) 17 Apr 1817 Hannah Frye of Ashburnham (d 8 Jun 1841 ae 76).
DIED: 22 Oct 1846 ae 87 Ashburnham.
CHILDREN (b Ashburnham):
    Phebe - d 4 Feb 1816 ae 13 Ashburnham
    Hannah - d 5 Sep 1816 ae 20 Ashburnham
    Mary - b 1799 m Thomas Rice 1819
REF: Lexington VR; Ashburnham VR; DARPI; DAR Lineage Bk 146 p 315; Pension Records 1832.

BOWERS, John

SERVICE: S&S Vol 2 p 335; BRR Resolve
1776 1 yr NY £3-12; MilAnn Lex Alarm;
MilAnn Canada Exped; MilAnn At Hull Capt
Wm Warner; MilAnn Saratoga 1777.
BORN: 2 Sep 1757 in Leominster s/o
Jerahmiel & Mary.
MARRIED: 11 Dec 1783 Leominster, Eliza-
beth Boutell.
DIED: 10 Aug 1808 Hancock NH GS Pine
Ridge Cem Hancock.
CHILDREN (b Leominster):
  Betsy - bpt 27 Feb 1785
  (Possiby) John - m Nancy Carter 1810
NOTE: also claimed by Leominster.
REF: Leominster VR; DARPI; Prelude to
Hancock's Second 100 Years, publ by
Tuttle, Hancock NH.

BREED, Ephraim

SERVICE: S&S Vol 2 p 457.
BORN : 26 May 1736 Lynn s/o Joseph &
Suzanah.
MARRIED: 22 Nov 1762 Lynn, Susannah
Mansfield.
DIED: 4 Apr 1812 ae 76 Lynn.
CHILDREN (b Lynn):
  Abigail - b 28 Nov 1765
  Susannah - b 8 May 1768
  Joseph - b 18 Dec 1771
REF: Lynn VR; DARPI.

BRIDGES, Corp James

SERVICE: S&S Vol 2 p 490 & 496; BHist
Lex Alarm; BHist Siege of Boston; BRR
Resolve 1776 1 yr £3-12-0; BHist 13th
Reg.
BORN: 18 Sep 1729 Southborough s/o Hack-
aliah & Sarah.
MARRIED: unk.
DIED: 9 Oct 1805 Southborough.
NOTE: Deserted during siege of Boston;
described "has large head of hair, al-
most black and very long, which is com-
monly cued with a black ribband. Wearing
an old blue surtout, clothcolored coat
and jacket, a pair of cotton breeches,
and 2 shirts, tow and linen." From Mass
Archives. However, he was later paid by
Bolton for 1 year's service agreeable to
the resolve of 1776, and was also in the
13th Reg of the Cont Army for Bolton.
REF: Southborough VR.

BRIGHAM, Sgt Abraham

SERVICE: S&S Vol 2 p 525; BRR Lex Alarm;
BHist 15th Reg.
BORN: 25 Feb 1720-21 Marlborough s/o
Jotham & Abigail.
MARRIED: 26 Feb 1752 Marlborough, Phebe

BRIGHAM, Sgt Abraham (Cont)

Martin (b 1727 d 1806 ae 77 Marl-
borough).
DIED: 10 Nov 1788 ae 67 Marlborough.
CHILDREN (b Marlborough):
  Lucy - b 30 oct 1753 m David Wyman
  Fortunatus - b 29 Sep 1759
  Anna - b 1 Mar 1763 m Sam'l Barnes
  Gardner - b 30 Apr 1766 d 1779
REF: History of the Brigham Family, W I
Tyler Brigham 1907; MVR.

BRIGHAM, Hosea also called Moses

SERVICE: S&S Vol 2 p 529.
BORN: 6 Sep 1750 Sudbury s/o Samuel &
Mary.
MARRIED: 17 Sep 1778 Holten, Catherine
Davis of Holden (d 19 Oct 1823 ae 74).
DIED: 17 Dec 1817 ae 67 Hubbardston GS
Center Cem.
CHILDREN (b Hubbardston):
  Hosea - b 2 Sep 1779
  Peter - b 2 Oct 1781
  Joseph - b 9 Aug 1785
  Samuel - b 12 May 1787
  ___ - 1 Mar 1790
  Betsy - b 19 Aug 1792 d 1851
  ___ - b 19 Aug 1793
REF: Sudbury VR; Hubbardston VR; History
of the Brigham Family, W I Tyler Brigham
1907.

BRIGHAM, John

SERVICE: S&S Vol 2 p 530; MilAnn p 158
RI 1778; MilAnn 27 ds Saratoga 1777.
BORN: 8 Aug 1758 Princeton s/o Stephen &
Betty (Betsy Weeks).
MARRIED: 24 Jan 1788 (int) "John of
Leicester, VT," Lydia How of Princeton
(d 1859).
DIED: 2 Apr 1841 Acworth NH.
CHILDREN (b Alstead NH):
  Joel - b 10 Jan 1790 d 2 Sep 1795
  Rufus - b 29 Jun 1791
  John - b 21 Apr 1793 m Mrs Eunice H
    Clark
  Lucy - b 6 Aug 1795 m Jared Beckwith
  Polly - b 16 Sep 1797
  Matilda - b 12 Jun 1800 m Martin Mason
  Silas - b 22 Jul 1802 m Sarah
    Manchester
  Lydia - b 21 Aug 1804 m Henry Clure
  Betsy - b 30 Oct 1808 m Almond
    Wetherbee
REF: Princeton VR; DARPI; History of the
Brigham Family, W I Tyler Brigham 1907.

BROWN, John

SERVICE: S&S Vol 2 p 636.
BORN: 14 Mar 1739/40 Stow s/o

11

BROWN, John (Cont)

Deliverance & Elizabeth.
MARRIED: 17 Dec 1764 Phebe Foskett.
DIED: Bolton before 17 May 1803 when Phebe was app't admx of estate.
CHILDREN (b Oakham):
  Phebe - b 15 Mar 1765
  Elizabeth - b 30 Aug 1770 m Calvin Pierce 1786
  Lydia - m John Walcott 1795
  Lucy - b 14 Sep 1773 m Asa Bride 1803
  Caty - m Otis Bruce
  Susanna - b 1783 m Levi Howe 1818
    (b Bolton):
  Mary - bpt 30 Oct 1785
NOTE: John Brown tythingman 1787, 1792 & 1796; above children listed in probate records; also claimed by Stow.
REF: Stow VR; BVR; Worc Co Probate Records; Soldiers of Oakham in the Revolution, Henry P Wright 1914.

BROWN, Jonas

SERVICE: S&S Vol 2 p 652.
BORN: 10 Mar 1731 Stow s/o Deliverance & Elizabeth.
MARRIED: 23 Nov 1751 Stow, Mary Graves.
DIED: 27 Oct 1810 ae 81 Waltham GS Grove Hill Cem.
CHILDREN (b Stow):
  Lydda - b 24 Mar 1752
  Sarah - b 1 Dec 1756
  Daniel - b 9 Mar 1758
REF: SVR; Waltham VR.

BRUCE, Benjamin Sr

SERVICE: S&S Vol 2 p 710; BerlHist Minute Man 1775; BRR 5 mos NY Jul 1776 Ł12; BHist Col Stearns Reg't 1777; BRR 2 mos RI 1777; BRR 30 ds Northern Army Oct 1777; BRR reinforce Cont Army 1780.
BORN: 24 Dec 1739 Marlborough s/o Daniel & Bathsheba (Bowker).
MARRIED: Dec 1768 Bolton, Nancy (Nanny) McBride.
DIED: 1831 ae 92 Bolton no stone.
CHILDREN (b Bolton):
  Mary - b 29 Apr 1769 m Jon'a Baker
  Cata - b 6 Mar 1771
  Otis - b 18 Apr 1773 m Caty Brown
  Calven - b 2 May 1775 m Ruth Priest
  Anna - b 6 Sep 1777 d 1857 unm
  William - b 5 Feb 1780 d 1811
  Oliver - b 6 May 1782 d 1813 m Sally Burnam
  Franklin - b 21 June 1784 went to VT
  Amos - b 16 Oct 1786 d 1824
REF: BVR; MVR; Berlin History, Rev W A Houghton 1895.

BRUCE, Benjamin Jr

SERVICE: S & S Vol 2 p 710; BHist to York Jul 1776 Ł10; BRR 3 mos NY 1776; BRR Resolve 1776 2 mos; DNR Dec 1776; BRR "a turn" to York pd by Wm Sawyer L 12; BRR Cont Army 1780.
BORN: 19 Aug 1759 Bolton s/o Timothy & Susannah (Joslin).
MARRIED: 10 May 1781 Philadelphia Wheeler.
DIED: 11 Sep 1839 ae 80 yr 22 ds Jay NY GS Center Cem.
CHILDREN:
  Jonah - b 11 Apr 1785
  Anna -
  Polly - m Oliver Cook
  Phila -
  Joseph - b Mar 1796 in War 1812 m Rebecca Houghton
  Howard -
NOTE: with Capt Mirick's men per Capt Nurses Journal.
REF: BVR; DARPI; DAR Lineage Book 37 p 226; pension application; History of Essex Co NY, H P Smith 1885.

BRUCE, Daniel Sr

SERVICE: S&S Vol 2 p 710 & 719; BRR Lex Alarm; BRR Siege of Boston; BRR money raised in Capt Nurse's Co for 3 yrs Ł3-10.
BORN: 22 Feb 1701 Marlborough s/o Roger & Elizabeth.
MARRIED: 1 Dec 1732 Bathsheba Bowker.
DIED: 13 Feb 1790 ae 89 Marlborough.
CHILDREN (b Marlborough):
  Ruth - b 22 May 1733 m Cyrus Gates 1753
  Abraham - b 23 Dec 1735
  Lucy - b 6 Nov 1737 d 8 May 1832 ae 95
  Benjamin - 24 Dec 1739
  John - b 25 May 1744 m Lois Wilkins
  Betty - b 22 Jan 1746
  Mary - b 9 Aug 1748 m John Brown Jr
  Daniel - b 21 Sep 1752 m Mary Bruce d/o Timothy
REF: Marlborough History, Chas Hudson 1862; Berlin History, Rev W A Houghton 1895.

BRUCE, Daniel, Jr

SERVICE: S&S Vol 2 p 710; BHist to York 5 mos July 1776 Ł10; BRR 1776 5 mos to York pd by Uriah Moore Ł5-3-4; BRR reinforce Cont Army 1780; BHist 15th Reg't.
BORN: 21 Sep 1752 Marlborough s/o Daniel & Bathsheba (Bowker).
MARRIED: 24 Feb 1785 Marlborough, Mary Bruce (b 1762 d/o Timothy).
DIED: 1805 (DARPI).
CHILDREN (b Berlin):

BRUCE, Daniel, Jr (Cont)

Abraham –
Lydia   – m   Timothy   Austin   of
  Marlborough 1816
Linda Mira – b 1798 m David Keyes
Lois – b 30 Oct 1802 m Ziba Keyes
Sally – m James Rich Jr
REF: Berlin History, Rev W A Houghton
1895; MVR; DARPI.

BRUCE, Isaiah

SERVICE: S&S Vol 2 p 711; BHist Lex
Alarm; BRR Capt Nurse's Co money raised
for 3 yrs Ł8-15; BRR 3 mos to Bennington
Aug 1777; DNR Dec 1776; BRR money depo-
sited in Capt Nurse's hands Ł1-19-0.
BORN: 18 Jan 1754 Bolton s/o Samuel &
Betty.
MARRIED: 12 Apr 1780 Stow, Mary Barnard
of Marlborough (d 1841 ae 78 d/o
Solomon).
DIED: 5 Feb 1837 ae 83 Marlborough.
CHILDREN (b Marlborough):
Caty – b 1790 d 15 Sep 1795 ae 5
Dexter – b 11 Aug 1791 d 1800 in West
  Boylston
Colling – b 1794 d 24 Feb 1826 ae 32
Mary Ann – b 1806 d 1845 ae 39
Emory – b 1808 d 28 May 1836 ae 28
REF: BVR; MVR; SVR.

BRUCE, John

SERVICE: S&S Vol 2 p 712; BHist Lex
Alarm; BRR York 2 mos Ł3 Sep 1776; BRR
Bennington Aug 1777.
BORN: 29 Mar or May 1744 Marlborough s/o
Daniel & Bathseba (Bowker).
MARRIED: 8 Feb 1770 Bolton, Martha Moore
(d Oct 1835 ae 85 Berlin).
DIED: 13 Feb 1843 ae 99 Berlin no stone.
CHILDREN (b Bolton):
Hugh – b 5 Aug 1770 m Sally Moore
Dorcas – b 25 Apr 1772
Nancy – b 30 Jun 1774 d young
Asenah – b 16 Sep 1776 m Luther Priest
Anna – b 6 Sep 1777 m Isaiah Coolidge
Eunice – b 1779 m Asa Sawyer
John – b 15 May 1781 m Prudence Priest
  (b Berlin):
Nancy – b Jun 1773 m ___ Lawrence
Dorcas – bpt 18 Dec 1785 m John Brewer
Parnell – b 31 May 1788 m Josiah
  Bennett
Sewell – b 15 Jul 1790 m Eunice
  Bennett
Sylvanus – b 15 Dec 1792 m Hannah Reed
Sophia – 10 Apr 1795 m Daniel Bacon
REF: BVR; MVR; Berlin History, Rev W A
Houghton 1895; DARPI.

BRUCE, Jonas

SERVICE: S&S Vol 2 p 712-3; BHist 5 mos
NY Jun 1776 Ł10; BRR 5 mos to York Jul
1776 Ł12; BRR Bennington Aug 1777; BRR
Northern Army Aug 1777; BRR Cont Army
1780.
BORN: 6 Oct 1753 Bolton s/o Sam'l Jr &
Marcy.
MARRIED: 14 Jun 1781 Marlborough, Lucy
Taylor of Marlborough (d 1810 Winchen-
don).
DIED: unk.
CHILDREN (listed Winchendon VR):
Ambrey – b Bolton 15 Jul 1781 m Daniel
  Day 1799
Charlotte – b Berlin 31 Jan 1783 m
  Capt Nath'l Holman 1805
David Taylor – b Bolton 15 Dec 1784
Dolly – b Marlborough 7 Jul 1787 m
  Eliel Sherman
Athalina – b Marlborough 1 Aug 1789
Linda Mira – d 1791 ae 1 yr
NOTE: Jonas Bruce was a silversmith in
Bolton 1783-4.
REF: BVR; Berl VR; MVR; Winchendon VR;
Worc Co Registry of Deeds.

BRUCE, Samuel

SERVICE: S&S Vol 2 p 715.
BORN: 5 March 1730 Woburn s/o Samuel &
Rebecca (Winn).
MARRIED: Marcy ___.
DIED: unk.
CHILDREN (b Bolton):
Jonas – b 6 Oct 1753 m Lucy Taylor,
  Marlborough
Joanna – b 30 Jan 1754
Lavinia – b 25 May 1755 m Sam'l Brown,
  Winchendon
Comfort – b 28 Jun 1757 d 1758 Bolton
Josiah – b 2 Oct 1759
Dolly – b 25 Jun 1761 m Francis
  Maynard, Winchendon
Silas – b 6 Oct 1763
NOTE: Military Annals calls him Lemuel
Bruce; in Marlborough in 1790 census.
REF: Woburn VR; BVR; MVR; Winchendon VR.

BRUCE, Samuel

SERVICE: S&S Vol 2 p 715; MilAnn Lex
Alarm; DNR 3 yrs Cont Army Ł50-15.
BORN: 4 Jul 1729 Southborough s/o Samuel
& Elizabeth (Townsend).
MARRIED: 1749 Betsy or Betty Whitney (d
1812 d/o Isaiah).
DIED: 1812 Bolton no stone.
CHILDREN (b Bolton):
Betty – b 14 Jul 1751 m Joseph Blood
Isaiah – b 18 Jan 1754 m Mary Barnard
Susannah – b 26 Nov 1756 m Jonas Smith
Jonathan – b 8 Jun 1759 d young

BRUCE, Samuel (Cont)

Abigail – b 1 Sep 1760
Jonathan – 1 Mar 1763
Sarah – b 15 Jan 1765 m Fortunatus
   Howe, Marlborough
Phebe – b 27 May 1768 m Benj Priest,
   Marlborough
Rebeckah – b 8 Aug 1770
Mary – b 8 Jan 1773
REF: Southborough VR; BVR; MVR.

BRUCE, Stephen

SERVICE: S&S Vol 2 p 715; BRR Bennington
3 mos Aug 1777.
BORN: 24 Jan 1764 Westborough s/o Jon´a
& Hannah (Beaman).
MARRIED: 4 Jun 1785 Elizabeth Baldwin of
Northborough.
DIED: 1803 Townsend.
CHILDREN: none.
REF: Westborough VR; Northborough VR;
Middlesex Co Probate Records; Townsend
VR.

BRUCE, Timothy

SERVICE: S&S Vol 2 p 716; BRR money
raised in Capt Nurse´s Co for 3 yrs £2.
BORN: 17 Feb 1731/2 Woburn s/o John &
Martha (Carter).
MARRIED: 13 Feb 1752 Marlborough, Susan-
nah Joslin of Marlborough (d 1832 ae
99).
DIED: 3 Jan 1787 Marlborough.
CHILDREN (prob b Marlborough):
Timothy – b 1752 m Matilda Wheeler
Benjamin – prob b Bolton ca1754 m
   Philadelphia Wheeler
Joseph – prob b Bolton 1759 m Ruth
   Lowell
Mary – b 1762-3 m Daniel Bruce Jr
Sally – b 1766 m Fortunatus Howe
Samuel – b before 1782
Elizabeth – b before 1782
John – b before 1782
NOTE: warned out of Bolton 20 Aug 1754
with wife Susannah & child Timothy;
warned out of Marlborough Nov 1782 with
wife Susannah & children Sam´l, John,
Elizabeth.
REF: Woburn VR; MVR; Marlborough His-
tory; DARPI; App to join DAR.

BUCK, Isaac Matross

SERVICE: S&S Vol 2 p 744; BHist Siege of
Boston; BHist 14th Reg.
BORN: 27 Sep 1757 Southborough s/o Isaac
& Mary (Richards).
MARRIED: 18 May 1780 Patty Phillips of
Lancaster.
DIED: 1840 bur Leg Cem Sterling.

BUCK, Isaac Matross (Cont)

CHILDREN (b Sterling):
Silas – d 1863 m Deborah Beaman
Isaac –
Pliny – b 1790 d 1874 m Betsy Dodd
   Perry
NOTE: Placed on pension roll 1840 for
service as priv & corp in Mass troops.
REF: Southborough VR; LVR; DARPI; Ster-
ling Rev Cemetery List; Worc Co Memoirs
Vol 2 p 363; DAR Lineage Bk 110 p 4.

BULLARD, Nathan

SERVICE: S&S Vol 2 p 786.
BORN: 17 Sep 1762 Medway s/o Nathan &
Ede (Rhoda) (Partridge).
MARRIED: 1) ___ ; 2) 15 Oct 1814 Medway,
Nancy Russell.
DIED: 21 May 1846 ae 84 yrs 6 mos Berlin
GSB.
CHILDREN (b Medway):
Joel – b Jun 1799 m Judith Brigham
Betsy – bpt 14 Feb 1816
NOTE: a Rev soldier from Medway buried
in Berlin, not credited to Bolton.
REF: Berlin History, Rev W A Houghton
1895; Medway VR; Berlin burial list.

BURGES, William also Burgess, Burgis

SERVICE: S&S Vol 2 p 838, 840 & 844; BRR
5 mos Canada 1776 £16-10s; BHist rein-
forcements 1778; BRR 9 mos Cont Army
1778 £37-10; BRR Fishkill 9 mos 1778;
BRR reinforce Cont Army 1779 £2-9-3; BRR
Claverack 1779 £50 per mo exclusive of
all other wages; BRR Cont Army 3 mos
1780 £20; BRR reinforce Cont Army RI 3
mos 1780 £12.
BORN: 5 Jan 1750/1 Harvard s/o Ebenezer
& Hannah.
MARRIED: 24 Mar 1774 Bolton, Elizabeth
Richardson.
DIED: Between 1780 & 1785 Bolton no
stone.
CHILDREN (b Bolton):
William – b 7 May 1777
Elizabeth Watts – b 25 Jan 1779
Achsah – bpt 13 Nov 1785 "dau. of
   Widow Elizabeth"
NOTE: Descriptive List – "1777, in Col.
Whitney´s Reg´t, Capt. Houghton´s &
Capt. Nurse´s Co., 27 years, 5´8" high;
lightish complexion, brown hair."
REF: HVR; BVR.

BURNAM, Jeremiah also Burnham, Burnum

SERVICE: S&S Vol 2 p 862, 876 & 886;
MilAnn 5th Reg´t.
BORN: 22 Jul 1759 (bpt) Ipswich s/o
Reuben & Elizabeth (Smith).

BURNAM, Jeremiah (Cont)

MARRIED: 1) Elizabeth ___; 2) 8 Jun 1791 per Bridgton ME records or 8 April 1791 per widow's statement, Mehitable Sanborn, Bridgton ME.
DIED: 23 Jun 1839 Athens Co OH.
CHILDREN (b Bridgton ME):
    Elizabeth - b 24 Jul 1786
    Jere - b 2 May 1788
            (b Bridgton ME):
    Ira - b 16 Jan 1792
    Bohemia - b 21 Mar 1793
    Phebe - b 13 May 1800
    Doly - b 20 Apr 1802 memtioned in
        Pension Appl
    Son - b 1809 mentioned in pension appl
    Dau - b 1812 mentioned on pension appl
NOTE: Jeremiah appl for pension 12 May 1818 Athens Co OH ae 59; widow Mehitable appl for bounty land 3 Aug 1855 ae 85 yrs; credited to Bolton, Boxford, Bridgton ME & Pearsontown ME.
REF: Ipswich VR; church records Bridgton ME; pension records GSA.

BURNAM, John also Burnham

SERVICE: S&S Vol 2 p 862, 876 & 877; BRR 3 mos NY 1776 £10; DNR Winter Campaign 1776-77; BHist 15th Reg't 1777-80; BHist 6 mos men 1780.
BORN: 1758 Lunenburg s/o Nathaniel & Elizabeth (Brown).
MARRIED: 1) 3 Jul 1782 Dummerston VT, Rhoda Wilson; 2) 14 Aug 1800 Dummerston VT, Roxanna Burnam.
DIED: 25 Dec 1828 Hadley Saratoga Co NY.
CHILDREN (b Dummerston VT):
    Mercy - b 13 Feb 1783
    Alvira - m Francis Spring
    Anna - b 1801
    Cromwell - b 1802
    Betsy - b 1804
    Washington - 1806
    Olive - b 1808
    Artemas - 1810
    Jefferson - b 1812
    Mary - b 1814
    Charles - b 1816
    Rody - b 1818
NOTE: DARPI says born 22 Jun 1760; Descriptive List 1780 - "Age 20, stature 5'10", complexion light, res. Bolton." Pensioned 1818; wid pensioned 1853.
REF: Early Records of Lunenburg; DARPI; DAR Lineage Bk 34 p 7 & Bk 133 p 271; VT Petitions for Land Grants.

BURNAM, Lemuel, Sr

SERVICE: S&S Vol 2 p 864; MilAnn Lex Alarm; BRR 5 mos to Canady 1776 £18.
BORN: 31 Jul 1748 (bpt) Boxford s/o

BURNAM, Lemuel, Sr (Cont)

Nathaniel & Ruth (Smith).
MARRIED: 29 Jun 1769 Bolton (Lemuel of Harvard), Hannah Pairce (listed as widow 1821, d Southborough 20 Feb 1828 ae 76).
DIED: before 1821.
CHILDREN (b Bolton):
    Hannah - b 12 Aug 1770 m Thomas
        Colburn
    Achsah - b 1 Oct 1772 m Luther Sawyer
        1797
NOTE: Descriptive List 1780 - ae 29 5'6", light complexion, hair sandy, res Bolton.
REF: Boxford VR; BVR; Southborough VR; DARPI.

BURNHAM, Lemuel, Jr

SERVICE: S&S Vol 2 p 878.
BORN: 2 Jun 1766 Bolton s/o Benjamin & Beulah (Holden).
MARRIED: 15 Nov 1798 Bolton, Sarah (Sally) Priest (d 1854 GS2).
DIED: 13 Feb 1852 Bolton ae 85 GS2.
CHILDREN (b Bolton):
    Lucinda - b 26 Jan 1799 d unm GS2
    Reuben - b 15 Nov 1800 m Roxanny
        Warner 1829
    Anna - b 1 Dec 1802
    Beulah - b 20 Oct 1804 m Amasa Lane of
        Bedford 1822
    Sally - b 19 Oct 1806 m William Barry
        1839
    Mary Ann - b 18 Jan 1809 m Leonard
        White of Bedford 1832
    Louisa - b 16 Apr 1811 m Nathan Fitch
        of Bedford 1834
    Lemuel - b 7 Sep 1813 d 1838 GS2
    Rachel - b 16 Apr 1817 m John Hatch
REF: BVR; Bolton Book of Deaths.

BURNAM, Corp Thomas also Burnham, Burnum

SERVICE: S&S Vol 2 p 867, 880 & 887; B Hist Bunker Hill & Siege of Boston; B Hist Col Stearns Reg 1777; BRR 2 mos RI 1777; Harv Hist 15th Reg 1778-1780; Harv Hist Col Tim'o Bigelow's Reg Valley Forge; Col Jason Duncan's Militia Dummerston VT.
BORN: 9 Sep 1756 Littleton s/o Nath'l Jr & Elizabeth (Brown).
MARRIED: 3 Jan 1782 Dummerston VT, Deliverance Graham (b Bolton 1755 d/o Andrew).
DIED: 1801 Baltimore Windsor Co VT.
CHILDREN:
    seven, all young at his death
NOTE: Capt Robert Longley's Co order for cartridge boxes 18 June 1775 (for Thomas Burnam) after Bunker Hill.
REF: Early Records of Lunenburg; Little-

BURNAM, Corp Thomas (Cont)

ton VR; BVR; VT Petitions for Land Grants; widow's pension W23740.

BURT, Sgt James

SERVICE: S & S Vol 2 p 916-7; MilAnn Capt Nurse's Co 1776 as carpenter; MilAnn Bennington 1777; MilAnn Cont Army Ticonderoga 1775; MilAnn Sgt J Drury's Co p 164.
BORN: ca 1755.
MARRIED: 9 Dec 1780 Taunton, Ruth Rine of Rehoboth (d 13 Apr 1821 ae 62).
DIED: 9 May 1806 ae 51 Taunton Plain Burying Ground.
REF: Taunton VR.

BUSH, Jonathan

SERVICE: S&S Vol 2 p 930; BRR service in RI; BRR list of those who rec bounty Ł4 mo; MilAnn Cont Army 3 mos 1779 Ł2-9-3; BRR reinf Cont Army 1780 RI Ł18; BRR Cont Army 1780 3 mos Ł19; BRR Claverack 3 mos 1780 bounty 20 bu rye & 36 bu Ind corn.
BORN: 29 Nov 1758 Marlborough s/o Micah & Dorothy (Whitcomb).
MARRIED: 2 Jun 1785 Bolton, Deborah Longley d/o Nathaniel.
DIED: 17 Dec 1836 ae 79 Bolton no stone.
CHILDREN (b Bolton):
  Sophia - b 7 Mar 1786
  Betsy - b 11 Jul 1790
  Elizabeth - bpt 11 Jan 1795
  Becca - b 31 May 1795
  Lucretia - bpt 28 Oct 1804
  Roanna - bpt 20 Sep 1807
REF: Marlborough History, Hon Charles Hudson 1862; BVR.

BUTLER, Ephraim Jr

SERVICE: Not in S&S under Bolton; BRR to Boston 1778 under Gen Heath.
BORN: 4 Jul 1759 Bolton s/o Ephraim & Comfort (Fay).
NOTE: Men of this name listed in S&S from Boston, Ervingshire & Leverett; 1790 census an Ephraim Butler listed in Edgartown.
REF: BVR.

CAMMEL, John

SERVICE: S&S Vol 3 p 44.
BORN: "In a foreign place" (Scotland), Shirley History ; parents unk.
MARRIED: 1) 6 Dec 1769 Hannah Nickless; 2) 27 Nov 1788 Martha Ivory d/o John & Sarah.
DIED: before Dec 1796 when will was

CAMMEL, John (Cont)

proved.
CHILDREN (b Tewksbury):
  John - m Nancy Rugg
        (b Shirley):
  Rogers - bpt 15 Jul 1777
  Elizabeth - bpt 15 Aug 1779
  Joseph - bpt 21 Oct 1781
  Elizabeth - bpt 16 Nov 1793
  Mary - under 16 in 1796
  Thomas - under 16 in 1796
  Sally - under 16 in 1796
  Job - under 16 in 1796
REF: Shirley History, Seth Chandler 1883; Uplands and Intervales, Ethel Stanwood Bolton 1914.

CAMPBALL, James also Campbell

SERVICE: S&S Vol 3 p 37 & 52; BHist First Reg.
BORN: "In a foreign place" (Scotland), Shirley History; parents unk.
MARRIED: 12 Jul 1764 Tewksbury, Elizabeth Nickless.
DIED: Rockingham VT GS Old Cem.
CHILDREN (b Tewksbury):
  Mary - bpt 6 Oct 1765
  James - bpt 20 Jul 1766
  Hannah -
  Jennie - m Richard Haseltine
  Nicholas -
  Polly - m Phineas Fletcher 1790
NOTE: "Settled outside of Mass.," Shirley History; enlisted for Bolton, also for New Gloucester ME; pensioned list of 1813 $15 Roll #48.
REF: Shirley History, Seth Chandler 1883; LVR; VR of Rockingham VT; Uplands and Intervales, Ethel Stanwood Bolton 1914.

CARRUTH, Ephraim also Corruth

SERVICE: S&S Vol 3 p 146 & 1019.
BORN: 14 Aug 1761 Westborough s/o John & Miriam (Maynard).
MARRIED: 3 Jun 1792 Northborough, Sally Sera (Sarah Sever?).
DIED: Paxton after 1811.
CHILDREN (b Northborough):
  Abigail - b 13 Oct 1793
        (b Paxton):
  Sarah -
  Lois - b 1804
  Augusta - b 1806 d 1863 unm
  Charles Edward - b 1808
  Edwin E - b 1811
NOTE: Carruth Family says Ephraim was a surveyor; moved to Paxton 1795.
REF: Westborough VR; Northborough VR; Carruth Family, Harold B Carruth 1953.

CARTER, Abel

SERVICE: S&S Vol 3 p 149.
BORN: 22 Dec 1761 Lancaster s/o Ephraim & Abigail.
MARRIED: unm.
DIED: 8 Nov 1790 ae 29 Lancaster.
NOTE: bpt 27 Aug 1786 Lancaster.
REF: LVR.

CARTER, Daniel

SERVICE: S&S Vol 3 p 150; BRR service in RI; BRR reinforce Cont Army RI 3 mos Jun 1780 Ł18; BRR Cont Army 3 mos 1780 Ł19.
BORN: 27 Nov 1762 Bolton s/o Stanton & Penina (Albert).
MARRIED: 22 Sep 1785 Dolly Jones d/o Samuel of Berlin.
DIED: 29 Jul 1824 GSB.
CHILDREN (b Berlin):
  Amory – b 14 Jun 1785
  Samuel – b 2 Oct 1788
  Daniel – b 1 Feb 1790
  Leonard – b 19 Mar 1792
  Dolly – b 14 Feb 1794
  Lewis – b 17 Jul 1796 d 1878 ae 82
  Anna – b 1 Jun 1798
  Mary – b 29 Mar 1800
  Danforth – b 19 May 1802 d 1852 ae 50
  Rufus – b 27 Feb 1804 d 1842 ae 39
  Sally – b 1806
  Chandler – 7 Oct 1808 d 1891 ae 82
REF: BVR; Berlin History, Rev W A Houghton 1895.

CARTER, Stanton

SERVICE: S&S Vol 3 p 161; BHist Lex Alarm; BRR 8 mos Cont Army 1778 Ł25; BRR 8 mos service 1778 Ł100.
BORN: 5 Feb 1738 Bolton s/o Samuel Jemima (Houghton).
MARRIED: 27 May 1762 Penina Albert d/o Daniel.
DIED: 1823 Berlin no stone.
CHILDREN (b Berlin):
  Daniel – b 27 Nov 1762
  Sanderson – b 17 Aug 1764 d 1841 settled Maine
  Jemima – b 29 May 1766
  Stanton – b 1768 settled Maine
  Mary – b 1770 m Levi Wheeler
  Sarah – b 1773 m Peregrin Wheeler
  Samuel – 1776 settled Maine
REF: BVR; Berlin History, Rev W A Houghton 1895; DARPI.

CHAMBERLAIN, Ephraim

SERVICE: S&S Vol 3 p 254; BHist Lex Alarm.
BORN: 29 Apr 1725 Chelmsford s/o Samuel & wid Rebecca (Wilder)(Whitcomb).

CHAMBERLAIN, Ephraim (Cont)

MARRIED: 1) 9 Jan 1752 Westford, Esther Boynton; 2) 26 Nov 1801 Westford, Sarah Harwood.
DIED: after 1790 DARPI, poss Waterford ME.
CHILDREN (b Westford):
  Hannah – b 14 Oct 1752
  Nathaniel – b 27 Jun 1758 went to Waterford ME
  Abigail – b 25 Jun 1760
  John – 24 May 1762 went to Waterford ME
  Thomas – b 10 Nov 1764
  James – b 13 Nov 1767
  Ephraim – b 14 Apr 1768 went to Waterford ME
  Elijah – b 14 Nov 1770
  Sarah – b 30 Sep 1776
REF: Chelmsford VR; DARPI; Westford VR; Waterford ME History, H P Warren 1879.

CHAMBERLAIN, Sgt Wilder

SERVICE: S&S Vol 3 p 290; BRR 3 mos to Claverack Ł32 per mo 1778; BRR reinforce Cont Army 1779 3 mos Ł2-9-3.
BORN: 11 Jul 1754 Westford s/o Samuel Jr & Sarah.
MARRIED: 1) 29 Apr 1782 Bolton, Lucretia Longley (d 1784 Bolton GS1); 2) 22 Nov 1787 Bolton, Rebecca Bush of Hollis NH (m2 ___ Wilder Hollis NH).
DIED: 27 Aug 1812 Hollis NH GS Church Cem.
CHILDREN (b Bolton):
  Nathaniel – b 31 Jan 1783 d 1783 Bolton GS1
REF: Westford VR; BVR; History of Hollis NH, Samuel T Worcester 1879.

CHOWEN, John

SERVICE: S&S Vol 3 p 433; BHist Siege of Boston; BRR Resolve 1776 1 yr Ł3-12; BHist 12th Reg.
NOTE: Lived in Lancaster, but enlisted for Bolton. Deserted during siege of Boston "A mulatto, but calls himself Indian; had on a dark-colored coat and a pair of breeches something lighter." MilAnn by Nurse. However, enlisted for 1 yr in 1776 and enlisted in the 12th Reg later.

CLERK, Jonathan

SERVICE: S & S Vol 3 p 629; MilAnn Bennington Alarm 1777.
BORN: 26 May 1733 Harvard s/o Juda & Eunis.
MARRIED: 12 Oct 1757 Mercy Hapgood (d 23 Oct 1815 ae 82).

CLERK, Jonathan (Cont)

DIED: 5 Apr 1810 ae 84 yr GS Old Cem Harvard.
CHILDREN (b Harvard):
   Jonathan – b 28 Jan 1759
   Hannah – b 19 Sep 1762 m Jonathan
     Symons
REF: HVR.

COOLEDGE, Isaiah

SERVICE: Not in S&S; List of Capt David Nurse's men per his journal; BRR Money raised in Capt Nurse's Co 3 yrs ₤7-18; BRR 1777 Capt Nurse's Co; BRR Money deposited in Capt Nurse's hands for benefit of Co ₤2-2-0.
BORN: ca 1733 Watertown s/o Obediah & Rachel (Goddard).
MARRIED: 27 March 1759 Roxbury, Hannah Harrington.
DIED: unk.
CHILDREN (b Bolton):
   Abigail – b 24 Apr 1760 m Nathan
     Foster 1786 Berlin
   Stephen – b 5 Jul 1762 m1 1785 Lavinia
     Jones m2 1818 Mrs Betsy Wetherbee
   Moses – b 19 Aug 1764 m 1795 Berlin,
     Lucy Crosby
   Silas – b 9 Sep 1767 m1 1787 Nabby
     Osburn m2 1799 Phebe Holder
   Obadiah – b 16 May 1769
   Hannah – b 4 Sep 1771
   Isaiah – b 2 Oct 1777 m 1799 Anna
     Bruce
   Sarah – b 17 Aug 1781
REF: BVR; History of Berlin, Rev W A Houghton 1895; Berl VR.

COOLIDGE, John

SERVICE: S&S Vol 3 p 956; BHist Lex Alarm; BHist Siege of Boston; BRR 3 mos NY 1776 ₤10; DNR Winter Campaign 1776-7; BRR Boston 1778 Gen Heath; BHist Service RI 1781.
BORN: 1756 Bolton s/o Josiah & Mary (Jones).
MARRIED: 8 Sep 1779 Lancaster, Hannah Priest d/o James of Marlboro.
DIED: 23 Mar 1822 Plymouth VT.
CHILDREN (b Plymouth VT – then Saltash):
   Calvin – b 27 Mar 1780 m Sally
     Thompson
   Luther – b 6 May 1782
   Catherine Elizabeth – b 4 Apr 1784 d
     1862
   Fanny – b 2 Feb 1786 d 1790
   Oliver – b 13 Aug 1787 d 1815
   Polly – b 22 May 1790 d 1868
   John – b 12 May 1795 d 1796
NOTE: Ancestor of Pres Calvin Coolidge.
REF: BVR; LVR; Coolidge Genealogy, Emma

COOLIDGE, John (Cont)

Downing Coolidge 1930; DARPI; Early Families of Plymouth VT, Blanche Bryant.

COOLEDGE, Josiah, also Cooleg

SERVICE: S&S Vol 3 p 957 & 958; BHist Lex Alarm; BHist Siege of Boston; DNR Dec 1776.
BORN: 17 Jul 1718 Watertown s/o Obadiah & Rachel (Goddard).
MARRIED: 26 Apr 1742 Bolton, Mary Jones (d 14 May 1794 Springfield VT VR).
DIED: 25 Dec 1780 Lancaster.
CHILDREN:
   Mary – b 5 Jun 1743 Brookline
   Josiah – b 6 Sep 1744 m Tabitha Fulham
   Obadiah – b 1754, Saltash VT 1790
     census
   John – b 1756 m Hannah Priest d/o
     James
   Isaac – b 1761 Bolton
   Jones – or Jonas
   Rachel – m 1780 Shrewsbury, Abel
     Houghton
NOTE: Warned out of Bolton 12 May 1747 with wife Mary and children Mary and Josiah.
REF: BVR; LVR; Coolidge Genealogy, Emma Downing Coolidge 1930.

COOLIDGE, Stephen

SERVICE: S & S Vol 3 p 958; BRR 3 mos Boston 1776; BRR reinforcement to RI 1777; BRR Service Boston 1778; BRR reinforce Cont Army 3 mos 1779 ₤2-9-3; B Hist 6 mos men 1780; BRR Oct 1779 3 mos at Claverack ₤32 per mo.
BORN: 5 Jul 1762 Bolton s/o Isaiah & Hannah (Harrington).
MARRIED: 1) 31 May 1785 Berlin, Lavinia Jones d/o Samuel Jr; 2) 1 Nov 1818 Berlin, Mrs Betsy Wetherbee.
DIED: after 1825.
CHILDREN (b Berlin):
   Luther – b 9 Jan 1786 d 1851 unm
   Caleb – b 21 Dec 1787
   Sally – b 29 Sep 1789
   John B – b 29 Aug 1791
   Merrick – b 13 Jan 1794
   Otis – bpt 3 Apr 1796
   Betsy – bpt 13 May 1798
NOTE: Descriptive List 1780 – "age 18, 5'11"tall;" deeded land to son Luther in 1825.
REF: BVR; Berlin History, Rev W A Houghton 1895; Coolidge Genealogy, Emma Downing Coolidge 1930, Worc Co Reg of Deeds.

COLLIDGE, William, also Cooledg, Cooledge, Coolidge

SERVICE: S&S Vol 3 p 809, 956, 958 & 968; BHist Lex Alarm; BRR to Bennington Aug 1777; BRR Northern Army Aug 1777; BRR reinforce Gen Sullivan RI; BRR 6 wks RI 1778; BHist First Reg Sep 1778; BRR Boston 3 mos 1778 £11-7-4; BRR 3 1/2 mos 1778 this State or elsewhere £20 per mo inc all other wages.
BORN: 25 Sep 1758 Bolton s/o Philip & Lydia (Foskett).
MARRIED: 1) 27 Jul 1779 Templeton, Phebe Skimmings (d 10 Jun 1799 ae 49); 2) 31 Oct 1799 Bolton, Anna Eames (d 1847 ae 74).
DIED: 15 mar 1826 ae 72 GS2.
CHILDREN:
  Lydia – b 15 Apr 1781 Templeton m ___ Dunton, Westport NY
  Daniel – b 18 Jan 1785 Bolton, publisher NY City 1826
NOTE: also served for Templeton.
REF: BVR; Templeton VR; Worc Co Probate Records.

COREY, Ephraim

SERVICE: S&S Vol 3 p 1002 & 1024; BRR reinforce Cont Army 1780 £19; BRR reinforce Cont Army 3 mos 1780; MilAnn RI 1781.
BORN: 13 Mar 1736 Lexington s/o Sam'l & Bethshua.
MARRIED: 1) 10 Nov 1764 Stow, Susannah Stephens; 2) Lois Chase.
DIED: 1820.
CHILDREN (b Stow):
  Sarah – b 26 Jan 1765
  Mary – b 4 Apr 1767
  Samuel – b 26 Feb 1769
NOTE: Also credited to Stow per Lex Alarm, and also served for Groton.
REF: Lex VR; SVR; DARPI; Groton During the Revolution, Sam'l Green Abbott 1900.

CROSMAN, James also Crosmon, Crossman

SERVICE: S&S Vol 4 p 161, 165 & 175; BHist 15th Reg.
NOTE: A James Crossman in Mason NH in 1790 census 2-0-1.

CROUCH, Fifer Isaac

SERVICE: S & S Vol 4 p 178; BHist Bennington 1777.
BORN: 1 May 1760 Harvard s/o David & Mary (Brown).
MARRIED: unm.
DIED: Joined the Harvard Shakers, d after 1791.
REF: HVR; Harvard Shaker Records.

CURTIS, Timothy

SERVICE: S & S Vol 4 p 276; BHist Enlisted Cont Army 3 yrs 1781.
BORN: 1759.
MARRIED: 20 Mar 1780 Bolton, Hannah Sawyer (b Bolton 1761).
DIED: 10 Dec 1836 ae 77 Newburyport.
CHILDREN: unk.
NOTE: Bolton Selectmen's Order Book – "paid Tim'o curtis 15s for teaching school, 29 Mar. 1784." Also letter informing him the selectmen disapprove of his keeping school in Bolton, "not qualified."
REF: BVR; Newburyport VR.

DAVIS, Samuel

SERVICE: S&S Vol 4 p 539; BHist Capt Hez Whitney's Co 1778; Lineage Book Lex Alarm; DNR Dec 1776 Jersey.
BORN: 5 mar 1746 s/o Ephraim & Rebecca (Danforth).
MARRIED: 4 Jan 1770 Rutland, Rebecca Williams.
DIED: 13 Sep 1800 per Hist Princeton, F E Blake; or 1798 per DARPI.
CHILDREN (b Rutland):
  Pattie – b 14 Nov 1770
  Lucy – b 18 Aug 1772
  Samuel – b 9 Sep 1774 d 1855 m Abigail Park
  Silas – b 11 Jun 1776
  ___ – b 16 Apr 1778
  John – b 12 Feb 1780
  Nabe – b 3 Feb 1782
NOTE: Capt David Nurse reported S Davis & Joseph Fay engaged under Wagon Master Thomas Wickers 1777. 1798 Assessors list in Princeton has description of house assessed to Sam'l Davis.
REF: Rutland VR; Princeton History, F E Blake 1915; DARPI; Lineage Bk 31 p 47.

DOLLASON, John

SERVICE: S&S Vol 4 p 860; MilAnn 13th Reg 5 mos 1777.
BORN: unk.
MARRIED: 4 Jul 1786 Sterling, Esther Sawyer of Lancaster d/o Darius.
DIED: Lived in Clinton, prob d there but no rec found.
CHILDREN (b Lancaster):
  Samuel – b 26 Aug 1786
  John – b 3 Mar 1788
  Elizabeth – b 29 Nov 1789
  Nancy – b 4 May 1792
  Esther – b 5 Apr 1794
  Daniel – b 20 Apr 1796 d 1801
  Lucy – b 23 Apr 1798 d 1802
  Barzillai – b 21 Feb 1800
  Daniel – b 2 Apr 1802

DOLLASON, John (Cont)

Mary Ann - b 6 Aug 1804
Margaret - b 12 June 1806
NOTE: Claimed by Stow; 1790 census John Dolenson, Lancaster; name also Dorrison.
REF: LVR; History of Clinton, Andrew E Ford 1896.

EAGER, Haran

SERVICE: S & S Vol 5 p 136; BHist Enlised 3 yrs 1781; MilAnn Serv in RI 1781 3 mos.
BORN: 3 Jul 1763 Lancaster s/o Nath'l.
MARRIED: 11 May 1797 Lancaster, Betsy Dunlap of Lancaster.
DIED: 10 Oct 1829 ae 66 Lancaster "a Rev. Pensioner."
CHILDREN:
Samuel - b 29 Aug 1803
Mercy - b 25 Aug 1805
NOTE: State Archives Vol 24 p 211 - receipt to Capt Jacob Moore dated Bolton 12 Jun 1781 for bounty pd Haran Eager by a class of the town of Bolton to serve in the Continental Army for 3 yrs.
REF: LVR.

EDWARDS, Josiah

SERVICE: S&S Vol 5 p 240; BHist Lex Alarm; BHist Siege of Boston.
BORN: 5 May 1756 Stow, Benjamin & Elizabeth (Fairbanks).
MARRIED: unm.
DIED: In siege of Boston, winter of 1775-6.
NOTE: Died in the war and father claimed bounty coat or value thereof.
REF: SVR.

EVANS, Asa

SERVICE: S&S Vol 5 p 339.
BORN: 4 Oct 1760 Leominster s/o Nathaniel & Mary.
MARRIED: 1) Dorothy Buss (d 24 dec 1807 Peterborough NH); 2) Margaret Stuart Moore wid/o John.
DIED: 16 Oct 1813 GS Old Street Road Cem Peterborough NH.
CHILDREN (b Leominster):
John - b 9 mar 1782 m Martha Stuart
Asaph - b 13 Jul 1784 m Betsy Ferguson (b Peterborough NH):
Samuel - b 2 May 1786 m Margaret Allison
Prudence - b 15 Aug 1788 m Dr Wm P Cutter
Dorothy - b 24 Apr 1798 m Timothy Ames
Artemas - b 29 Jan 1792 m Widow Wiggins
Luke - b 13 Sep 1793

EVANS, Asa (Cont)

Nathaniel - b 22 Dec 1795 m Harriet Wiggin
Alpha - b 3 Jul 1797 m Hannah Emery
Stephen - b 3 Nov 1799
Mary - b 27 Sep 1801 m Capt Chas Chase
Louisa - b 10 Aug 1803 d 1826
REF: Leominster VR; Peterborough History, Smith 1876; Peterborough Soldiers in the Revolution, Hildreth Allison.

FAIRBANKS, Corp Ephraim, Sr

SERVICE: S&S Vol 5 p 454 & 462; MilAnn Lex Alarm; BHist 5 mos Capt Nurse 1775 "a turn;" MilAnn 3 mos 14 ds to Goose L 5.
BORN: 1721 Lancaster s/o Jabez & Hepsibah (Sawyer).
MARRIED: Achsah Goeth.
DIED: 18 nov 1799 in 75th yr "Esq" GS1.
CHILDREN (b Bolton):
Thankful - b 31 Jan 1746-7
Mary - b 14 Feb 1748-9 d 1765
Achsah - b 18 Mar 1751 m Jonathan Whitcomb 1772
Ephraim - b 28 Jun 1753 m Prudence Wilder
Jabez - b 27 Nov 1755 m Betsy Baker
Hepsibah - b 26 Feb 1758 m Edward Baker 1778
Jonathan - b 26 Feb 1761 m Parna Howe
Keziah - b 26 Apr 1763 m Nat'l Longley
Manassah - b 20 Dec 1765 m Abigail How
Caleb - b 30 Jul 1768 m Mary Goddard
NOTE: On coat rolls 1776; DARPI gives birthdate as 1724.
REF: LVR; BVR; DARPI; Mass Archives Vol LVI p 144.

FAIRBANK, Sgt Ephraim, Jr

SERVICE: S&S Vol 5 p 454; BHist Lex Alarm; BHist Siege of Boston; BRR reinforce Cont Army RI 3 mos Jun 1780 £12; BRR Cont Army 3 mos 1780; Mil ann RI 1781; BRR to Goose 3 mos 14 ds £5.
BORN: 28 jun 1753 Bolton s/o Ephraim & Achsah (Goeth).
MARRIED: 1) 21 Nov 1774 Bolton, Prudence Wilder; 2) 19 Nov 1815 Bolton (Int), Sarah Austin of Lunenburg; 3) 11 Feb 1821 Bolton, Betsy Brooks.
DIED: 12 Jan 1849 ae 83 GS3.
CHILDREN (b Bolton):
Molly - b 7 Jan 1776
Ephraim - b 11 Jun 1778 d 1831 m Lucy Babcock
NOTE: DARPI notes death of Ephraim Jr as "In the year 1831." This is an error; that was death of Ephraim 3rd. BRR calls him Deacon.
REF: BVR; Berl VR; DARPI.

FAIRBANK, Drummer Jabez, Jr

SERVICE: S&S Vol 5 p 454; BHist Lex Alarm drummer; BRR Resolv Dec 1775 6 wks; BRR Resolve Jan 1776 2 mos; BRR 5 mos NY Nov 1776; BRR 3 mos to NY 1776; BRR 3 mos 14 ds to Goose 1777 "a turn;" BRR RI May 1777; MilAnn In the Jerseys 1776-7; BRR 30ds reinforce North Army Sep 1777.
BORN: 22 Nov 1755 Bolton s/o Ephraim & Achsah (Goeth).
MARRIED: 1) 23 Jul 1778 Bolton, Lucy Bailey d/o Col Silas; 2) 19 Jul 1786 Berlin, Betty Baker d/o Judge Samuel.
DIED: 1794 Westminster.
CHILDREN (b Berlin to Lucy):
  Lucy - b before 1786
  Silas - b before 1786
  Jabez - b before 1786
        (b Berlin to Betty):
  Jabez -
  Polly - bpt 8 May 1796 Berlin "dau of Widow Betty"
REF: BVR; History of Berlin, Rev W A Houghton 1895; Berl VR; Westminster VR.

FAIRBANK, John

SERVICE: S&S Vol 5 p 464; BRR 2 mos men 1776.
BORN: 4 May 1731 Lancaster s/o Thomas & Dorothy.
MARRIED: 1) 10 Jul 1751 Lancaster, Relief Houghton (d 29 Oct 1795 ae 69 Athol); 2) Mrs Tabitha White DARPI.
DIED: 9 Feb 1817 in 86th yr Athol.
CHILDREN (b Lancaster):
  Relief - bpt 8 Mar 1752
  Nahum - b 9 Sep 1753
  Seth - b 28 Dec 1755
  Samuel - bpt 20 Mar 1757 d 3 Jun 1777 ae 20
        (b Athol):
  John - b 6 May 1755
  Benjamin - b 1 Aug 1759
  Dolly - b 14 May 1761 twin
  Dorotha - b 14 May 1761 twin d 27 Aug 1790 Charlemont
  Ephraim - b 2 Nov 1765 d 23 Dec 1844 ae 79
  Rhoda - b 11 May 1768
NOTE: Lancaster Church records - "Dismissed and recommended to the church in Pequog (Athol) 15 Aug 1759." Date of birth of son John 1755 must be an error.
REF: LVR; Athol VR; DARPI.

FAIRBANK, Jonathan

SERVICE: S&S Vol 5 p 455; BRR Bennington 1777; BRR Northern Army 1777; BRR reinforce Cont Army 3 mos 1779 ₤2-9-3; BRR 3 mos Claverack ₤32 per mo.

FAIRBANK, Jonathan (Cont)

BORN: 26 Feb 1761 Bolton s/o Ephraim & Achsah (Goeth).
MARRIED: 1) 12 Jan 1786 Berlin, Parna Howe (d 1793); 2) 7 May 1795 Berlin, Susan Cahoon of Waterford ME.
DIED: Waterford ME GS family lot.
CHILDREN (b Berlin):
  Jonathan - b 18 Apr 1787 Methodist preacher
  Phineas - b 6 Feb 1789
  Achsah - b 31 mar 1790 d young
  Parnel - b 3 Aug 1791 twin
  Acsah - b 3 Aug 1791 twin
  Lucretia (Cressy) - b 26 Nov 1796 m Bowdoin Wood
  Sophia - b 16 Aug 1799 m Josiah Pride
        (b Waterford ME):
  Susan - m ___ Norcross
  Ephraim -
REF: BVR; Berl VR; History of Waterford ME, H F Warren 1879.

FAY, Asa

SERVICE: S&S Vol 5 p 572; BHist Lex Alarm.
BORN: 19 Sep 1761 Northboro s/o Paul & Rebekah.
MARRIED: 7 Sep 1794 Grace (Mahan) Harrington.
DIED: 17 Apr 1837 ae 75 yr 6 mos 29 ds Northboro.
CHILDREN:
  Lewis - b 5 Nov 1794 m Anna Tilton
  Abraham - b 3 Nov 1797
REF: Northboro VR; DARPI; DAR Lineage Bk 52 p 428.

FAY, Corp John, Jr

SERVICE: S & S Vol 5 p 577; MilAnn reinforce Cont Army.
BORN: 23 may 1756 Southborough s/o John & Thankful.
MARRIED: 16 Dec 1779 Marlborough, Lavinia Brigham of Marlborough.
DIED: 14 Jun 1839 DAR.
CHILDREN (b Marlborough):
  Windsor - b 15 Jul 1780 d Bolton over 100 yrs old.
REF: MVR; DARPI; Southborough VR.

FERRIN, Michael

SERVICE: S&S Vol 5 p 629; BHist First Reg; MilAnn under Capt Jeremiah Hill.
BORN: ca 1758.
NOTE: Reported a stroller. Descriptive List 1780 - ae 22 5'8" light complexion red hair. Engaged for Bolton. Deserted from First Reg. See P 190 MilAnn. 1790 census North Yarmouth ME.

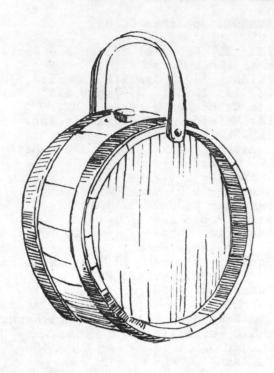

Eighteenth Century Wooden Canteen

FIFE, James

SERVICE: S & S Vol 5 p 658; MilAnn 8 mos
Dorchester Hghts 1776; BRR to Boston 3
mos 1776; BRR to Bennington Aug 1777.
BORN: 1719 Scotland.
MARRIED: 1742 Patience Butler (d 1816 ae
90).
DIED: 25 Jun 1779 ae 60 GSB.
CHILDREN (b Bolton):
  James - b Nov 1742 d young
  Silas - b 4 Oct 1743
  Molly - b 24 Feb 1745-6 m Robert
      Hudson
  Robert - b 11 Mar 1747-8
  Relief - b 27 Jan 1750 m Jonathan
      Whitcomb
  Patience - b 1751 d young
  Susannah - b 21 Mar 1752 m Capt Sam'l
      Woods
  Patience - b 1 Nov 1757 m William Fife
  James - b 24 Aug 1760 d 1790 unm
  Deliverance - b 22 Jul 1763 m Israel
      Maynard
  Samuel - b 16 Aug 1764 d young
  Sarah - b 7 Mar 1766 d 1782
  Martha - b 2 Oct 1767 m James Britain
REF: BVR; Berlin History, Rev W A Hough-
ton 1895; Berlin Grave List.

FIFE, James, Jr

SERVICE: S&S Vol 5 p 658; BRR 5 mos
Canady Jul 1776 ₤3-8-8; MilAnn Bennington 1777; BRR Northern Army Aug

FIFE, James, Jr (Cont)

1777;   BRR 30 ds Northern Army Sep 1777;
BHist Capt Hez Whitney's Co 1778.
BORN: 24 aug 1760 Bolton s/o James &
Patience (Butler).
MARRIED: unm.
DIED: 21 Nov 1790 ae 31 GSB.
NOTE: BRR spells name Feife
REF: BVR; Berlin History, Rev W A Hough-
ton 1895, Berlin Grave List.

MARRIED: unm.
DIED: 21 Nov 1790 ae 31 GSB.
NOTE: BRR spells name Feife
REF: BVR; Berlin History, Rev W A Hough-
ton 1895, Berlin Grave List.

BORN: 11 Mar 1747 Bolton s/o James &
Patience.
MARRIED: 11 Jul 1776 Hepsibah Bush of
Marlboro (m2 Wm Babcock).
DIED: 22 Apr 1787 ae 40 Berlin GSB.
CHILDREN (b Bolton):
  Lucy - b Nov 1777 d young
  Hannah - b 29 Jul 1778 m S Moore,
      Hillsboro NH
  Lucy - b 18 May 1780 m Curtis Pollard,
      Bolton
  Hepsibah - b 30 Sep 1781 m Asa Goss,
      Sterling
  Robert - b 3 Sep 1783 went to Florida
      MA
  Jesse - b 3 Aug 1785 m Lydia Kemp &
      went to Florida MA
  Sarah - b 1787 d 1803
REF: BVR; Berlin History, Rev W A Hough-
ton 1895.

FIFE, William

SERVICE: Not in S&S; BRR 5 mos Capt D
Nurse's Co 1775 ₤5-7-0; BRR 6 wks RI
1778; BRR Tower to Providence.
BORN: 10 May 1759 Bolton s/o William &
Abigail.
MARRIED: 1) 26 Dec 1786 Bolton, his
cousin Patience Fife (d 1830 ae 73); 2)
28 Jun 1832 Bolton, Anna Wheeler (d 1849
ae 80).
DIED: 28 Nov 1835 ae 76 Bolton GS3.
CHILDREN (b Bolton):
  Joseph - b 21 Oct 1788 d 1810
  Nancy - b 15 Apr 1792 m Josiah
      Billings 1824
  Patience - b 5 Jan 1794 m Abram
      Babcock 1838
  William - bpt 11 May 1794 m Mrs Sarah
      Brewer 1835
  Mary Ann - b 9 Nov 1796 d young
  Mary - b 1 Jan 1797 m Barnabus Brigham
      1824
REF: BVR.

FLOOD, James

SERVICE: S&S Vol 5 p 803; BHist Lex Alarm.
BORN: ca 1740.
MARRIED: 15 May 1764 Bolton, Betty Whitcomb d/o Israel & Azuba.
DIED: 24 Jun 1790 Marlboro, NH GS Center Cem "Deacon."
CHILDREN (b Bolton):
  Sarah - b 4 Sep 1765 m Henry Hunt
  James - b 16 Jul 1767 m Lois Hunt of Dublin NH
  Betsy - b 12 Nov 1771 d unm
  Israel - b 24 Jan 1776 m Lydia Porter (b Marlboro NH):
  Joseph - b 10 Oct 1779 m Betsy Priest
  Abigail - b 27 Jul 1782 m Daniel Priest
  Rufus - b 4 mar 1784
REF: BVR; History of Marlboro NH, Charles A Bemis 1881.

FOSGATE, Ezekiel

SERVICE: Not in S&S; BRR Resolve Sep 1776 2 mos to York; BRR to Canada £15-10; BRR £3 pd by John Bruce for "a turn."
BORN: 24 May 1744 Bolton s/o Robert & Sarah (Howe).
MARRIED: 30 Sep 1770 Leicester, Hannah Harrington (d 1823 at home of son Bela, Auburn, NY).
DIED: after 1817, possibly Herkimer Co NY.
CHILDREN (b Bolton):
  Bela - b 28 Jul 1773
  Greata - b 11 May 1775
  Ezekiel - probably
  Josiah - probably
NOTE: BRR spells name Fosgat; sold land to James Bruce 1785 (Worc Co Reg Deeds); 1790 census in Mohawk, Montgomery Co NY; 1800 census in Dutchess Co NY; 1817 was in Herkimer Co NY.
REF: BVR; Leicester VR; Berlin History, Rev W A Houghton 1895; Worc Co Reg Deeds.

FOSKETT, Joel

SERVICE: S&S Vol 5 p 881; BHist Lex Alarm; BRR Jul 1776 to York £2-13-6; BRR Paid E Johnson Jr for quarter turn; BRR Jul 1778 6 wks to RI; BRR Tower to Providence.
BORN: 16 Mar 1751 Bolton s/o Robert & Sarah (Howe).
MARRIED: 11 Dec 1777 Bolton, Naoma Gilbert of Brookfield (d Berlin 1839).
DIED: 21 Mar 1824 ae 73 GSB.
CHILDREN (b Bolton):
  Luke - b 12 Feb 1778 d young

FOSKETT, Joel (Cont)

  Robert - b 15 Aug 1779 m Hannah Sawyer
  Mendall - b 13 Jun 1781 m Sally Spofford
  Gilbert - b 15 Feb 1783 d 1811 (b Berlin):
  Joel - b 18 Dec 1784 d young
  Luke - b 5 Aug 1787 m Mary Rice joined Shakers 1844
  Betsy - b 5 Jan 1789 m Sam'l Spofford
  Sally - b 2 Apr 1791 m Stephen Puffer
  Sophia - b 4 Aug 1793 m Jas Maynard
  Susannah - b 28 Jul 1795 m Moses Brigham
  Lucy - b 16 Aug 1798 m Thomas Holder
REF: BVR; History of Berlin, Rev W A Houghton 1895.

FOSKETT, Robert, also Fosgate

SERVICE: Not in S&S; BRR to Goose w/Capt D Nurse 3 mos 14 ds 1777 L-7-6-6; BRR Donation £7-6-6 to hire men for Cont Army.
BORN: 1 Apr 1704 Charlestown s/o Robert & Mercy (Goodwin).
MARRIED: 1 Dec 1730 Newbury, Sarah Howe (b Marlborough 1714 d/o Josiah & Mary).
DIED: no record, probably after 1790.
CHILDREN:
  Sarah - b 24 Oct 1731 Marlborough
  Sarah - bpt 12 Oct 1735 Harvard m Sam'l White
  Mercy - bpt 12 Oct 1735 Harvard
  Mary - bpt 9 May 1736 Harvard
  Josiah - bpt 21 Sep 1740 Marlborough
  Robert - 21 Sep 1740 Marlborough
  Elizabeth - bpt 22 Aug 1742 Marlborough m John B Moulton
  Ezekiel - bpt 4 Nov 1744 Marlborough
  Patience - bpt 24 Aug 1746 Marlborough m Josiah Wilson
  Keturah - b 19 Aug 1748 Bolton m Sylvanus Billings
  Joel - b 16 Mar 1751 Bolton
  Olive - b 13 Oct 1755 Bolton m Asa Nourse
  Anna - b 24 Apr 1758 Bolton m John Hosmer
NOTE: Children bpt in Marlborough were b Bolton. In 1790 census Robert & wife were probably living with Joel, BRR spells name Fosgat.
REF: MVR; Charlestown VR; Newbury VR; HVR; BVR; Berlin History, Rev W A Houghton 1895.

FOSTER, Elijah, Sr

SERVICE: S&S Vol 5 p 897; BHist Lex Alarm.
BORN: 11 Mar or Nov 1727 Andover s/o Aaron & Martha (Smith).

FOSTER, Elijah, Sr (Cont)

MARRIED: 1) Elizabeth ___; 2) 4 Dec 1769
Elizabeth Knights.
DIED: 1790 DARPI.
CHILDREN (b Bolton):
  Israel - b 26 Dec 1752
  Elijah - b 23 Jun 1758 (1753?)
  Abner - b 10 Sep 1770
  Aaron - b 19 Jul 1773
REF: The Foster Family, E J Forster
1876; BVR; DARPI; Worc Co Reg Deeds.

FOSTER, Elijah, Jr

SERVICE: S&S Vol 5 p 897; BHist 15th
Reg; BRR Resolve Jan 1776 2 mos; BRR
July 1776 5 mos to Canada £3-5; BRR 1776
Canada £13-10; DNR engaged for 3 yrs
1777 £30-15.
BORN: 23 Jun 1758 (1753?) Bolton s/o
Elijah & 1st wife Elizabeth.
MARRIED: 4 May 1773 Ipswich, Elizabeth
Dresser.
DIED: unk.
CHILDREN (bpt Ipswich):
  Elizabeth - bpt 6 Mar 1774
  Elijah - bpt 16 Nov 1777
     (bpt Berlin):
  Jedediah - bpt 27 Jun 1784
  Joel - bpt 27 Jun 1784
  Ruth - bpt 2 Sep 1787
  Penelope - bpt 28 Sep 1788
  Aaron - bpt 26 Jun 1791
NOTE: Lex Alarm for Ipswich.
REF: BVR; Berl VR; Ipswich VR.

FOSTER, Israel

SERVICE: S&S Vol 5 p 904; BHist Lex
Alarm; BRR 5 mos to Canada Jul 1776 £3-
5; BRR Tower to Boston 3 mos 1776.
BORN: 26 Dec 1752 Bolton s/o Elijah &
1st wife Elizabeth.
MARRIED: Susannah ___.
DIED: unk.
CHILDREN (b Bolton):
  Timothy - b 30 Jan 1776
  Lucretia - b 9 mar 1777
NOTE: 1790 census in Washington, Ches-
hire Co NH.
REF: BVR.

FRENCH, Jacob

SERVICE: S & S Vol 6 p 4; BHist Lex
Alarm; BHist Siege Boston.
BORN: 20 Jan 1741-2 Billerica s/o Jacob
& Sarah.
MARRIED: 24 Feb 1767 Billerica, Eliza-
beth Kittredge of Tewksbury.
DIED: unk.
CHILDREN (b Billerica):
  Silent - b 7 Dec 1767 d 1767

FRENCH, Jacob (Cont)

  Elizabeth - b 6 Aug 1769
  Jacob - b 9 Apr 1771
  Hannah - b 16 Jan 1774
  Judah - b 28 Jan 1776
  Anna - b 27 Nov 1777
  Joel - b 30 Jan 1780
  Sarah - b 22 Dec 1782 m Benj Dowse
NOTE: Rec'd cartridge box 18 Jun 1775
(day after Bunker Hill). Lost his in
battle. 1790 census shows men of his
name in Berkley, Concord, Orange, Tewks-
bury, Walpole, Williamsburg, Seabrook
NH, Weathersfield VT.
REF: Billerica Hist.

FRENCH, James

SERVICE: S&S Vol 6 p 75; BRR Resolve
1776 1 yr £3-12.
BORN: 2 Aug 1746 Berkley.
MARRIED: 3 Nov 1774 Tabitha Crane.
DIED: 22 Feb 1828 Berkley bur fam lot
Berkley Community Cem.
CHILDREN:
  Ephraim - b 1775 d 1842 m Silence
     Hathaway 1795
REF: Berkley VR; DARPI; DAR Lineage Bk
151 p 217.

FRENCH, Corp John, Jr

SERVICE: S&S Vol 6 p 77; MilAnn Cont
Army 3rd Reg 1777-79.
BORN: 8 Apr 1757 Hollis NH s/o John &
Mary (Whitcomb).
MARRIED: Susannah White of Northfield.
DIED: unk.
NOTE: Dublin NH History says "a large
family" but gives no names. "A stroller
hired," MilAnn H S Nourse. Descriptive
List 1781 - ae 24, 5'9", light complex-
ion, sandy hair, blue eyes.
REF: Hollis NH VR; History of Dublin NH,
Rev Levi W Leonard and Rev Josiah L
Seward 1920.

FULLER, Amos (Amoz)

SERVICE: S&S Vol 6 p 148; BHist Lex
Alarm.
BORN: 1732.
MARRIED: 25 Mar 1762 Bolton (Amos of
Marlborough), Mary Coolidge of Bolton (b
1742 d/o Josiah).
DIED: 17 May 1810 Needham.
CHILDREN (b Bolton):
  Hannah - b 7 Oct 1762
  Molly - b 30 Sep 1764 prob d young
  Lucy - b 9 Nov 1766
  Rachel - b 9 Sep 1769
  Silas - b 5 Sep 1774
NOTE: Warned out of Bolton 21 May 1765

FULLER, Amos (Amoz) (Cont)

with wife Mary and dau Hannah.
REF: BVR; DARPI; Needham VR.

GALE, Jonathan

SERVICE: S & S Vol 6 p 232; MilAnn
reinforce Cont Army 1778.
BORN: 26 Sep 1762 Shrewsbury s/o Jona-
than & Margaret.
MARRIED: 11 May 1786 Royalston, Rhoda
Baker.
DIED: 19 Aug 1833 ae 71 Royalston.
CHILDREN (b Royalston):
   Isaac – b 23 Feb 1787
   Abigail – b 27 Jun 1789
   Jonathan – b 16 Jul 1800 m Patty
       Pierce 1817
REF: Shrewsbury VR; Royalston VR.

GATES, Cyrus

SERVICE: S&S Vol 6 p 311; BHist Lex
Alarm; BRR 2 mos 10ds York Sep 1776 £2.
BORN: 1 Apr 1732 Stow s/o Ephraim & Mary
(Hale).
MARRIED: 8 Jan 1753 Bolton, Ruth Bruce
of Bolton.
DIED: 8 Jul 1813 Boston.
CHILDREN (b Bolton):
   Cyrus Lovewell – b 30 Aug 1754 d 1770
   Ruth – b 5 May 1757 m Philip Atwood
   Eunice – b 12 Aug 1759
   Hannah – 25 Feb 1762
   Laban – b 16 Sep 1764 d 1837
   Ebenezer – b 14 Mar 1767
   Abiather b 20 Aug 1769 d 1841
   Lovel – b 19 Sep 1772
   Luther – b 17 mar 1775 d 1777
   Ephraim – b 1777
REF: BVR; DARPI; Stephen Gates of Hing-
ham & Lancaster and his Descendants,
Charles O Gates 1898.

GATES, Joseph

SERVICE: S&S Vol 6 p 317.
BORN: 7 Dec 1759 Framingham s/o Samuel &
Abigail (Blodgett).
MARRIED: 1) 15 Feb 1789 Rutland, Sarah
Roper of Rutland; 2) 12 Jun 1814 Sarah
Fiske of Holden (d 1820 Rutland); 3) ca
1820-30 Martha ___.
DIED: 4 Sep 1830 ae 70 Rutland.
CHILDREN (b Rutland):
   Lydia – b 6 Dec 1789 m ___ Wheeler
   Sally – b 4 Dec 1792 m ___ Hodges
   Joseph – b 29 Jan 1794
   Samuel – b 29 Aug 1797 physician
REF: Framingham VR; DARPI; The Ropers of
Sterling & Rutland, Ella E Roper 1904;
Rutland VR; Worc Co Probate Records.

GATES, Levi

SERVICE: S&S Vol 6 p 318; MilAnn Boston
1776 8 mos.
BORN: 27 Aug 1756 Stow s/o Samuel &
Margaret.
MARRIED: 7 oct 1779 Betty Brooks of
Stow.
DIED: 27 Oct 1827 Sterling.
CHILDREN (b Stow):
   Betty – b 12 Jan 1781 d 1843 ae 62
   Reuben – b 29 Jul 1783
   Margaret – b 13 Feb 1791 d young
   Lois – b 28 Dec 1793
   Sam'l – b 20 Feb 1797 twin d 1797
   Levi – b 19 Feb 1797 twin
NOTE: also served for Stow.
REF: SVR; Worc Co Probate Records; Ster-
ling VR.

GEORGE, Gideon

SERVICE: S&S Vol 6 p 356 & 643.
BORN: 8 Nov 1760 Kingston NH s/o Gideon
& Deborah (Stevens).
MARRIED: Apr 1782 Anna Chase of Brent-
wood NH.
DIED: 23 Feb 1817 Bradford VT.
CHILDREN (b Brentwood NH):
   Sarah – b 13 Aug 1784 m Peter Cross
   Susannah – b 1 Aug 1786 m Timothy
       Heath
   John – b 9 Apr 1789 m Amanda Kaye
       (b Bradford VT):
   Gideon – b 2 Jun 1791 d young
   Stephen – b 15 Jun 1793 m Lydia
       Leighton
   Dorothy – b 10 Apr 1795 m Timothy
       Heath (2nd wife)
   Gideon – b 11 May 1797 m Mart
       Highlands
   Ebenezer – b 12 Jul 1802 d 10 Jul 1814
NOTE: Descriptive List 26 Jan 1781 –
Capt Turner's Co Col Benj Tupper's 10th
Reg, 20 yrs, 5'9", dark complexion, dark
hair, residence Bolton.
REF: Concord NH VR; Family Records of
Charles A George 1982; Family Records of
Louis E George 1982.

GEORGES, Gideon

SERVICE: S&S Vol 6 p 361.
NOTE: Claimed by both Bolton and Lancaster. Descriptive List West Point 23 Feb
1780 – 1st Co 10th Mass Reg gives age 17
yrs, 5'4", black complexion, black hair,
residence Lancaster, term during the
war. The only other Georges who was
black claimed "The Bermudas" as his
birthplace and Freetown as his res.

GERRALL, John

SERVICE: S&S Vol 6 p 365.
BORN: ca 1765 Boston.
NOTE: Descriptive List 1782 - gives age 17 (also as 18), 5´4", light complexion, brown hair (also called light), farmer, born Boston, residence Bolton (also given as Shelburne). Also found in 1790 census in Boscawen, Hillsboro Co NH.

GIBBS, Daniel, alias Jonathan Gary

SERVICE: S&S Vol 6 p 380; MilAnn Capt D Nurse's Co 1776 p 148.
BORN: "came from Ashburnham" per History of Peterborough NH.
MARRIED: 15 May 1777 (Int) Princeton, Lidia Wood of Ashburnham (d 1836).
DIED: 25 Sep 1824 ae 74 Peterborough NH "In accident while carrying the mail" GS Old Street Rd Cem.
CHILDREN (b Peterborough NH):
 Polly - b 1 Apr 1780 d 1795
 Asa - b 29 Aug 1783 m1 Polly Gregg m2 Sally Porter
 Abel - b 18 Jul 1787 m Nancy Porter
 Lydia - b 29 Aug 1798 m John Gardner
 Sally - b 1800 d 1820
REF: Princeton VR; History of Peterborough NH, Albert Smith 1876.

GIBBS, Hezekiah, Jr

SERVICE: S&S Vol 6 p 381; BHist Lex Alarm; BRR Resolve 1776 to Canada ₤8-13-4; BRR 2 mos 10 ds NY Sep 1776 "a turn;" BRR 30 ds reinforce Northern Army Sep 1777; BRR Northern Army Oct 1777.
BORN: 18 Aug 1752 Bolton s/o Hezekiah & Elizabeth (Pratt).
MARRIED: 4 May 1775 Miriam Powers of Littleton.
DIED: Living in 1792 (father's will); died after 1800.
CHILDREN (b Bolton):
 Jonathan - b 18 Dec 1775
 Merriam - b 1778 m Sam'l Heard 1797
 Hezekiah - b before 1792 (g'father's will)
NOTE: Guardian appointed 1785 because of Hezekiah becoming "a drunkard and a spendthrift." Guardianship Case #23449A Worc Co Probate. Guardianship renewed 1800.
REF: BVR; Worc Co Probate Records.

GIBBS, Joseph, Jr

SERVICE: S & S Vol 6 p 385 & 386; MilAnn Capt Nurse's Co in the Jerseys 1776-1777.
BORN: 12 Oct 1756 Narragansett #2 (Templeton) s/o Joseph & Hannah (Howe).

GIBBS, Joseph, Jr (Cont)

MARRIED: 1) 1781 Princeton, Wid Abigail Richards; 2) Sally ___.
DIED: 20 Nov 1825 Ashburnham.
CHILDREN:
 Jonathan D -
 Azuba - m Allison Lake
 Betsy - m Jonathan Sampson
 Leavitt -
NOTE: Princeton History memtions that there were nine children.
REF: Templeton VR; Princeton VR; Ashburnham VR; Worc Co Probate Records.

GODDARD, Gardner

SERVICE: S&S Vol 6 p 519; MilAnn 10th Reg 9 mos 1779; BRR 6 mos RI 1779 ₤12-3-8.
BORN: 15 Apr 1763 Northborough s/o Josiah & Lydia (Ball).
MARRIED: 1) 11 Dec 1782 Holden, Sophia Rice of Worcester; 2) Anna Perry (d 1822 Paxton).
DIED: After 1832 per Probate Records.
CHILDREN (by Sophia):
 Ezra - b 2 Jun 1783
 Lydia - b 1785 m Nathaniel Crocker of Paxton
    (by Anna):
 William - d 1813 physician
 Anna - b 22 Nov 1793 d 1800 Wiscassett ME
 Luther - b 12 Mar 1796 Leicester
 Assenath - b Leicester
 Tyler - b Paxton
NOTE: Westborough VR calls him Garner; guardian appointed 1832 "Drunkard and Spendthrift" Case #24272A.
REF: Westborough VR; Northborough VR; Paxton VR; DARPI; Worc Co Probate Records.

GODDARD, James

SERVICE: S&S Vol 6 p 519; BRR Tower to Providence; BRR RI 1778; BRR to Canaday see note.
BORN: 6 Jan 1731 Marlborough s/o William & Keziah (Cloyes).
MARRIED: 11 Oct 1755 Westborough, Hannah Rice (b 1735).
DIED: 13 Jan 1815 ae 84 Berlin GSB "Deacon."
CHILDREN (b Bolton):
 Jacob - b 24 Jan 1757
 William - b 2 Aug 1758 d young
 Hannah - 27 Oct 1761 m Reuben Babcock
 James - b 15 Apr 1763
 Eunice - b 1765 m Capt Sam'l Spofford
 Molly - b 14 Dec 1769 m Caleb Fairbank
 Sarah - b 8 Jun 1772 m Alvin Sawyer
 Betsy - b 9 mar 1774 m Wm Barnes

26

GODDARD, James (Cont)

NOTE: from BRR "1 Aug 1776, then rec´d of Goddard Ł8 for 1/2 a turn of soldiering agoing to Canaday. Ezekeel Fosgate."
REF: MVR; Westborough VR; BVR; Berlin Grave Records; DARPI.

GODDARD, James, Jr

SERVICE: S&S Vol 6 p 519; BRR reinforce RI 1778 Ł4-8-10; BRR 6 wks RI 1778 Ł4-8-10.
BORN: 15 Apr 1763 Bolton s/o James & Hannah (Rice).
MARRIED: 28 Jul 1785 Berlin, Keziah Fairbank (d 19 Jul 1848 ae 85).
DIED: 19 Jan 1842 ae 79 GSB "Deacon."
CHILDREN (b Berlin):
  James - b 6 Feb 1786 d 1801 ae 16
  Betsy - b 25 Oct 1787 d 1808 ae 20
  William - b 22 Feb 1789 d 1808 ae 19
  Jacob - b 6 May 1791 m Abigail Morse
  Ephraim - b 19 Jan 1793 m Mary Bigelow
  Keziah - b 4 Jul 1795 d 1796 a 8 mo
  Keziah - b 26 Feb 1796 d 1807 ae 11
  Jabez - 20 Aug 1798 d 1807 ae 9
  Rebeckah - b 18 Jan 1801 m Theodore Morse
  Euseba - b 5 May 1804 m Calvin Smith
  James - b 8 Mar 1806 m Betsy Spafford
REF: BVR; BerlVR; Berlin Grave Records.

GODDARD, Josiah

SERVICE: S&S Vol 6 p 520; BHist 10th Reg 1777-9.
BORN: 29 Jul 1759 Northborough s/o Josiah & Lydia (Ball).
MARRIED: 8 Nov 1774(?) Athol, Ruth Raymond.
DIED: 23 Oct 1801 ae 55 "Esq" Brookfield.
CHILDREN (b Athol):
  Henry - b 5 Mar 1778
  Nathan - b 22 Jun 1780
  Susannah - b 1 Dec 1781 m Rufus Taylor
  Sally - b 4 Mar 1784
  Ashbel - b 13 Dec 1788
  Eber - b 27 Apr 1791 m Lucinda Fisk
  Daniel - b 14 May 1793
  Rhoda - b 17 Jun 1795
  Nabby - 22 Jun 1797
REF: Northborough VR; Athol VR; Brookfield VR.

GODDARD, Levi

SERVICE: S&S Vol 6 p 521; BRR to Canady 5 mos bounty Ł8.
BORN: 9 Sep 1762 Northborough s/o Solomon & Thankful.
MARRIED: 16 May 1799 Grafton, Polly Goddard of Grafton (d 24 Aug 1833 ae

GODDARD, Levi (Cont)

57).
DIED: 31 Jul 1848 ae 76 Grafton "worn out."
CHILDREN (b Grafton):
  Benjamin - b 14 Mar 1800
  Sally - b 30 Nov 1801
  John Flagg - b 11 Dec 1803
  Hulda Chandler - b 1 May 1805
  Levi - b 2 May 1807
  Mary Elizabeth - b 10 Apr 1809
  Loiza - b 10 Apr 1811
  Clarinda - b 24 Feb 1813
  Lucy Emeline - b 17 Feb 1815
  Martha E - b 4 Jul 1817
  Susan C - b 3 Oct 1819
NOTE: Engaged for town of Northborough. Descriptive List 1780 - gives age 17 yrs, 5´9". Patriot Index says d 1805 but he had 8 children after 1803; either date or age on gravestone is wrong.
REF: Northborough VR; Grafton VR; DARPI.

GODDARD, Moses

SERVICE: S&S Vol 6 p 521; BRR Resolve 1776 1 yr Ł3-12-10; BRR to Bennington Sep 1777; BRR 3 mos to Northward 1777 L 6-14-4; BRR Northern Army 1777 Ł6-3-4; BRR Bennington Alarm Aug 1777 Ł10.
BORN: 1742 Bolton s/o William & Keziah (Cloyes).
MARRIED: 1765 Molly Walker of Stukely Canada.
DIED: Removed to Conn & d there after 1795 per Berl Hist.
CHILDREN:
  Eber - b 5 Apr 1766 Marlborough
  Abel - b 22 Sep 1767 Northborough
  Moses - b 23 Feb 1771 Monadnock #5
  Elijah - b 17 Mar 1773 Monadnock #5
  Archelaus - b 13 May 1775 Northborough
  Silas - b 7 Mar 1778 Bolton
  Abram - b 22 May 1780 Bolton
  Solomon - b 16 Jul 1782 Bolton
  Molly - b 30 Oct 1785 Berlin
  Lydia - b Berlin m Aaron Green
  Calvin - bpt 30 Jan 1791 Berlin
REF: BVR; Berlin History, Rev W A Houghton 1895.

GOLD, Sgt Benjamin, also Gould

SERVICE: S&S Vol 6 p 541 & 662-664; BHist Lex Alarm; BHist Siege of Boston; BRR 5 mos York Jul 1776 Ł12; BRR reinforce Cont Army 1779 Ł2-9-3; BRR to Claverack 3 mos 1779 Ł50 exclusive of all other wages; BRR reinforce Cont Army 3 mos 1780 Ł12.
BORN: 29 Aug 1742 Chelmsford s/o Adam & Elizabeth.
MARRIED: 8 Jul 1767 Silence Atherton (b

GOLD, Sgt Benjamin (Cont)

1745 d/o Capt Benjamin).
DIED: 10 Jan 1818 Bolton no stone
CHILDREN (b Bolton):
  Silence - b 2 Jan 1768
  Benjamin - b 7 oct 1769 d young
  Benjamin - b 4 Mar 1772 m Betsy Parker
    removed to Princeton
  Moses - b 18 Sep 1774
  John - b 8 Mar 1777
  Samuel - b 27 Feb 1782
  Betsy - b 27 May 1785 d young
  Betsy - b 8 Apr 1787
NOTE: Capt Benj Hastings ordered cart-
ridge boxes 18 Jun 1775, the day after
Bunker Hill, incl one for Sgt Gould.
Also served for Stow, and as a black-
smith for Marlborough.
REF: Chelmsford VR; BVR; DARPI.

GOSS, Elihu

SERVICE: S&S Vol 6 p 653; MilAnn Capt
Richardson's Co; Mil Ann Capt Smith
1777.
BORN: 16 Mar 1760 Lancaster s/o Ephraim
& Keziah (Gary).
MARRIED: unm.
DIED: 6 Jul 1778 in Army.
REF: LVR.

GREENLEAF, Calvin, Sr

SERVICE: Not in S&S; MilAnn Guard at
Rutland; BRR Guard Rutland Sep 1779 Ł6-
16.
BORN: 31 mar 1740 Bolton s/o Dr Daniel
Sr & Silence (Nichols)(Marsh).
MARRIED: 17 Nov 1762 Becky Whitcomb (d
1787 ae 41 GS1 d/o Gen John & Becca).
DIED: 12 Aug 1812 ae 72 Bolton GS1.
CHILDREN (b Bolton):
  Calvin - b 1 Nov 1763 d 1785 Templeton
  Becke - b 10 Jun 1765 d 1776
  John - b 20 Mar 1767 m Abigail
    Townsend
  Dolly - b 1 Sep 1769 d 1776
  Daniel - b 2 Nov 1771
  Sarah - b 11 Jan 1774 d 1775
  Betsy - b 1 Apr 1776 m Levi Moore
  Asa - b 29 Sep 1778 d 1778
  Moses - bpt 12 Mar 1786 m1 Experience
    Sawyer m2 Mrs Lucy Sawyer
NOTE: Town Records 1783: "To see if the
Town will come into any method to re-
cover the wages that Calvin Greenleaf
drew for his son Calvin's service at
Rutland Guards, which was relinquished
by him to the Town. They are hereby
directed that in case sd Greenleaf will
not deliver up the certificate he drew
for his son Calvin's wages at Rutland
Guards that they bring an action against

GREENLEAF, Calvin (Cont)

him.
REF: BVR; DARPI; Greenleaf Genealogy,
Jonathan Greenleaf 1854.

GREENLEAF, Calvin, Jr

SERVICE: S&S Vol 6 p 786; Mass Archives
Muster Rolls XVV 120; MilAnn Guard at
Rutland; BRR Guard Oct 1779 Apr 1780 Ł6-
16; BRR Rutland 6 mos 1779 Ł25 per mo
including all other wages.
BORN: 1 Nov 1763 Bolton s/o Calvin &
Becky (Whitcomb).
MARRIED: unm.
DIED: 1 Jun 1785 ae 21 yrs 7 mos
Templeton.
NOTE: See note under Calvin Sr re wages.
REF: BVR; Templeton VR; Greenleaf Gene-
alogy, Jonathan Greenleaf 1854.

GREENLEAF, Dr Daniel, Jr

SERVICE: S&S Vol 6 p 848; BHist Resolve
Jun 1776; BRR 5 mos to York, Surgeon,
Jul 1776.
BORN: 2 Jul 1732 Hingham s/o Dr Daniel
Sr & Silence (Nichols, Marsh).
MARRIED: 4 Jun 1763 England, Anna (Nan-
cy) Burrell.
DIED: 18 Jan 1777 ae 44 yrs 4 mos 16 ds
Bolton GS1.
CHILDREN (b Harvard):
  Silence - b 8 Apr 1764
    (b Bolton):
  Eleanor - b 23 May 1766
  Daniel - b 20 Jul 1769
NOTE: Warned out of Bolton 11 May 1766
with wife Nancy and dau Silence from
Harvard. After Dr Daniel's death his
widow returned to England with her chil-
dren per Greenleaf Genealogy. He died
in the war.
REF: Hingham VR; HVR; BVR; Worc Co Pro-
bate Records; Greenleaf Genealogy, Jona-
than Greenleaf 1854; Worc Co Reg Deeds.

GREENLEAF, Daniel, 3rd

SERVICE: Not in S&S; Mass Archives Mus-
ter Rolls XVV 120; MilAnn Guard at Rut-
land Oct 1779 - Apr 1780.
BORN: 16 Jan 1764 Bolton s/o Stephen &
Eunice (Fairbank).
MARRIED: 22 Jul 1792 Sarah Townsend d/o
Joshua Jr.
DIED: 30 Dec 1845.
CHILDREN (b Bolton):
  Sarah - bpt 16 Nov 1794 m Tim'o
    Switcher
  Theophilus - bpt 8 Feb 1795
  Rebecca - bpt 15 Oct 1797 m John
    Greenleaf

Home of Dr. Daniel Greenleaf, Jr., on the Marlborough Road (Route 85). Razed ca. 1920.   Dr. Greenleaf was killed or died in the Revolution.

GREENLEAF, Daniel, 3rd (Cont)

(b Templeton):
Arad – d 6 Jun 1799 ae 6 mos
Daniel – bpt 5 Sep 1802 m Pamilla Greenleaf 1823
Mary Townsend – bpt 21 Oct 1804 m Levi Hill 1826
REF: BVR; Templeton VR; Greenleaf Genealogy, Jonathan Greenleaf 1854.

GREENLEAF, David

SERVICE: S&S Vol 6 p 848; BRR reinforce Army RI 1778; BRR 6 wks RI Jul 1778; BRR 6 mos Guards 1779 Ь6-16; BRR Rutland 6mos 1779 Ь25 per mo including all other wages.
BORN: 13 ul 1737 Bolton s/o Dr Daniel & Silence.
MARRIED: 2 Jun 1763 Mary Johnson of Coventry CT.
DIED: 11 Dec 1800 Coventry CT.
CHILDREN (b Lancaster):
David – b 1765 d 1835 m Anna N Jones
Daniel – b 1767 d 1842 m Abigail Forsyth
Annis – b 17 Jun 1770
Susannah – b 5 Jan 1772
John – b 1774 d 1851 m Catherine Dubois
REF: BVR; LVR; Greenleaf Genealogy, Jonathan Greeneaf 1854; DARPI; DAR Lineage Bk 127 p 98 & Bk 150 p 103.

GREENLEAF, John

SERVICE: S&S Vol 6 p 850; BRR 5 mos NY Jul 1776 Ь10.
BORN: 26 Mar 1760 Bolton s/o Israel & Prudence (Whitcomb).
MARRIED: 1) 3 Apr 1788 Rebecca Lewis; 2) Ann Millington.
DIED: 1827 Volney NY.
CHIILDREN: unk.
REF: BVR; Greenleaf Genealogy, Jonathan Greenleaf 1854.

HARRIS, Sgt Daniel

SERVICE: S&S Vol 7 p 339; BRR Service in RI 1780 Ь18; BRR reinforce Cont Army 1780 Ь19; BHist West Point Exped 1781.
BORN: 1758 Bolton s/o Jonathan & Annis (Houghton).
MARRIED: 1 Jan 1783 Northborough, Abigail Reed (d Lancaster 26 Mar 1842 ae 78).
DIED: 22 Oct 1838 ae 80 Lancaster GS Middle Cem "A Revolutionary Pensioner."
CHILDREN (b Northborough):
Betsy – bpt 1 Jul 1783
(b Boylston):
Polly – b 13 Aug 1785 d 1806
Emory – b 13 Aug 1788
Reed – b 23 Apr 1791 d 1794
Asahel – b 15 Oct 1793

HARRIS, Sgt Daniel

      (b Lancaster):
Reed - b 22 Sep 1795 d 1805
Maria - b 28 Jan 1798 m Alanson Chace
Sidney - b 23 Sep 1800 d 1802
Sidney - b 4 Oct 1804 m Sally Kilburn
REF: BVR; Worc Co History Vol 4 p 396;
LVR; Northborough VR; DARPI.

HASELTINE, Daniel

SERVICE: S&S Vol 7 p 645; MilAnn Rutland
Guards 1779.
BORN: 20 Dec 1761 s/o Abner & Martha
(Robbins) Goss.
MARRIED: Susannah Jones of Dover VT.
DIED: 26 June 1828 prob Busti NY.
CHILDREN (b Wardsboro VT):
Laban - b 7 Aug 1789 m ___ Flagel &
    settled in Jamestown NY physician
Chloe - b 8 Jun 1791 m David Dexter 2
    Feb 1815
Abner - b 3 June 1793 m1 21 Sep 1819
    Polly Kidder m2 21 Jul 1834
    Matilda Hayward
Daniel - b 9 Mar 1795 m 1818 Mehetabel
    Bemus Jamestown NY
Abraham - b 10 Jan 1797
Susannah -
Pardon - b 29 May 1801 m Abigail
    Wheelock & settled in Busti NY &
    later Worcester MA
Clark - b 24 Jun 1804
Edwin - b Mar 1807
Hardin - b Apr 1810
NOTE: 1790 census Wardsboro South (now
Dover) VT 1-1-1; 1800 census Wardsboro
North VT 1m 26-45, 1m 10-16, 3m -10, 1f
26-45, 2f -10. Abner Hazeltine grad-
uated from Williams College in 1815 at
the age of 22 yrs. Commenced the prac-
tice of law in Jamestown NY. He served
two terms in Congress & was for several
years district attorney and county judge
for four years (Return to Yesterday).
REF: DARPI; Wardsboro VT Town Records;
Genealogy of Robert & John Hazelton, W B
Lapham; Return to Yesterday, A History
of Wardsboro VT, Clarence S Streeter
1980; History of Chautauqua Co NY, Andrew W Young 1875.

HASELTINE, Corp Richard, also Hazeltine

SERVICE: S&S Vol 7 p 418 & 646; BHist
Lex Alarm; BHist Siege of Boston; BRR
Bennington 1777.
BORN: 28 Apr 1757 Lunenburg s/o Amos &
Eunice (Gilson).
MARRIED: 1) 30 Apr 1781 Dorothy (Dolly)
Walker d/o John of New Ipswich NH (d 22
Aug 1784 ae 25 yrs 11 mos; 2) 14 Nov
1787 Rockingham VT, Jane (Jennie) Camp-

HASELTINE, Corp Richard (Cont)

bell d/o James of Rockingham VT (d 30
Aug 1845 ae 81).
DIED: 20 Aug 1810 ae 54 bur Old Rocking-
ham Cemetery "wid. pensioned."
CHILDREN (b Rockingham VT):
Uriel - b 6 Jun 1788 m Amu Eddy
Dolley - b 28 Mar 1790 m Ezekiel
    Weston
David Baverly - b 18 Jan 1792 m Lucy
    Parker
Richard - b 23 Jun 1794 m Olive Eddy
Betsy - b 10 Jan 1798 m Phineas White
    Jr
Amos - b 26 May 1800 m Louisa Weston
James - b 1802 d 14 Jun 1807 ae 4 yr 9
    mo 2 ds
NOTE: There was another Richard Hazelton
in Westmoreland NH at the same time; he
went to Orford NH. Westmoreland History
gives info as if one man.
REF: Early Records of Lunenburg; History
of Westmoreland NH, Westmorelan Hist Com
1976; History of Rockingham VT, Lyman S
Hayes 1907; Old Rockingham Cemetery
Inscriptions in "The Detroit Society for
Genealogical Research Magazine," 1956-7;
DARPI.

HASKELL, Benjamin

SERVICE: S&S Vol 7 p 432; BRR NY 1776;
BRR Boston 1778 with Gen Heath; BRR 6
mos RI 1779 ₤12-3-8; BHist 9 mos men
1779; BRR Reinforce Cont Army RI 3 mos
1780 ₤12; MilAnn RI 1781.
BORN: 20 Aug 1747 Gloucester s/o William
5th and Elizabeth (Haskell).
MARRIED: 29 Oct 1775 New Salem, Sarah
Foster (d 18 Jun 1838 ae 83).
DIED: 8 Oct 1804 ae 58 GS Center Cem New
Salem.
CHILDREN (b New Salem):
Rebecca - bpt Sep 1779
Samuel - bpt Sep 1779
Jonathan - bpt May 1781 d 1784
Sally - b 4 Aug 1787
Benjamin - bpt 11 Oct 1789 m Lidia
    Adams
REF: Gloucester VR; New Salem VR.

HASKELL, Moses

SERVICE: S&S Vol 7 p 441; BHist 9 mos
men 1779; BRR 6 mos RI 1779 ₤12-3-8; B
Hist 6 mos men 1780; BHist Enlisted 3
yrs 1781.
BORN: 25 May 1760 Lancaster s/o Ezekiel
& Rebecca (Howard).
MARRIED: 6 Sep 1791 Harvard, Sarah Wil-
lard.
DIED: after 4 May 1818 when he applied
for pension in Marietta Township,

HASKELL, Moses (Cont)

Washington Co OH.
CHILDREN: unk.
NOTE: Descriptive List 1780 - lists Moses Haskell 20 yrs, 5´7" per State Archives Vol 34 p 203; An acc´t dated Bolton 25 Jun 1781 rendered by Selectmen of bounties pd sd Haskell & others to serve in Cont Army for a term of 3 yrs says sd H rec´d 10 silver dollars, 2500 Continental dollars, and 18 3 yr old cattle equivalent to ₺85 specie. He is reported as having marched without giving a receipt.
REF: LVR; HVR; Official Roster of Soldiers of the Army of the Am Rev of Ohio; Chronicles of the Haskell Family, Ira J Haskell.

HASKELL, Sgt William

SERVICE: S&S Vol 7 p 445; BHist Capt Hez Whitney´s Co 1778.
BORN: 20 Sep 1751 Harvard s/o Samuel & Sibel (Willard).
MARRIED: 8 May 1779 (Int) Harvard, Mercy Farnsworth.
DIED: 1815 Bolton no stone.
CHILDREN:
  Mercy - b 3 Sep 1788 Fitchburg
  Sarah Marble - b 18 Jun 1793 Fitchburg
  Ephraim - b 23 Sep 1797 Harvard
  Mary - b 7 May 1800 Lancaster
REF: HVR; BVR; Chronicles of the Haskell Family, Ira J Haskell.

HASTINGS, Capt Benjamin

SERVICE: S&S Vol 7 p 463; BHist Lex Alarm; BHist Siege of Boston; MilAnn Bunker Hill at the rail fence; BRR 3 1/2 mos 1778 this state or elsewhere ₺20 per mo including all other wages.
BORN: ca 1720 Watertown (town records missing 1702-1724).
MARRIED: 1743 Watertown, Abigail Sawtel.
DIED: 1808 or 1809 per tax records of Bolton, no stone.
CHILDREN (b Bolton):
  John - b 5 Oct 1744 d 1825 m Submit Russell
  Abigail - b 14 Nov 1746 m Samuel Moor 1776
  Susannah - b 1 Feb 1748-9 m Nath´l Oak Jr
  Elizabeth - b 25 Jan 1750 m Abner Moor 1769
  Ruth - b 26 Feb 1753 m Ezekiel Russell
  Edmund - b 24 Dec 1755 d 1769
  Grace - b 12 Apr 1757
  Benjamin - b 1763
NOTE: In French and Indian War as Ensign in 1755; was at Ft William Henry; a Lt

HASTINGS, Capt Benjamin (Cont)

in a reg´t for the reduction of Canada; Capt of a Co in Col Abijah Willard´s Reg; in 1759 "dismessed ye Servis with Disgrace for mutinous behavior." Was at "the rail fence" at Battle of Bunker Hill. His men were finally obliged to flee for lack of ammunition. Many lost most of their possessions. The next day, 18 Jun, Capt Hastings requisitioned a number of cartridge boxes for his men who had to leave theirs behind on the battlefield. No death recorded, however he is listed on the Bolton tax records up to 1808 but not in 1809 or thereafter. A brave and popular captain.
REF: BVR; Military Annals, H S Nurse; Bolton Tax Records; Watertown Records 1894; History of Sullivan NH, Rev Josiah H Seward 1921.

HASTINGS, Benjamin, Jr

SERVICE: S&S Vol 7 p 463; BRR 3 mos Boston 1778 ₺11-7-4; BHist Cont Army 9 mos RI 1779 ₺37-16; BRR reinforce Cont Army Jun 1780 3 mos ₺12; BRR Continental Army 1780; BRR 3 mos service 50 bu rye or money equivalent.
BORN: 1763 Bolton s/o Capt Benjamin & Abigail (Sawtelle).
MARRIED: 30 Jul 1782 Lancaster, Experience Ball d/o Nathan "both of Lancaster."
DIED: 9 Nov 1845 Sullivan NH GS Four Corners Cem.
CHILDREN (b Bolton):
  Lucy - b 26 Feb 1783 m John Foster 6 children
  Thomas - b 17 Dec 1784 drowned in Still River 4 Jul 1813 ae 28 bur Lancaster
  Nancy - b 3 Apr 1787 m John MacDonald of Boston
  Betsey - m ___ Barrett
  ___ - d young
  ___ - d young
  Lucretia - b 1796 m John Saunders
  Benjamin - b 1797 drowned in Still River 4 Jul 1813 ae 16 bur Lancaster
  Hannah - b 1799 m George Graves d Keene NH 1869 2 children
  Abijah - b 1801 prob Sullivan NH ml Sarah Hale 4 children m2 Sarah Richardson
  William - b 1805 d Sullivan NH 1866 m Lestina Emerson 11 children
  ___ - an infant "buried under the shade of the first tree n.w. of the house"
NOTE: Descriptive List 1779 - gives age 17, 5´9", light complexion. Benj Hast-

HASTINGS, Benjamin, Jr (Cont)

ings Jr was Overseer of Poor 1799 Bolton. "Thomas & Benjamin sons of Benjamin of Sullivan, NH drowned in Still River, Sabbath morning 4 July 1813. Funeral next day from First Church, buried Lancaster Middle Cem." History of Sullivan NH has picture of house Benj built at ae 80; he was pensioned.
REF: Shrewsbury VR; BVR; LVR; History of Sullivan NH, Rev Josiah Seward 1921; DARPI.

HASTINGS, John

SERVICE: S&S Vol 7 p 468; BHist Lex Alarm; BHist Siege of Boston; BRR 5 mos NY Jul 1776 L2; BHist 14th Reg 1777-9.
BORN: 5 Oct 1744 Bolton s/o Capt Benjamin & Abigail (Sawtel).
MARRIED: 31 Dec 1767 Bolton, Submit Russell (d 31 Oct 1816 GS1).
DIED: 4 Mar 1825 ae 80 Bolton no stone.
CHILDREN (b Bolton):
  Sarah - m ___ Tobias
  Mary - bpt 17 Sep 1786
  John - bpt 17 Sep 1786 m Eliz Moore
  Thomas - bpt 17 Sep 1786
  Annah - bpt 18 Sep 1791
NOTE: In 59th DAR report to Smithsonian a GS in Old Cemetery, Bolton, is reported. Not there in 1982.
REF: BVR; Berl VR.

HASTINGS, Nathaniel, also Hasting

SERVICE: S&S Vol 7 p 462 & 473; BHist Lex Alarm; BRR Resolve Sep 1776 to York 2 mos 10 ds; BRR 3 mos Boston 1776 L10.
BORN: 21 May 1738 (bpt) Lancaster s/o Nathaniel.
MARRIED: 8 March 1764 Lancaster, Elizabeth Goodnow (d 1830 ae 87).
DIED: 1820 ae 82 GSB.
CHILDREN:
  Francis - went west
  Abel - d young
  Parney - m Moses Chase of Groton
  Nathaniel - went to Canada
  Sylvanus - went to Wardsboro VT
  Elizabeth - d young
  Nahum - b 1779 settled Oakham
  Reuben - b 5 Aug 1781 m Hannah Puffer
  Benjamin - b 1783 m Abigail Hager
  Thomas - b 8 Jan 1786 d 1813
REF: LVR; Berlin History, Rev W A Houghton 1895.

HASTINGS, William

SERVICE: S&S Vol 7 p 478.
BORN: ca 1764 possibly s/o Capt Benjamin & Abigail.

HASTINGS, William (Cont)

MARRIED: 13 Dec 1787 Bolton, Mary (Polly) Gwinn.
DIED: 16 Dec 1836 ae 72 Bolton GS1.
CHILDREN (b Bolton):
  Abigail - b 24 Mar 1788
  Sally - b 25 Feb 1791
  Debby - b 18 Dec 1793
  William - b 18 Jul 1796
  Mary - b 8 Oct 1798
NOTE: Marched for Gov't in Shays Rebellion.
REF: BVR.

HATEN, James

SERVICE: S&S Vol 7 p 507; MilAnn West Point Exp 1781; MilAnn Butts Hill 1781.
BORN: 3 Jul 1758 Bolton s/o Daniel & Experience.
MARRIED: unk.
NOTE: Birth listed as Houghton; no further record.
REF: BVR.

HAUGHTON, Jacob, also Houghton

SERVICE: S&S Vol 7 p 535 & Vol 8 p 301; BHist Lex Alarm; BHist Col Wade's Reg 1777; BRR RI 1778 6 mos L12-10.
BORN: 7 Dec 1757 Bolton s/o Timothy & Eunice.
MARRIED: 17 Feb 1785 Olive Houghton of Harvard (d 1825).
DIED: 26 Dec 1836 ae 79 Bolton no stone.
CHILDREN (b Bolton):
  Elizabeth - b 18 Nov 1785
  Jacob - b 25 Oct 1787
  Levi - b 5 Jul 1789
  Asa - b 18 Dec 1791
  Eunice - b 13 May 1794
REF: BVR.

HAWKS, John

SERVICE: S&S Vol 7 p 562; BRR 3 mos to Northward 1777; BRR 3 mos Northern Army 1777.
BORN: 14 Jul 1754 Lynn.
MARRIED: 1) Hannah ___; 2) Rachel Bancroft.
DIED: 26 Jan 1827 Lancaster "Old Age."
CHILDREN:
  Polly - b 4 Nov 1775
  Polly - b 13 Nov 1776
  John - b 6 Dec 1777
  Rachel - b 25 Sep 1779 m James LaKeman 1798
  Sally - b 6 Nov 1780 d 1814 m Lemuel Whiting
  Pamela - b 11 Nov 1781 d 1794
  Adam - b 26 Apr 1798 d 1869 m Dolly Carter, Mansfield

HAWKS, John (Cont)

NOTE: DARPI says John Hawks died 3 May 1811. Speech of Joseph Willard, Esq., Lancaster 1826 mentions "John Hawks, one of 6 Revolutionary soldiers still living."
REF: Lyn VR; BVR; LVR; Lynnfield VR; DARPI; DAR Lineage Bk 109 p 308.

HAZARD, Levi, also Hazzard

SERVICE: S&S Vol 7 p 643 & 650; MilAnn Enlisted 1781 3 yrs.
BORN: ca 1756
NOTE: Descriptive List 1780 - gives 24 yrs, 5´8", black complexion, farmer. Many Hazzards lived in Harvard and Shirley.

HAZELTINE, Nathaniel, also Hazelton

SERVICE: S&S Vol 7 p 648; MilAnn to RI 1779 2 mos.
BORN: 1738 Lunenburg s/o Nathaniel.
MARRIED: 30 May 1758 Harvard, Patience Whitcomb.
DIED: 9 Jul 1829 ae 91 Hancock NH GS Pine Ridge Cemetery.
CHILDREN (b Harvard):
  Sarah - b 22 Apr 1759 m Phineas Taylor
  Hannah - b 29 May 1760 m Gabriel
     Priest Jr in Harvard
  Patience - bpt 21 Feb 1762 m Wm
     Willard Jr in Harvard
  Nathaniel - bpt 23 Dec 1763
REF: Lunenburg VR; HVR; Prelude to Hancock´s Second Hundred Years, Ptd by Tuttle, Hancock NH; List Rev Soldiers bur Hancock NH.

HEMENWAY, Corp Joshua

SERVICE: S&S Vol 7 p 703; BRR 30 ds reinforce Northern Army; BRR Northern Army Oct 1777.
BORN: 28 Apr 1755 Framingham s/o Sylvanus & Hephsibah (Frost).
MARRIED: Melicent ___.
DIED: 18 Mar 1817 Sudbury "A native of Framingham" by law, but "an inhabitant of Bolton" per Sudbury records.
CHILDREN (b Bolton):
  Jesse - b 16 Dec 1783
  Rebeckah - b 13 Jan 1788
  Susannah - b 9 Jun 1792
  Betsy - b 18 Dec 1794
NOTE: Warned out of Bolton 6 Jan 1767, Joshua from Concord; a schoolmaster per Framingham History; also claimed by Stow.
REF: Framingham VR; Framingham History, William Barry 1847; Sudbury VR; BVR; DARPI.

HEMENWAY, Simeon

SERVICE: S&S Vol 7 p 705; MilAnn Lex Alarm; MilAnn Siege of Boston.
BORN: 4 Oct 1752 Framingham s/o Jonathan & Mary (Foster).
MARRIED: 4 May 1777 Bolton, Mary Goss d/o Rev Thomas.
DIED: 3 May 1818 Framingham.
CHILDREN (b Bolton):
  Francis - b 11 Aug 1777
  Judith - b 28 May 1780
  Sopha - b 20 Nov 1787
  Phineas - bpt 6 Sep 1794
  Thaddeus - bpt 6 Sep 1794
  Abigail - bpt Nov 1797
NOTE: Also credited to Lancaster; he was a tanner & built Harvard Rd tannery in Bolton.
REF: Framingham VR; Framingham History, William Barry 1847; BVR; Ralph Hemenway´s Descendants, Clair A H Newton 1943; Files of Bolton Hist Society.

HEMINGWAY, David, also Hemmenway & Hemmingway

SERVICE: S&S Vol 7 p 706, 712 & 713; MilAnn Dorchester Hts 1776; MilAnn reinforce Cont Army 1778.
BORN: 23 Jul 1758 (bpt) Framingham s/o Ralph Jr & Lydia (Trowbridge).
MARRIED: 30 May 1787 (int) Holden, Polly Davis of Holden.
DIED: in Heath "by the fall of a tree" before 1797.
CHILDREN (b Hubbardston):
  son - b 17 Aug 1788
  son - b 24 Mar 1791
  David - bpt 10 Sep 1797 "s of wid
     Polly" in Heath
REF: Framingham VR; Holden VR; Hubbardston VR; Ralph Hemenway of Roxbury and his Descendants, Clair A H Newton 1943; Heath VR.

HILE, John, also Hill

SERVICE: S&S Vol 7 p 861 & 887; DNR 1776; BHist Capt Hezekiah Whitney´s Co 1778; BHist Enlisted 3 yrs 1781.
BORN: 11 Sep 1763 (bpt) Harvard s/o John.
MARRIED: 27 Nov 1782 Sarah Davis of Groton.
DIED: 11 Apr 1832 Harvard GS Old Cem.
CHILDREN (b Harvard):
  John - b 25 Oct 1785 m Betsy Chaffin
     1817
NOTE: Descriptive List 2 Dec 1780 - gives age 16 yrs, 5´2", light complexion, farmer; Descriptive List 20 Feb 1782 - gives age 16 (also 17), 5´4" (also 5´3"), light compexion (also

HILE, John (Cont)

dark), hair brown (also dark), laborer.
REF: HVR; Groton VR.

HINESTON, Roberto, also Hinesman
& Kinsman

SERVICE: Not in S&S; BRR NY 2 mos 1776
bounty ₤4.

HOAR, Joseph

SERVICE: S&S Vol 8 p 5; BHist Siege of
Boston; MilAnn Battle Kips Bay 1776;
MilAnn 5th Reg Cont Army 3 yrs 1777.
BORN: 20 Feb 1735-6 Littleton s/o Benja-
min & Esther.
MARRIED: 1) 18 Dec 1760 Littleton, Lucy
Ruggles; 2) Mary Farwell of Littleton (d
1820 Brimfield).
DIED: 5 Feb 1816 Brimfield ae 75 "Capt."
CHILDREN (by Mary):
  Betty – b 16 Jul 1765 Littleton
  Joseph – b 7 Oct 1767 Littleton
  Luther – b 31 Dec 1769 Leominster
  David – bpt 16 Aug 1772 Leominster
REF: Littleton VR; Leominster VR; Brim-
field VR; Hoar Family in America, H S
Nourse 1899.

HOBSON, Stephan also Holman, Homans

SERVICE: S&S Vol 8 p 24, 158 & 204; BRR
Bennington Sep 1777; BRR reinforce Nor-
thern Army 30 ds; BRR 3 mos to Northward
1777 ₤10-17; BRR Guard at Rutland 6 mos
1778 ₤8-4-8.
BORN: 6 Jul 1762 Templeton s/o Nathaniel
Jr & Abigail (Atherton).
MARRIED: 3 Oct 1793 Groton, Rhoda Rus-
sell d/o Ephraim (d 1845 Caanan ME).
DIED: unk.
CHILDREN (b Groton):
  Abigail – b 1793 d 1814
        (b Caanan ME):
  Levi – b 1796 d 1870
  Merrick – b 1797 d 1816
  Aisah – b 1800
  Sullivan – b 1801 d 1841
  John Pitts – b 1803
  Jonas Welsh – b 1805 d 1873
  Nathaniel – b 1807 d 1834
  Bowin – b 1809 d 1898
  Sophia Abigail – b 1813
NOTE: Pensioned; DARPI gives birth as 20
Oct 1763 & death as 19 Feb 1850.
REF: Templeton VR; Groton VR; Skowhegan
on the Kennebec, Coburn; DARPI.

HODSON, Corp Elisha

SERVICE: S&S Vol 8 p 56; BHist Lex
Alarm.

HODSON, Corp Elisha (Cont)

BORN: 24 Sep 1744 Bolton s/o John &
Elizabeth (McAllister).
MARRIED: 4 Oct 1770 Susannah Brigham d/o
Dr Samuel & Anna (Gott).
DIED: 17 Apr 1815 Newport, Compton Co
Quebec Canada.
CHILDREN:
  Benjamin – b 1 Sep 1773
  William – b 29 Mar 1776 m Anna Morse
  Samuel Brigham – b 25 Dec 1777 m1
      Submit Rice m2 Polly Abbott
  Charles – b 1783 m1 Anna Abbott m2
      Ruth Tibbetts
  Robert Breck – b 1785
  Susannah – b 17 Aug 1791
  Nancy –
  Eliza – b 1798
  Achsah – m ___ Farnsworth
  Reuben – lived Ontario Canada
REF: BVR; Marlborough History, Charles
Hudson 1862; DARPI; DAR Lineage Book 148
p 249.

HOLLAND, Ephraim

SERVICE: S&S Vol 8 p 127; MilAnn Cont
Army 1778.
BORN: 21 Jun 1714 Marlborough.
MARRIED: 11 Dec 1739 Shrewsbury, Thank-
ful Howe of Worcester (d 1792 Boylston).
DIED: 20 Aug 1786 Boylston.
CHILDREN (b Shrewsbury):
  Tabitha – b 23 Apr 1742 m Benj Hinds
      Shrewsbury
  Eunice – b 24 Sep 1744 m Abel Osgood
  Levinah – b 14 Feb 17-- m Joshua Morse
  Thankful – b 24 Oct 1748 m Josiah
      Randall
  Ephraim – b 22 Oct 1755 m Eunice
      Newton
  Joseph – b 19 Oct 1756 m Eliz Gleason
  James – b 5 Jun 1758
  Nathaniel – b 11 May 1761 d 1784
REF: MVR; DARPI; Shrewsbury VR; Boylston
VR.

HOLMAN, Abraham, Sr

SERVICE: S&S Vol 8 p 153; BHist Lex
Alarm.
BORN: prob 1730 Lexington s/o Nathaniel
& Elizabeth (Knight) d/o Jonathan.
MARRIED: 1) Abigail Atherton d/o Capt
Benjamin (d 1777); 2) 21 Oct 1780 Pru-
dence Mills (m2 Thaddeus How, Marl-
borough).
DIED: Nov 1782 ae 52 GS1 (error in BVR,
will dated 1783).
CHILDREN (b Bolton):
  Calvin – b 20 Dec 1757 d 1778 or later
  Silas – b 2 Aug 1760 m Betsy Atherton
  Abraham – b 30 Aug 1762 m Abigail

HOLMAN, Abraham, Sr (Cont)

Nurse d/o Capt Samuel 1784
Jonathan - b 26 Dec 1764 m Eunice Bush 1792
Nathaniel - b 5 Jul 1767
John - b 5 Sep 1769 m Abigail Nurse d/o Capt David 1793
Betty - b 29 Jun 1772 m Robert Townsend
Oliver - b 29 Aug 1774 ml Caty Nurse d 1804 m2 Sarah Nurse
Asa - b 15 Aug 1777 m Becca Houghton 1799
NOTE: Abraham made will 10 Sep 1783, filed 1784. Will gave Silas his oldest living son only one share because son Calvin, the oldest, died after he became of age. To Betty, only daughter, only 11 years old "ħ60, all her mother's things and remainder of my estate by law of Commonwealth." Oliver Barrett, sole executor refused app't. Jonathan Whitcomb & Caleb Sawyer made oath that sd Abraham was not capable of making a valid will because of his illness. Judge refused to probate. Silas and step-mother Prudence app'ted co-admin.
REF: BVR; Atherton Genealogy, F L Lewis; Worc Co Probate Records.

HOLMAN, Calvin

SERVICE: S&S Vol 8 p 153; BHist Lex Alarm; BRR 5 mos NY 1776; BRR 2 mos NY 1776 ħ4.
BORN: 20 Dec 1757 Bolton s/o Abraham & Abigail (Atherton).
MARRIED: unk.
DIED: after 1778 according to father's will, but before 1782 when father died.
NOTE: There is no stone for him in family lot in Bolton; did he die in war?
REF: BVR; Worc Co Probate Records.

HOLMAN, Nathaniel, Jr

SERVICE: S&S Vol 8 p156; BHist Lex Alarm; BRR 3 mos Northward 1777 ħ10-6-8; BRR RI 6 mos 1778 ħ12-10; BRR 2 mos RI 1779 ħ5-6-8; BRR Bennington Sep 1777.
BORN: 30 Aug 1733 Lancaster s/o Nathaniel & Elizabeth (Knight) d/o Jonathan.
MARRIED: Abigail Atherton (m2 Levi Houghton of Lunenburg & d 1819 GS1).
DIED: 14 Jan 1805 ae 70 GS1.
CHILDREN:
Nathaniel - b 24 Nov 1760
Stephen - b 6 Jul 1762
Charles - b 6 Jul 1765
Jonas - b 6 Jul 1767
Molly - bpt 8 Aug 1769
Levi - b 26 Jul 1777 d 22 Aug 1796
REF: LVR; BVR; Templeton VR; DARPI.

HOLMAN, Nathaniel, 3rd

SERVICE: S&S Vol 8 p 156; BHist Wade's Reg 1777; BRR 3 mos to Northward 1777; BRR Bennington Exped 1777; BRR Service RI 1778; BRR service RI 1779; BRR reinforce Northern Army 30 ds; B Hist West Pt Exped 1781.
BORN: 24 Nov 1760 Bolton s/o Nathaniel Jr & Abigail (Atherton).
MARRIED: 13 Feb 1792 Bolton, Abigail Houghton (d 1844 ae 77).
DIED: 1830 Bolton no stone.
CHILDREN:
Nathaniel - b 1801 d 1842 ae 41
REF: BVR.

HOLMAN, Silas

SERVICE: S&S Vol 8 p 158; MilAnn 6 wks RI 1778; BRR 1778 reinforce Gen Sullivan RI.
BORN: 2 Aug 1760 Bolton s/o Abraham & Abigail (Atherton).
MARRIED: 6 Sep 1785 Bolton, Betsy Atherton (d 11 Mar 1844, d/o Eliakim & Elizabeth (Sawyer)).
DIED: 25 Apr 1846 ae 86 bur fam lot Pan Cem no stone.
CHILDREN (b Bolton):
Betsy - b 30 Jan 1787 d unm 1825 GS2
Silas - b 21 Jan 1789 physician in ME
Sally - b 1 May 1791 m Rev Nath'l Whitman of Billerica
Amory - b 15 Apr 1793 d 1794
Amory - b 17 Jan 1796 m Fanny Whitcomb
Eliakim Atherton - b 20 Apr 1799 m Lucinda Whitcomb physician
Louisa - b 30 Nov 1803 d 1809
Horatio Nelson - b 21 Dec 1806 d 1809
Martha - b 26 Aug 1811 m John Eveleth
NOTE: General in Militia.
REF: BVR.

HOLT, Thomas

SERVICE: S&S Vol 8 p 196.
BORN: 1 March 1749 Lancaster s/o Thomas & Susannah (Parker).
MARRIED: 13 Dec 1770 Bolton "both of Lancaster" Molly Corey of Lancaster (d 1803).
DIED: 29 Sep 1808 Bolton GS1.
CHILDREN (b Lancaster):
Molly - bpt 23 Aug 1772
Lucy - bpt 15 Nov 1772
Sarah - bpt 8 Sep 1776
NOTE: credited to Andover.
REF: LVR; BVR.

HOPPING, John

SERVICE: S&S Vol 8 p 250; MilAnn 2nd Worc Reg to RI 1778; BRR reinforce Army

HOPPING, John (Cont)

to RI 1778.
BORN: 1762 per DARPI.
MARRIED: Elizabeth Hoppin (d 10 Dec 1836 ae 73 Templeton).
DIED: 1839 per DARPI.
CHILDREN:
   Asa - m Betsy Stockwell 1828
NOTE: Tything man in Bolton 1798. Sold land in Bolton 1784, 1792, 1793, 1803. Living in Bolton 1809-1817, took care of paupers. Assessed in Bolton for house $1000 in 1820 but not in 1821. Sold land in Templeton 1821.
REF: Worc co Reg Deeds; DARPI; Templeton VR; Sterling VR; Bolton Selectmen's Order Books.

HOUGHTON, James

SERVICE: S&S Vol8 p 301; Town Records, service in RI pd ₤1 1783.
BORN: 25 Aug 1764 Bolton s/o John & Keziah (Ross).
MARRIED: 8 Sep 1789 (Int) Beckey (Rebecca) Dunton.
DIED: 1811 Bolton per Worc Co Probate, no stone.
CHILDREN (b Bolton):
   Asenath - b 24 Mar 1790 d Jul 1790
   John - b 12 Dec 1791
   Ziba - b 9 Dec 1793
   Rebecca Liscomb - b 29 May 1795
   Europe - b 26 Mar 1797
   Melinda - b 29 Apr 1799 d Mar 1816
   Thos Jefferson - b 1 Aug 1801
   Norman - b 17 Mar 1804
   Zenas - b 5 May 1806 d 1840
   Jonathan - b 26 Aug 1808 d 1808
   James - d 24 July 1810
REF: BVR; Worc Co Probate Records; Bolton Selectmen's Order Book.

HOUGHTON, Lt John

SERVICE: S&S Vol 8 p 301; BHist Lex Alarm; BHist Siege of Boston; BRR Resolve Jun 1776 5 mos ₤12; BRR 5 mos NY Jul 1776; BRR Service in RI 1781 as Lt.
BORN: 14 Sep 1739 Bolton s/o John & Hepzibah (Priest).
MARRIED: 14 Jun 1763 Sudbury, Keziah Ross d/o John & Submit.
DIED: 1807 Bolton no stone.
CHILDREN (b Bolton):
   James - b 25 Aug 1764 m Becky Dunton
   Keziah - b 27 Apr 1767 unm d 1859(?)
   John - b 1 May 1770
   Judith - b 6 Aug 1774 m John Kimmens
REF: BVR; Sudbury VR; DARPI.

HOUGHTON, Capt Jonas

SERVICE: S&S Vol 8 p 302.
BORN: 1728 Lancaster s/o Capt Jonas & Mary (Brigham).
MARRIED: 1) Rebecca Nichols (d 1772 ae 43); 2) Lucy Johnson (d 1794 ae 44).
DIED: 21 Nov 1801 ae 73 Bolton GS1.
CHILDREN (b Bolton to Rebecca):
   Jaazaniah - b 3 Jan 1754 d 1828 m Ruth Tower
   Sarah - b 25 Oct 1756
   Jonas - b 24 Apr 1760 twin
   Rebecca - b 24 Apr 1760 twin
      (b Bolton to Lucy):
   Eleazar - b 13 Mar 1776
   Silas - b 17 Sep 1777
   Lucy - b 30 Jun 1780
   Levi - b 3 Sep 1783
   Sabra - b 30 Sep 1786
REF: LVR; BVR; DARPI.

HOUGHTON, Jonas, Jr, also Haughton & Haugton

SERVICE: S&S Vol 7 p 535 & Vol 8 p 302; MilAnn Dorchester Hts 1776; BRR Service in NY 1776; MilAnn Service RI 6 mos 1778 ₤12-10; BRR reinforce Cont Army 1780 L 19; BRR reinforce Cont Army RI 3 mos Jun 1780 ₤12.
BORN: 23 Apr 1760 Bolton s/o Jonas & Rebecca (Nichols).
MARRIED: 10 May 1781 Bolton, Eunice Houghton (d 1842 ae 78).
DIED: 1 Dec 1847 ae 87 yrs 7 mos 7 ds "Major" GS3.
CHILDREN (b Bolton):
   Phineas - b 17 Jun 1782 d 1833
   Eunice - 18 May 1784 m Thomas Moore
   Emery - b 9 Sep 1787
   Mary Sawyer - b 5 Sep 1792 m Jacob Goddard
   Achsah - b 8 May 1795 d 1839
   Lucinda - b 2 Sep 1797 m Abraham Wilder
   Jonas - b 9 Feb 1800 d 1804
   Sanford - b 22 Feb 1803 m1 Emily Moore m2 Miriam Houghton
NOTE: In 1840 was a pensioner ae 80. Major in Bolton Militia after Rev.
REF: BVR.

HOUGHTON, Capt Jonathan

SERVICE: S&S Vol 8 p 303; BHist Lex Alarm; BHist Siege of Boston; BHist Resolve Jun 1776; BRR 5 mos NY Jul 1776 as Capt.
BORN: 7 Nov 1737 Lancaster s/o Jonathan & Mary (Houghton).
MARRIED: 24 Nov 1759 Bolton, Susannah Moore of Cambridge (d 19 Sep 1809 "widow Susannah").

HOUGHTON, Capt Jonathan (Cont)

DIED: 29 Oct 1780 Bolton no stone.
CHILDREN (b Bolton):
 Susannah - b 6 Jan 1761
 Unity - b 19 Sep 1762
 Abigail - b 1763
 Jonathan - b 5 Apr 1765 m Jane Bigelow
  d/o Wm
 Abigail - b 26 Sep 1767
 Rufus - b 6 Dec 1769
NOTE: Military Service p 317 Houghton Genealogy, J W Houghton.
REF: BVR; DARPI; Houghton Genealogy, J W Houghton 1912.

HOUGHTON, Joseph

SERVICE: S&S Vol 8 p 304; BHist Siege of Boston; BRR 3 mos NY 1776 ₤13-8-8; B Hist Col John Jacobs' Reg; DNR carpenter Winter campaign 1776-7.
BORN: 24 Jan 1746-7 Bolton s/o Benjamin & Mary.
MARRIED: 29 Nov 1770 Lancaster, Lois Ross (b 13 Aug 1745 Scotland d 1812 "widow").
DIED: before 1812.
CHILDREN (b Bolton):
 Benjamin - b 22 Jan 1770
 Joseph - b 29 Sep 1772
 Betsy -
 Mary -
 Nancy -
 Thomas - b 10 Feb 1781
NOTE: Capt Benj Hastings requisitioned cartridge boxes on 18 Jun 1775, the day after Bunker Hill; one was needed by Joseph Houghton.
REF: BVR; LVR.

HOUGHTON, Rufus

SERVICE: S&S Vol 8 p 307; BHist 6 mos men 1780; BHist Cont Army 16th Reg 1781; BRR Cert of Bounty 1780.
BORN: 8 May 1764 NH s/o Lt Jonathan & Sarah.
MARRIED: 1 Feb 1788 Pittstown, Rensalear Co NY, Mary Gleason (b 1766 d/o Moses).
DIED: 25 Jul 1814 in battle of Lundy's Lane, Canada War of 1812.
CHILDREN:
 Keziah - b 1788 m ___ Ogden d
  Galesburg IL
 Rufus - b 6 Jul 1791 d 1865 in Shaker
  Comm, Cleveland OH
 Luther - b 1800 wounded in War of 1812
  pensioned rest of life
NOTE: Certificate signed by Paul Whitcomb 1780 "Pd Rufus Houghton Bounty to serve in the Continental Army, 1780. ₤3 hard money ₤750 paper money. Obligation to deliver 18 3-year-old cattle if he

HOUGHTON, Rufus (Cont)

serves 3 years. If 1 year, 1-year-old cattle." per Bolton records. Descriptive List 1780 - gives age 17 (and 18), 5′5″, light complexion, light hair, farmer, born NH, res Bolton. Pension records show widow Mary applied 1854 ae 88 living Brantford, Can. Received $3.50 a month.
REF: Houghton Genealogy, J W Houghton 1912, DARPI; Pension Records GSA, Wash DC.

HOUGHTON, Sanderson, also Hougton

SERVICE: S&S Vol 8 p 308 & 310; BHist Lex Alarm.
BORN: 1716 Woburn s/o Henry & Abigail (Barron).
MARRIED: unm.
DIED: 24 Nov 1799 ae 93 GS1.
REF: Woburn VR; BVR.

HOUGHTON, Silas

SERVICE: S&S Vol 8 p 308; BRR Money raised in Capt Nurse's Co for 3 yrs ₤5.
BORN: 7 Oct 1742 Lancaster, Chockset Parish, s/o Benjamin & Zerviah.
MARRIED: 1) 26 Oct 1768 Lancaster, Eunice Sawyer "both of Lancaster;" 2) 20 May 1773 Bolton, Sarah Wyman of Harvard; 3) 22 Jun 1778 Lancaster, Mary Knight "both of Lancaster" (d 1 Nov 1778); 4) 19 Sep 1781 Lancaster, Juda Houghton "both of Bolton."
DIED: 9 Jun 1797 Brattleboro VT.
CHILDREN: unk.
REF: LVR; BVR; Brattleboro VT VR.

HOUGHTON, Simon, also Hougton

SERVICE: S&S Vol 8 p 309 & 310; BHist Lex Alarm; MilAnn Bennington Alarm 1777; BHist Capt Hez Whitney's Co 1778.
BORN: 13 Nov 1737 Lancaster s/o Jacob Jr & Mary.
MARRIED: 6 Dec 1770 Martha Stearns (d 1823 GS Old Common Cem).
DIED: 25 March 1814 ae 76 yrs 5 mos 10 ds Bolton GS Old Common Cem Lancaster, DAR marker.
CHILDREN (b Bolton):
 Timothy - b 12 Sep 1771 m Olive Moore
 Simon - b 19 Feb 1773 d Weare NH 1814
  ae 41
 Asa - b 3 Feb 1775 GS Old Common Cem
 Jacob - b 15 Feb 1777
 Dinah - b 28 May 1779 d 1786 ae 7
 Martha - b 16 Oct 1781 m Orsamus
  Willard
 Mary - b 11 Apr 1784
 Sam'l Stearns - b 20 Aug 1786 m Nancy

HOUGHTON, Simon (Cont)

Pollard
Daniel - b 25 Nov 1788
Josiah - b 3 Nov 1790
Abigail - b 4 Dec 1792
NOTE: DAR says b 13 May 1737.
REF: DARPI; LVR; BVR.

HOW, Capt Artemas

SERVICE: S&S Vol 8 p 327; BHist Lex Alarm.
BORN: 23 Mar 1734 Bolton s/o David & Mary (Reed).
MARRIED: Abigail ___.
DIED: after 1790 prob Westford, Otsego Co NY.
CHILDREN (b Bolton):
David - b 7 Nov 1757
Joseph - b 21 Jul 1759
Abigail - b 9 Sep 1761
Moses - b 2 Oct 1763
Silas - b 27 Apr 1766
Levi - b 23 Jul 1768
Jonathan - b 5 May 1771
Mary - b 9 Jun 1773
Artemas - b 22 Oct 1775
NOTE: removed to Brattleboro VT about 1777. Served in army from VT. About 1790 removed to Westford, Otsego Co NY with sons David, Joseph, Moses, Silas & Levi. Built first mill in town. No record of death.
REF: BVR; LVR; DARPI; Howe Genealogies, G B Howe 1929.

HOW, David

SERVICE: S&S Vol 8 p 338; BHist Siege of Boston.
BORN: 7 Nov 1757 in Bolton s/o Artemas & Abigail.
MARRIED: Eunice Earl in Brattleboro VT.
DIED: 7 Sep 1834 Camillus, Onondaga Co NY.
CHILDREN:
Stephen - b 5 Feb 1785
Jonathan - b 11 Aug 1789
James - b 23 Nov 1793 d 1812
Phineas - b 3 Aug 1796 d 1817
Waite - b 13 Jul 1798 m Stephen Britten
Ardilla - b 3 Nov 1801 d 1818
NOTE: Went with his farther to Brattleboro VT, then to Westford, Otsego Co NY, then to Camillus, Onondaga Co NY.
REF: BVR; Howe Genealogies, G B Howe 1929.

HOW, 2nd Lt Joseph

SERVICE: S&S Vol 8 p 340-1; BHist Lex Alarm; BRR Resolve 1775 6 wks; BRR Re-

HOW, 2nd Lt Joseph (Cont)

solve Jan 1776 2 mos; BRR 5 Mos to York 1776; BRR Sep 1776 2 mos NY "a turn;" BRR reinforce Northern Army 30 ds 1777; BRR Northern Army 1777.
BORN: 1 Feb 1728 Marlborough s/o Joseph & Ruth (Brigham).
MARRIED: 21 May 1751 Marlborough, Grace Rice d/o Simon & Grace.
DIED: 26 Sep 1800 ae 72 Marlborough.
CHILDREN (b Marlborough):
Levinah - b 19 Jul 1751 m Peter Rice
Ruben - b 12 Oct 1752
Simon - b 14 Aug 1754
Samuel - b 2 Oct 1756
Lucy - b 18 Sep 1758 m Thomas Tileston
Eli - b 20 Jul 1760 d in Army
Hepsibeth - b 15 Sep 1762 d 1773
Daniel - b 4 Aug 1764
Joseph - b 20 Sep 1768 d 1773
Miriam - b 16 Oct 1770 m John Coats
Hepsibah - b 5 Apr 1773 m Jacob Barnes
Joseph - b!8 May 1775
REF: MVR; DARPI; Howe Genealogies, G B Howe 1929.

HOW, Levi

SERVICE: Not in S&S; BRR 6 wks men 1775; BRR 2 mos to York 1776; BRR Feb 1776 2 mos.
BORN: 20 Oct 1764 Lancaster s/o Silas & Abigail (Moore) d/o Isaac.
MARRIED: 13 Feb 1787 Molly Ross of Boylston (d 1842).
DIED: 9 Jun 1826 Boylston.
CHILDREN (b Boylston):
Micah - b 4 Aug 1787 d 1795
Levi - b 27 Jun 1789
Abel - 5 Jul 1791 d 1793
Thina - b 11 Aug 1795 m Sam'l Brigham Jr
Jotham - b 22 Nov 1797
Micah - b 26 May 1800
REF: LVR; Boylston VR.

HOW, Paul

SERVICE: Not in S&S; BRR 5 mos to Canady 1776 bounty L8-13-7.
BORN: 8 Jun 1715 Marlborough s/o John Jr & Deliverance.
MARRIED: Elizabeth Howe d/o Jon'a & Sarah.
DIED: 31 Oct 1789 Paxton.
CHILDREN (b Marlborough):
Susannah - b 8 Feb 1738-9 d 1739
Millicent - b 11 Mar 1740 m Abel Brown (b Paxton):
Martha - b 14 May 1742 m Ephraim Davis
Elizabeth - b 10 Jun 1744 m Jeduthan Stone
Jonah - b 2 Jul 1746 m Sarah Newton

HOW, Paul (Cont)

Delia - b 24 Sep 1748 m Silas Newton
Windsor - b 27 Mar 1751
Sarah - b 25 May 1753 d 1760
John - b 19 Mar 1756 m Lucy Hubbard
Francis - b 9 Sep 1758 d 1760
Jonathan - bpt 4 Oct 1761 d 1835
REF: MVR; Paxton VR.

HOW, Phineas

SERVICE: S&S Vol 8 p 346; BRR Tower to
Providence; BRR Jul 1776 5 mos Canady Ł
8-13-7.
BORN: 1733 Marlborough s/o Phineas &
Abigail (Bennett).
MARRIED: Experience Pollard of Bolton.
DIED: 14 Mar 1832 ae 94 prob Concord NH
(lived with dau Polly Baker).
CHILDREN (b Bolton):
Silas - b 28 Apr 1760
Lucrece - b 4 Oct 1761 m Sam'l Goss
Mary (Polly) - b 10 Nov 1763 m Abel
Baker, moved to Concord NH
Parne - b 24 May 1765 m Jon'a Fairbank
Sarah - b 1 Mar 1767 m Silas Sawyer
Phineas - b 25 Mar 1769
Experience - b 1 Apr 1771 d young
Betty - b 19 Apr 1773
Abraham - b 24 Jun 1776
NOTE: BRR names Phineas as ensign.
REF: MVR; BVR; Berlin History, Rev W A
Houghton 1895.

HOW, Silas

SERVICE: S&S Vol 8 p 347; BRR Northern
Army Aug 1777; BRR Money raised in Capt
Nurse's Co for 3 yrs Ł10; BRR to Ben-
nington Aug 1777.
BORN: 28 Apr 1760 Bolton s/o Phineas &
Experience (Pollard).
MARRIED: 2 Nov 1780 Silence Moor d/o
Abraham & Silence.
DIED: Prob Rumford ME.
CHILDREN (b Bolton):
Jaazaniah NIchols - b 14 Mar 1781
Rebecca - b 1782
Becca Hubbard - b 22 Sep 1783
Samson - b 1786
Sophia - b 6 Feb 1791
Sally - b 15 Feb 1795 twin
Siley - b 15 Feb 1795 twin
(b Rumford ME):
Hannah - b 1798
Lydia - b 1802
NOTE: Silas How of Concord NH was warned
out of Bolton 1790 with wife & four
children.
REF: BVR; Berlin History, Rev W A Hough-
ton 1895.

HOWARD, Sgt Edward Jr

SERVICE: S&S Vol 8 p 360; MilAnn 15th
Reg 1777.
BORN: 24 Jan 1756 W Bridgewater s/o Col
Edward & Susannah (Howard).
MARRIED: 25 Sep 1780 W Bridgewater,
Melly Howard of Braintree.
DIED: 18 Jan 1842 Detroit MI GS Woodmere
Cem.
CHILDREN (b Bridgewater):
Walter - b 8 Dec 1780
(per Hist Bridgewater):
Church? -
Warren -
Cyrus -
Joshua -
Edward -
2 daughters
REF: DARPI; Bridgewater VR; History
Bridgewater, Nahum Mitchell 1840.

HOWARD, Job

SERVICE: S&S Vol 8 p 366.
BORN: 20 May 1758 W Bridgewater s/o
George.
MARRIED: Hannah Capen (d Bolton 1848 ae
84).
DIED: 1 Oct 1844 ae 86 yrs 4 mos 12 ds
GS3 Rev marker.
CHILDREN (b Bolton):
Barnard - b 23 Dec 1783 m Hannah ___ d
1816
Levi - b 6 Dec 1788 m Mary Houghton
Amasa - b 13 Jul 1790
Hannah -
Daniel -
NOTE: Served for Bridgewater; came to
Bolton about 1783.
REF: W Bridgewater VR; BVR; DARPI.

HUDSON, Charles

SERVICE: S&S Vol 8 p 455.
BORN: 1759 Marlborough s/o John & Eliza-
beth (McAllister).
MARRIED: unm.
DIED: killed in Continental service.
NOTE: Accidentally killed by "friendly
fire." "Two scouting parties met in the
night time, each mistaking the other for
the enemy, fired and killed Charles
Hudson and another man." Berlin History.
REF: MVR; Marlborough History, Charles
Hudson 1862; Berlin History, Rev W A
Houghton 1895.

HUDSON, John, Sr

SERVICE: S&S Vol 8 p 459; BHist Siege of
Boston.
BORN: 1713 Marlborough s/o Nathaniel &
Jane (Bannister).

HUDSON, John, Sr (Cont)

MARRIED: Elizabeth McAllister of Northboro.
DIED: 6 Aug 1799 Berlin no stone.
CHILDREN:
  Elijah – b 11 May 1740 m Hannah Goodnow in Northboro
  Elizabeth – b 1 Nov 1742 m Levi Fay
  Elisha – b 24 Sep 1744 m Susanna Brigham
  Miriam – b Apr 1746 m Jonas Babcock
  Moses – b 4 Jan 1749 d Bolton unm.
  Aaron – b 24 Aug 1750 killed Lex Alarm from Marlborough
  Hannah – b 20 Jul 1752 d Berlin unm
  Ebenezer – b 16 May 1755 d Rev Army while serving for Marlborough
  John – b 9 May 1757 m Bethia Woods 1787, moved to Oxford
  Charles – b 1759 killed Rev Army while serving for Bolton
  Stephen – b 12 Jun 1761
NOTE: Warned out of Bolton 1762, ´63, ´64, ´65. John Hudson and 2 sons were in French and Indian war as well as in Revolution.
REF: Marlborough History, Charles Hudson 1862; Berlin History, Rev W A Houghton 1895; DARPI.

HUDSON, Moses also Hutsen

SERVICE: S&S Vol 8 p 460 & 591; BHist Siege of Boston; BRR Resolve 1776 1 yr ₤ 3-6; MilAnn 4th Reg; BRR RI Jun 1780 ₤ 18; BRR reinforce Cont Army 3 mos 1780 ₤ 19.
BORN: 4 Jan 1749 Marlborough s/o John & Elizabeth (McAllister).
MARRIED: unm.
DIED: Bolton no stone.
REF: Marlborough History, Charles Hudson 1862; BVR; Berlin History, Rev W A Houghton 1895.

HUNT, Sgt Sherebiah

SERVICE: S&S Vol 8 p 539; MilAnn 2 mos RI 1779.
BORN: 30 Jul 1758 Lancaster s/o Lt Sherebiah & Deborah (Wilder).
MARRIED: 1) 16 May 1780 (int) Ruth White (d 30 Oct 1794); 2) 12 Apr 1796 Princeton, Dorothy (Mirick) Garfield (d 1846 ae 83).
DIED: 6 Mar 1826 Ashburnham ae 67 "Dea."
CHILDREN (b Ashburnham):
  Deborah – b 21 Jul 1780 m John Stearns
  Dorothy – b 9 Apr 1797
  Ruth – b 3 Jun 1799
  Sherebiah – b 9 Jan 1802
REF: LVR; Princeton VR; Ashburnham VR; DARPI.

JAY, Drummer Richard, also Jey

SERVICE: S & S Vol 8 p 728 & 800; MilAnn 16th Reg; MilAnn Cont Army 1781 3 yrs.
BORN: ca 1763
NOTE: "Engaged for Bolton, 1777, Credited to Bolton, 1779;" decriptive list gives age 18 5´7" light complexion light hair yeoman res Bolton.

JEWEL, Jonathan, also Jewell, Juel

SERVICE: S&S Vol 8 p 786, 789 & 1026.
BORN: 12 May 1762 Stow s/o William & Lucy (Gibson).
MARRIED: 1785 Elizabeth Whitcomb of Stow.
DIED: unk.
NOTE: Enlisted for town of Bolton. Descriptive list 1778 gives age 17 5´4" light complexion res Stow. Also claimed by Stow. In Adams in 1790 census.
REF: SVR.

JEWETT, Jesse, also Jewet

SERVICE: S&S Vol 8 p 791 & 795.
BORN: 17 Nov 1753 Pepperell s/o Edward & Susan (Farmer).
MARRIED: 10 Dec 1778 Bolton, Hannah Johnson (d 1849 ae 94).
DIED: 5 Feb 1829 ae 76 Berlin GSB.
CHILDREN (b Berlin):
  Joshua – b 4 Apr 1782 d 1804 ae 22
  Jesse – b 30 May 1792 m Myra Cotting
  Hannah – b 2 Sep 1793
REF: BVR; Berl VR; Jewetts of America, Frederic Clark Jewett MD 1908.

JEWETT, Lt John, also Jewet

SERVICE: S & S Vol8 p 791 & 1026; BRR Bennington Sgt 1777; BRR Northern Army; BRR 3 mos to Northward 1777.
BORN: 6 Nov 1749 Pepperell s/o Edward & Sarah (Farmer).
MARRIED: 27 Aug 1776 Stow, Eunice Patch of Stow (d 30 Dec 1843).
DIED: 8 Feb 1802 ae 52 Bolton GS1.
CHILDREN (b Bolton):
  Eunice – b 19 Jun 1777 d unm
  Josiah – b 12 Oct 1778
  Sarah – b 13 Jun 1780 d unm 1830
  Lydia – b 11 Nov 1781 d unm
  Rachel – b 27 Feb 1783 m Daniel Sawyer
  Benjamin – b 14 Mar 1785 d 1809
  Relief – b 4 Nov 1787 m ___ Robbins
  Joseph – b 17 Aug 1790 d 1804
  Asenath – b 20 Oct 1793 m Eli Davis
REF: Jewetts of America, Frederic Clark Jewett MD 1908; BVR; Pepperell VR; Stow VR.

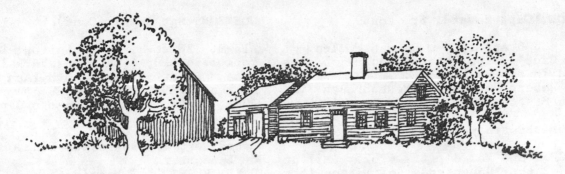

Home of John Jewett on the Great Road.   Built   in
1749; torn down in 1954, when the road was rebuilt.

JEWETT, Joseph, also Jewit

SERVICE: S&S Vol 8 p 796 & 799; BRR 8
mos Cont Army 1778 Ь25; BRR 7 mos ser-
vice 1778 Ь100; BRR reinforce Cont Army
3 mos 1779 Ь2-9-3; BRR Claverack 1779 L
50 per mo exclusive of all other wages.
BORN: 10 May 1761 Pepperell s/o Edward &
Sarah (Farmer).
MARRIED: 11 Apr 1786 Sarah Woods of
Princeton (d 1852).
DIED: 3 May 1846 Ashburnham.
CHILDREN (b Princeton):
  Ivers – b 7 May 1788
  Joseph – b 30 Apr 1790
  Milton – b 31 May 1793
  Polly Gibbs – b 4 Mar 1796
  Merrick Augustus – b 26 Aug 1798
  Sarah Farmer – b 4 Sep 1803
REF: Peperrell VR; Princeton VR; Ash-
burnham VR; Jewetts of America, Frederic
Clark Jewett MD 1908.

JEWETT, Sgt Oliver, also Jewet, Jewitt

SERVICE: S&S Vol 8 p 791, 797 & 799; B
Hist Lex Alarm; BHist Siege of Boston.
BORN: 24 Feb 1747 Pepperell s/o Edward &
Sarah (Farmer).
MARRIED: 1) 23 Jan 1772 Betty Houghton;
2) 28 Apr 1780 Bolton (int), Keziah Snow
(d 20 Jul 1797 ae 39); 3) 15 Nov 1801
Bolton (int), Sarah (Snow) McBride (d
widow 9 Dec 1830 ae 81).
DIED: 22 Aug 1829 ae 82 yrs 6 mos Bolton
GS1.
CHILDREN:
  Oliver – b 3 Nov 1772 m Polly Slead
  Jonathan – b 2 Apr 1775 m Phebe
    Underwood
  Samuel – b 6 Jan 1781 d young
  Betsy – b 13 Dec 1782
  Samuel – b 10 Feb 1785
  Edward – b 4 Jun 1787
  Sally – b 18 Aug 1789
  Keziah – b 18 Nov 1792 m James Bride
  Mersylvia – b 10 Jul 1795 m Hollis
    Ward

JEWETT, Sgt Oliver (Cont)

REF: Pepperell VR; BVR; Jewetts of America, Frederic Clark Jewett MD 1908.

JOHNSON, Amos

SERVICE: S&S Vol 8 p 814.
BORN: 13 Oct 1750 Bolton s/o Joshua &
Hannah (Ball).
MARRIED: 1) 15 Jan 1782 Elizabeth Pol-
lard (d 1813 Berlin); 2) 22 Apr 1814
Maverick (Houghton) Cotting (d 1852).
DIED: 12 Jul 1825 ae 74 Berlin GSB.
CHILDREN (b Berlin):
  Lewis – b 16 Mar 1783
REF: BVR; Berl VR; Berlin History, Rev W
A Houghton 1895.

JOHNSON, Asa

SERVICE: S&S Vol 8 p 815; BHist Lex
Alarm; BHist 15th Reg.
BORN: 6 Apr 1759 Bolton s/o Capt Edward
& Mary (Ball).
MARRIED: 2 Jul 1778 Holliston, Hannah
Mellen.
DIED: 28 Oct 1801 ae 73 Sterling GS Old
Cem.
REF: BVR; Holliston VR; Sterling Grave
Records.

JOHNSON, Capt Edward, Sr

SERVICE: S&S Vol 8 p 824.
BORN: 28 Sep 1715 Woburn s/o Edward &
Rebecca.
MARRIED: 13 Jun 1744 Westborough, Mary
Ball (d 1810).
DIED: 9 Oct 1784 ae 70 GSB.
CHILDREN (b Bolton):
  Edward – b 21 Oct 1745 m Relief ___
  Nathan – b 19 Jul 1748 m Beulah Wood
  Jemima – b 25 Nov 1750 m James Welder
    1772
  Jotham – b 20 Nov 1753 m Eunice Reed
  Jonas – b 4 Feb 1757 m1 Damaris Rugg
    m2 Mary Lyon

JOHNSON, Capt Edward, Sr (Cont)

Asa – b 6 Apr 1759 m Hannah Mellen
NOTE: Capt of the Train Band; all 5 sons served in the Revolution.
REF: Woburn VR; BVR; Westborough VR; Berlin History, Rev W A Houghton 1895.

JOHNSON, Edward, Jr

SERVICE: S&S Vol 8 p 824 & 825; MilAnn Capt Jonathan Houghton's Co; MilAnn 15th Reg; BRR Qtr turn NY 1776 for Joel Fosgate ₤2-13-5; BRR 5 mos York Jul 1776 L 10; BRR 5 mos York 1776 see note.
BORN: 21 Oct 1745 s/o Capt Edward & Mary (Ball).
MARRIED: Relief ___.
DIED: 21 Jul 1828 Sterling GS Old Cem.
CHILDREN (b Lancaster, Chocsett Parish):
    Clarissa – bpt 1 Jul 1781 d 1801
    Luther – bpt 4 May 1783 m Sophia Lincoln
    Oliver – bpt 1 May 1785
    Fanny – bpt 2 Sep 1787 M Jon´a Burpee
    Abel – bpt 2 May 1790 d 1791
    Peleg – b 19 Apr 1792 d 1822
    Lucy – b 11 Jun 1794 m Richard Hildreth
    Relief – b 22 Jun 1796
    Edward – b 23 Dec 1798 d 1800
    Mary – b 12 Oct 1801
NOTE: 5 mos to York 1776 pd by Joel Fosgate-2-13-6, Eben Worcester ₤2-13-4, William Fife ₤4-6.
REF: BVR; Berlin History, Rev W A Houghton 1895; Sterling VR.

JOHNSON, Eliezar

SERVICE: S&S Vol 8 p 826; BRR to Goose 3 mos 14 ds 1777 ₤5; BRR money raised in Capt Nurse's Co for 3 yrs ₤10.
JOHNSON, Eliezar (Cont)

BORN: 27 Feb 1718 Woburn s/o Edward & Rebecca.
MARRIED: 1750 Lucy Ball d/o Nathan of Northborough.
DIED: 31 Jul 1791 ae 71 Berlin GSB.
CHILDREN (b Bolton):
    Lucy – b 10 Mar 1749-50 m Jonas Houghton
    Elizabeth – b 7 Oct 1751 m Ephraim Barnard
    Lydia – b 3 Jul 1754 m Abram Wood
NOTE: DAR gives 1719 as birth year.
REF: Woburn VR; Northborough VR; BVR; Berlin History, Rev W A Houghton 1895; DARPI.

JOHNSON, Sgt Jonas

SERVICE: S&S Vol 8 p 849; BHist Lex

JOHNSON, Sgt Jonas (Cont)

Alarm; BHist Siege of Boston; BRR 5 mos York 1776 ₤10; BRR 5 mos York 1778 see note; BHist 15th Reg; MilAnn Guard at Rutland 1779.
BORN: 4 Feb 1757 Bolton s/o Capt Edward & Mary (Ball).
MARRIED: 1) 17 Oct 1777 Damaris Rugg of Lancaster; 2) 1 Mar 1802 (int) Mary Lyon of Lancaster.
DIED: 8 Jul 1823 Leominster.
CHILDREN (b Lancaster):
    Lucy – b Harvard 23 Mar 1779
    Jonas – b 31 Dec 1804
    Rollen – b 26 Sep 1809
    Mary – b 22 Nov 1812
NOTE: 5 mos at York 1778 pb by F Barnes, ₤4, Wm Badcock, ₤3; gave receipt for ₤30 for engaging in Cont service for 3 yrs; pension S32904.
REF: BVR; LVR; HVR; Leominster VR; Berlin History, Rev W A Houghton 1895.

JOHNSON, Corp Joshua, Jr

SERVICE: S&S Vol 8 p 855; BHist Lex Alarm; BRR money raised in Capt Nurse's Co 3 yrs ₤10; BRR 5 mos men ₤2-12-6.
BORN: 20 Aug 1745 Bolton s/o Joshua & Hannah (Ball).
MARRIED: unm.
DIED: 25 Jan 1832 ae 86 GSB.
REF: BVR; Berlin History, Rev W A Houghton 1895.

JOHNSON, Jotham

SERVICE: S&S Vol 8 p 856; BRR 3 mos NY Nov 1776 ₤10; BRR 5 mos NY 1776; BRR 2 mos 10 ds York 1776 "a turn;" DNR Winter Campaign 1776-7.
BORN: 20 Nov 1753 Bolton s/o Capt Edward & Mary (Ball).
MARRIED: 23 Feb 1775 Lexington "both of Woburn," Eunice Reed d/o Samuel & Eunice.
DIED: 16 Jun 1827
CHILDREN (b Woburn):
    Eunice – b 29 Sep 1775
    Jotham – b 6 May 1778
    Lucy – b 8 Mar 1785 d young
    Susannah – b 9 Aug 1787
    Lucy – b 6 Mar 1790
    Edward – b 12 Jul 1794
REF: BVR; Woburn VR; DARPI.

JOHNSON, Nathan

SERVICE: S & S Vol 8 p 860; BerlHist Bunker Hill; BRR reinforce Northern Army 30 ds Sep 1777.
BORN: 19 Jul 1748 Bolton s/o Capt Edward & Mary (Ball).

JOHNSON, Nathan (Cont)

MARRIED: 18 Dec 1781 Beulah Wood (d 1830).
DIED: 23 Dec 1832 Berlin GSB.
CHILDREN:
  Beulah - b 23 Mar 1783 m David Newton
  Edward - b 4 May 1785
  Zenas - b 8 May 1787
  Susan - b 2 Sep 1789 unm
  Amelia - b 5 Feb 1793 unm
REF: BVR; Berl VR; Berlin History, Rev W A Houghton 1895.

JONES, 2nd Lt Ichabod

SERVICE: S&S Vol 8 p 921.
BORN: 11 Mar 1735-6 Marlborough s/o Samuel & Susannah (Johnson).
MARRIED: unm.
DIED: 1778 Bolton of smallpox GSB.
NOTE: Credited to Marlborough.
REF: MVR; Berlin History, Rev W A Houghton 1895.

JONES, Nathan

SERVICE: S&S Vol 8 p 945; BHist Lex Alarm; BRR ₤5 raised in Capt Nurse's Co for 3 yrs; BRR money deposited in Capt Nurse's hands ₤0-6-0.
BORN: 1 Aug 1742 Marlborough s/o Samuel & Susannah (Johnson).
MARRIED: 1) Nov 1767 Bolton, Mary Bruce; 2) 4 Oct 1774 Princeton, Mercy Parminter of Rutland.
DIED: 8 April 1827 Ashburnham.
CHILDREN (b Princeton):
  Nathan - b 13 Apr 1775
  Mary - b 17 Oct 1777
  Benjamin Gibbs - b 11 Dec 1779
  Lucy - b 2 Jun 1782
  John - b 24 Nov 1783
  Anna - b 21 Jan 1787
  Ebenezer - b 26 Jul 1789
  Abel Parminter - b 13 Mar 1792
REF: MVR; BVR; History of Princeton, F E Blake 1915; Ashburnham VR.

JONES, Samuel, Jr

SERVICE: S&S Vol 8 p 952; BHist Lex Alarm; BHist Siege of Boston; BRR 30 ds reinforce Northern Army; BRR Northern Army Oct 1777.
BORN: 24 Aug 1725 Woburn s/o Samuel & Susannah (Johnson).
MARRIED: 1) 1748 Mehitable Brigham of Marlborough (d 1762); 2) 14 Dec 1763 Dorothy (Carter) Whitcomb (d 1818).
DIED: 23 Jan 1797 GSB.
CHILDREN (b Bolton):
  Samuel - b 22 Mar 1751 d young
  Solomon - b 25 Mar 1753 d young

JONES, Samuel, Jr (Cont)

  Samuel - b 14 Feb 1757
  Sally - b 19 Aug 1758 twin
  Solomon - b 19 Aug 1758 twin
  Lavina - b 19 Feb 1761
  Nancy - b 14 Sep 1764
  Dolly - 25 Mar 1766
  Silas - 12 Feb 1768
  Persis - 12 Mar 1770
  Sullivan - b 13 Nov 1775
NOTE: Also known as "Landlord Jones;" proprietor of the local inn, an ardent patriot, had a gun prepared to give warning of any approaching crisis. When the courier arrived giving news of the approach of the British on 19 April 1775, the gun was fired and a group of men left for the scene of battle.
REF: Woburn VR; BVR; Berlin History, Rev W A Houghton 1895; Berl VR.

JONES, Samuel, Jr (or 3rd) also Johns & Jons

SERVICE: &S Vol 8 p 812, 952, 955 & 972; BHist Lex Alarm fifer; BRR 5 mos York Jul 1776; BRR Northern Army 30 ds Sep 1777.
BORN: 14 Feb 1757 Bolton s/o Samuel Jr & Mehitable (Brigham).
MARRIED: 1777 Woburn, Martha Fay of Woburn (d 1831).
DIED: 22 Sep 1811 Berlin GSB.
CHILDREN (b Bolton):
  Samuel - b 20 May 1778
  William - b 23 Dec 1779
  Patty - b 10 Jan 1782 m Silas Fairbanks
      (b Berlin):
  Betty - b 7 Jul 1784 m Jonathan Tenney
  Timothy - b 18 Mar 1787
  Susannah - b 7 May 1789 m Archie Tenney
  Esther - b 12 Dec 1791 m Aaron Stow
  Sally - b 16 Jan 1796 d young
  Hannah - b 7 Jan 1798 m Abel Rugg
  Sally - b 4 Feb 1800 m Lemuel Howe
  Jonathan- b 25 Jun 1802
REF: BVR; Berl VR; Berlin History, Rev W A Houghton 1895.

JONES, Solomon

SERVICE: S&S Vol 8 p 958; BHist Lex Alarm; BHist Siege of Boston; BRR 5 mos NY 1776 ₤10-10; BHist 15th Reg; BRR RI 1781; BRR 5 mos York Jul 1776 see note.
BORN: 10 Aug 1758 Bolton s/o Samuel Jr & Mehitable (Brigham).
MARRIED: 23 Oct 1782 Bolton, Hannah Gates.
DIED: After 1801 Waterford ME.
CHILDREN (b Berlin):

JONES, Solomon (Cont)

Rosamond – b 22 Oct 1784 m Luther
   Brigham d Waterford ME
Pelatiah – b 18 Mar 1787 m Persis
   Barnes
Solomon – b 27 Apr 1789 m Molly Bruce
   d Ogdenburg NY
Timothy – b 25 Aug 1791 d Ogdenburg NY
Lucy – b 12 Aug 1797 d Auburn NY
Jonathan – b 1802
NOTE: Paid to Solomon Jones for 5 mos to
York Jul 1776 - John Nurse, Amaziah
Knight, Capt Sam'l Nurse, & Benjamin
Bailey, ₤2-12-6 each.
REF: BVR; Berlin History, Rev W A Hough-
ton 1895; DARPI; DAR Lineage Bk 140 p
249.

JONES, Lt Timothy

SERVICE: S&S Vol 8 p 966; BRR 2 mos 10
ds NY 1776 "a turn;" BRR 1 yr to York
1776 ₤3-6; BRR 30ds reinforce Northern
Army 1777; BRR Northern Army 1777.
BORN: 1740 Woburn s/o Samuel & Susannah
(Johnson).
MARRIED: unm.
DIED: 7 Jul 1822 ae 82 GSB.
REF: Woburn VR; Berlin History, Rev W A
Houghton 1895.

JONES, Sgt William

SERVICE: S&S Vol 8 p 967; BHist Lex
Alarm.
BORN: 23 Aug 1724 Woburn s/o Jonathan &
Elizabeth.
MARRIED: 1) Margaret Huston; 2) Mrs
Jane (Rogers) Young. Margaret Huston.
DIED: 28 Sep 1811 Walpole ME bur Old
Walpole Cem "Col."
REF: Woburn VR; DARPI; DAR 59th Report
to Smithsonian p 135.

KEYS, Joseph

SERVICE: S & S Vol 9 p 155; BRR 5 mos
York Jul 1776 ₤10; BRR 3 mos York 1776 ₤
10; DNR Winter Campaign 1776-7; MilAnn
Capt N Longley's Order Bk 1777; MilAnn
in the Jerseys 1777.
BORN: 5 Nov 1726 Lancaster s/o Matthias
& Sarah.
MARRIED: Elizabeth ____.
DIED: 1790 Westford.
CHILDREN (b Bolton):
   Dorothea – b 9 May 1750
   Leles – b 7 Dec 1751
   Joseph Annis – b 16 May 1754
   Christopher – b 4 Sep 1757
   Charles – b 17 Jul 1761
   Hannah – b 17 Sep 1764

KEYS, Joseph (Cont)

NOTE: In Westford in 1790 census. J
Keys paid his wages rec'd for last cam-
paign in Jersey to David Moor.
REF: BVR; LVR; Westford VR.

KNIGHT, Amaziah

SERVICE: Not in S&S; BRR to York Jul
1776 bounty ₤2-12-6; BRR Capt Nurse's Co
for 2 mos ₤10.
BORN: unk.
MARRIED: 17 May 1753 Bolton, Jane Smith
of Marlboro.
DIED: 1812 Bolton no stone.
CHILDREN (b Bolton):
   Unice – b 11 Apr 1755
   Aaron – b 30 Jul 1759 bpt Marborough
      22 May 1759
   Unice – b 20 Apr 1764 bpt Marlborough
      22 Apr 1764
   Anna – b 8 May 1766 bpt Marlborough 1
      May 1766
   Keziah – b 14 May 1768 bpt Marlborough
      22 May 1768
   David – b 4 Jun 1779 m Mary Wilkins
      1812
NOTE: Conflicts in dates of births and
baptisms are given just as they appear
in BVR and MVR.
REF: BVR; MVR.

KNIGHT, Carter

SERVICE: S & S Vol 9 p 343; DNR Dec
1776.
BORN: 16 Jan 1757 Lancaster s/o Russell
& Mary (Bruce).
MARRIED: unk.
DIED: 1 Dec 1834 ae 76 Bolton GS3 Rev
marker.
NOTE: Credited to both Lancaster &
Harvard.
REF: LVR; BVR.

KNOLTON, Asa

SERVICE: S&S Vol 9 p 365.
BORN: 21 Sep 1752 Shrewsbury s/o Joseph
Jr & Mary.
MARRIED: 1) 28 Feb 1782 Sarah Hadley of
Sterling; 2) 2 Feb 1789 Worcester, Olive
Wait of Shrewsbury; 3) 24 Dec 1805 Alice
Divoll "both of Lancaster;" 4) 4 Oct
1818 Damaris Howe.
DIED: unk.
CHILDREN (b Shrewsbury):
   Damaris –
   Edeline – b 2 Jun 1820
   Charles – b 4 Jul 1822
NOTE: Descriptive List 1781 - gives age
23, 5'11", dark complexion, 1 eye, en-
listed for 3 yrs; on muster list for

KNOLTON, Asa (Cont)

Sterling 1781.
REF: Shrewsbury VR; LVR; Sterling VR.

LANGLEY, Eli also Longely, Longley

SERVICE: S&S Vol 8 p 493, Vol 9 p 922 & 925; MilAnn Cont Service at claverack 1779; MilAnn 6 mos men 1780; BRR reinforce Cont Army 3 mos 1779 Ŀ2-9-3.
BORN: 13 Dec 1762 Bolton s/o Col Robert & Anna (Whitcomb).
MARRIED: 7 Mar 1785 Harvard "both of Bolton" Mary Whitcomb (b 1767).
DIED: Raymond ME 1839.
CHILDREN (b Bolton):
   Polly - b 15 Jul 1785
   Eli - b 19 Mar 1787 ml Betsy Barker m2
      Laura McWain
        (b Waterford ME):
   Sally - b 1790 m Stephen Sanborn
   Lucy - b 1792 d young
   Geo W - b 1794 m Abigail Spurr
   Sophia - b 1796 twin m Winthrop Brown
      MD
   Lucinda - b 1796 twin ml Eben Cross m2
      John Mead
   Lucy - b 1799
   Rebecca - b 1802 m Hon John Sawyer
   Laurinda - b 1805 m Dea James Walker
   Fanny - b 1807
   Mary A - b 1808 m Daniel Cook
   Fisher A - b 1812
NOTE: Descriptive List 1780 - gives age 18 yrs, 5´6"; on Pension Roll for Cumberland Co ME 1831 Vol 29 p 357; in Waterford he had 1st store, 1st tavern, 1st potash works, was 1st postmaster & 1st town treasurer.
REF: BVR; HVR; DARPI; History of Waterford ME, Warren & Warren 1879.

LANGLEY, Col Robert also Longley, Longly

SERVICE: S&S Vol 9 p 494, 929 & 931; B Hist Lex Alarm; BHist Siege of Boston; BRR Resolve Jun 1776; BRR 5 mos NY Jul 1776.
BORN: 11 Mar 1733-4 Groton s/o John & Deborah.
MARRIED: 17 Mar 1756 Anna Whitcomb (d 10 Dec 1815 GS1).
DIED: 10 Aug 1802 Bolton ae 70 GS1.
CHILDREN (b Bolton):
   Rachel - b 13 Jul 1757 m A Gibson 1778
      Stow
   John - b 22 Jan 1759 m Sarah Longley
      in Littleton
   Lucy - b 21 Oct 1760
   Eli - b 13 Dec 1762 m Mary Whitcomb &
      moved to Waterford ME
   Becke - b 6 Feb 1765 d 1787
   Rhoday - b 31 May 1768 m Oliver

LANGLEY, Col Robert

      Pollard 1789
   Robert - b 10 May 1770 ml Elizabeth
      Whitman 1797 & moved to Kentucky
      m2 Nancy Barnes
   Tille - b 22 Sep 1772 d 1790
   Jonathan - b 24 Nov 1774 m Susan
      Barker at Waterford ME, all killed by Indians in Kentucky
NOTE: R Longley was in French & Indian War; Crown Point 1756, Campaign of 1760.
REF: Groton VR; BVR; Worc Co Probate Records; DARPI.

LARKIN, Ephraim

SERVICE: S&S Vol 9 p 514; MilAnn RI 1779; MilAnn 6 mos men 1780; MilAnn RI 1781.
BORN: 29 Mar 1763 Lancaster s/o Peter & Azuba (Wheeler).
MARRIED: 11 Feb 1784 Bolton, Dinah Baker d/o Jonathan.
DIED: 8 Oct 1846 prob Rome NY.
CHILDREN (b Berlin):
   John - b 18 Sep 1784
   Meriam - b 6 Mar 1786
   Ephraim - b 10 Jun 1788
   Lucretia - b 29 Jul 1790
   Asa Goodenow - b 3 Jul 1792
   Dinah - b 18 Sep 1794
   Baker - b 8 Feb 1797
   Peter - b 9 Jun 1799
   Huldah - b 28 Sep 1801
   Persis - b 26 Aug 1806
NOTE: DARPI gives date of birth as 28 Mar 1753; Descriptive List 1781 - gives age 18, height 5´11", dark complexion, farmer; also on muster list for Sterling 1781.
REF: LVR; BVR; Berl VR; Berlin History, Rev W A Houghton 1895; DARPI.

LARKIN, John

SERVICE: S&S Vol 9 p 515; MilAnn Cont Army 1778.
BORN: 27 Jan 1761 Lancaster s/o Peter & Azuba (Wheeler).
MARRIED: 1 Jun 1786 Sarah Robinson (d 1843 ae 82).
DIED: 12 Apr 1841 ae 80 GSB.
CHILDREN (b Berlin):
   Peter - b 16 Oct 1787 d 1812
   Lucy - b 8 May 1789 d 1815
   Sally - b 8 May 1791
   Hezediah - b 3 Jun 1794 m Amory Harris
      1813
   John Flavel - b 15 Feb 1796
   Catherine - b 5 Aug 1798 d 1884
REF: LVR; Berlin History, Rev W A Houghton 1895; Berl VR.

LARKIN, Corp Peter

SERVICE: S & S Vol 9 p 516; BerlHist Lex Alarm.
BORN: 29 Jul 1727 Lancaster s/o Philip & Mary.
MARRIED: 28 Feb 1750 Lancaster (int), Azuba Wheeler of Shrewsbury (d 1805 ae 74).
DIED: 13 Apr 1815 ae 88 GSB.
CHILDREN (b Lancaster):
  Betty - b 27 Dec 1751
  Persis - b 18 Feb 1753
  Hezediah - b 29 Dec 1755
  Mary - b 27 Sep 1757
  Azuba - b 22 May 1759
  John - b 27 Jan 1761 m Sarah Robinson 1786
  Ephraim - b 29 Mar 1763 m Dinah Baker
  Lucy - b 22 May 1765 d 1778
  Lucretia - b 4 Apr 1767
  Caty - b 22 May 1769 d 1778
  Peter - b 8 Jan 1773 d 1778
NOTE: Credited to Lancaster.
REF: LVR; Berlin History, Rev W A Houghton 1895; DARPI.

LONGLEY, Abraham (or Abram)

SERVICE: S&S Vol 9 p 493; MilAnn cont Army 1779 Claverack.

LONGLEY, James

SERVICE: S&S Vol 9 p 926; BRR Resolve of 1776 1 yr bounty L3-0-0.
BORN: 4 Nov 1753 Shirley s/o William & Mary.
MARRIED: 15 Jan 1784 Northboro, Molly Bartlett of Northboro.
DIED: 15 Jan 1837 ae 83 Boylston.
CHILDREN (b Boylston):
  Otis - m Lydia Patch
  Mary - b 18 Feb 1786 m Abijah Flagg
  Jonas - b 11 Nov 1787
  Jonathan - b 21 Jun 1789 minister
  James - b 22 Jun 1791 d 1793
  Israel - b 21 Nov 1792 d 1793
  James - b 3 Sep 1794 m Sally Eustis
  Israel - b 8 Nov 1795 d 1812
  Betsy - b 22 May 1799 m Daniel Barnes
  Parker - b 22 Nov 1800
  Lois - b 26 May 1805 m Joseph Dudley
NOTE: Claimed by Boylston; was in privateering service under Commodore Moody; then joined land forces & served under Gen Sullivan (Kip's Bay); was at the battle of Saratoga & capture of Burgoyne; in gov forces against Shay's Rebellion per "Boylston Centennial."
REF: Shirley VR; Northborough VR; DARPI; Boylston Centennial 1887.

LONGLEY, John also Longly

SERVICE: S&S Vol 9 p 926 & 930; Mil Ann Siege of Boston; BHist Resolve Jun 1776; BRR 5 mos NY Jul 1776 L10; BRR 2 mos RI 1777; BHist Col Stearns Reg 1777.
BORN: 22 Jan 1759 Bolton s/o Col Robert & Anna (Whitcomb).
MARRIED: 25 Oct 1780 Sarah Longley of Littleton.
DIED: after 1802; will of his father states his whereabouts unknown.
CHILDREN (b Bolton):
  John - b 17 Mar 1781 bpt 25 Feb 1787 d 1824 ae 43
NOTE: Descriptive List 1780 - gives age 22, height 5'6", light complexion, brown hair, gray eyes, farmer, engaged for Littleton; also reported deserted 20 Aug 1782.
REF: BVR; Littleton VR; Worc Co Probate Records.

Pewter Mug Once the Property
of Nathaniel Longley, Jr

LONGLEY, Nathaniel, Jr also Longly

SERVICE: S&S Vol 9 p 928, 929 & 931; B Hist Lex Alarm; BRR Resolve 1775 6 wks; BRR Resolve 1776 2 mos; BRR reinforce N Army 1777; BRR 5 mos York Jul 1776 "a turn;" BRR Tower to Rutland to guard prisoners; BRR Northern Army Oct 1777; MilAnn Capt Hez Whitney's Co 1777; BRR Bennington 1777; BRR Guard at Rutland 6 mos 1778 L8-4-8 per mo.
BORN: 17 Oct 1756 Bolton s/o Nathaniel & Beulah (Fairbank).

LONGLEY, Nathaniel, Jr (Cont)

MARRIED: 5 Mar 1781 Harvard, Keziah Fairbank (d 1812 Bolton).
DIED: 11 Nov 1842 ae 86 Bolton no stone.
CHILDREN (b Harvard):
  Betsy - b 18 Jun 1782
  Nathaniel - b 24 Apr 1784
  Polly - b 30 Jul 1786
  Henry - b 28 Nov 1788
REF: BVR; HVR.

McBRIDE, Alexander

SERVICE: Not in S&S; BRR to Goose 1777 3 mos 14 ds ₤3.
BORN: ca 1707 Ireland.
MARRIED: Mary ___.
DIED: Sep 1779 Bolton.
CHILDREN (b Lancaster):
  John - b 1727
  William - b 6 Jun 1734 m Susannah Bailey
  Agnus - b 1 Nov 1736 d young
         (b Bolton):
  Thomas - b 23 Mar 1739 d young
  Thomas - b 7 Feb 1741-2 m Sarah Snow
  Agnus - b 19 Jul 1744 m Benj Bruce
  James - m Lydia Wilson 1763
  Alexander - d young
  Mary - d young
REF: LVR; BVR; Berlin History, Rev W A Houghton 1895.

McBRIDE, Thomas

SERVICE: S&S Vol 10 p 415; MilAnn Lex Alarm; BRR Resolve Jan 1776 2 mos; BRR to York Sep 1776; BRR 2 mos 10 ds York Sep 1776 "a turn."
BORN: 7 Feb 1741-2 Bolton s/o Alexander & Mary.
MARRIED: 19 Apr 1769 Bolton, Sarah Snow of Bolton.
DIED: 1793 Berlin no stone.
CHILDREN (b Bolton):
  William - b 30 Jul 1769
  Prudence - b 15 Jan 1771 m Rufus Whitcomb
  Keziah - b 9 Jul 1773
  Gardner - b 17 Jul 1775 d 1810
  Sarah - b 22 Dec 1780
        (b Berlin):
  Thomas - bpt 15 Jun 1783
  John - bpt 11 Mar 1787
  Ruth - bpt 28 Feb 1790
REF: BVR; Berl VR; DARPI.

McBRIDE, William

SERVICE: S & S Vol 10 p 416; BRR reinforce Cont Army 3 mos; BRR service in RI 1780 ₤18; BRR reinforce Cont Army 1780 ₤ 19; MilAnn RI 1781.

McBRIDE, William (Cont)

BORN: 6 Jun 1734 Lancaster s/o Alexander & Mary.
MARRIED: 20 Jul 1781 Bolton, Susannah Bailey.
DIED: About 1801 Bolton per Selectmen's Order Book.
NOTE: 12 Jun 1786 Abr Wheeler for providing for Wm McBride & family, ₤1-3-1; 11 Jul 1786 same, ₤3-5-5; Oct 1786 same, L 4-8-9; May 1787 Jona Jewell for McBride family ₤0-5-8; Feb 1801 Benj Burnham, part pay for Wm McBride & family 7 wks, $4; Burnham for McBride's wife $3.46 per Bolton Selectmen's Order Book.
REF: LVR; BVR.

McDANIEL, Daniel, also McDonald

SERVICE: S & S Vol 10 p 460 & 467; B Hist 16th Reg.
NOTE: Residence Boston, hired for Bolton; may be same man who served in 4th Hampshire Reg, residence Pelham, birthplace Medford; Descriptive List 1778 - gives age 19 (or 18), height 5'2" (or 5'4"), complexion light (or sandy), farmer; deserted 23 May 1778; deserted 6 Apr 1781, retaken May 1782 at Boston; tried by martial & sentenced to receive 100 lashes; court martialed for insubordination, sentenced to fatigue for 1 wk; discharged 10 Jun 1783 enlistment having expired.

MCELWAIN, Andrew, also McIlwain, McWain & McWines

SERVICE: S&S Vol 10 p 476, 545, 573 & 574; BHist Lex Alarm; BHist 10th Reg.
BORN: 8 Jun 1742 Bolton s/o Andrew & Hezediah (Moor).
MARRIED: 1 Feb 1764 Bolton, Rebecca Cever (Seaver?) of Lancaster.
DIED: 29 Jul 1837 "age 99 yrs 1 mo 18 days" Woodstock VT GS Woodstock Cem.
CHILDREN:
  ?Jerusha? - d 1857 ae 68 GS Woodstock VT Cem
NOTE: 1790 census has Andrew McWain in Putney VT.
REF: BVR; Berlin History, Rev W A Houghton 1895; Records of Woodstock VT Hist Soc.

McINTIER, James, also McIntire, McIntyre

SERVICE: S&S Vol 10 p 502, 507 & 514; BHist Enl Cont Army 3 yrs 1781 ₤120 silver; MilAnn 16th Reg Cont Army.
NOTE: Descriptive List returned by Seth Washburn, Supt, 1781 - gives age 40, height 5'3", light cmplexion, occupation

McINTIER, James (Cont)

sailor; engaged for town of Bolton for 3 yrs.

MARBEL, Benjamin

SERVICE: S&S Vol 10 p 209; BHist Lex Alarm.
BORN: unk.
MARRIED: 5 Oct 1749 Bolton, Martha Goss.
DIED: unk.
CHILDREN (b Bolton):
  Sarah - b 10 Nov 1750
  Joseph - b 23 Oct 1752 d 26 Oct 1797 a Shaker, lived Shaker Village
  Hannah - b 23 Dec 1755 m Josiah Rice Jr of Northboro
  Martha - b 6 Oct 1758
  Benjamin - b 25 Apr 1761
  Levi - b 1 May 1763
  Patience - b 2 Apr 1765
  Oliver - b 7 mar 1767
  John - b 9 Aug 1769 twin
  Mary - b 9 Aug 1769 twin
  Elizabeth - b 11 Jun 1771
NOTE: Men of this name found in 1790 census in Hartland VT and Westmoreland NH; also in Westmoreland in 1790 were Joseph and Levi.
REF: BVR.

MARTIN, Lt Edward

SERVICE: S&S Vol 10 p 282; BRR Resolve of 1775 6 wks; BRR 2 mos 10 ds at York 1776 "a turn;" BRR a Tower to Providence; BRR Bennington Sep 1777; BRR Northern Army 1777; BRR 3 mos to Northward 1777 £9-8-6; BHist Capt Hez Whitney's Co 1778; BRR 6 wks RI 1778; BRR reinforcements RI 1778.
BORN: 7 dec 1746.
MARRIED: Deborah Brown.
DIED: 27 Mar 1782 Rehoboth GS Burial Place Hill.
REF: Rehoboth VR; DARPI.

MASON, Lt Thomas

SERVICE: S & S Vol 10 p 334; BHist Bennington Alarm 1777; MilAnn in the Jerseys 1776; DNR Winter Campaign Dec 1776; DNR £27-3-6 wages, sauce money, prize money pd Apr 1777.
BORN: 14 Jun 1733 s/o Thomas & Mary (Sadey).
MARRIED: 21 Jul 1763 (int) Mary Baxter of Medfield (d 1824 ae 87 Princeton).
DIED: 28 Nov 1814 81st yr Princeton.
CHILDREN (b Princeton):
  William - b 19 Nov 1764
  Sarah - b 23 May 1767 m John Eustis 1793

MASON, Lt Thomas (Cont)

  Thomas - b 28 may 1769 grad Harvard, settled Northfield
  Mary - b 16 oct 1771 m Capt John Read 1793
  Elizabeth - b 17 Mar 1774 m Joseph Clark
  Horation - b 30 Jul 1776
  Joseph - b 3 Jul 1778 m Sally Foster
  John - b 19 Dec 1780 d 1795 ae 15
REF: Princeton VR; History of Princeton, F E Blake 1915; DARPI.

MAYNARD, David

SERVICE: S & S Vol 10 p 393; MilAnn Capt Jona Houghton's Co 1776; BRR 5 mos NY 1776 "a turn."
BORN: 16 Feb 1758 Bolton s/o Jotham & Abiel.
MARRIED: unm.
DIED: 19 Jan 1777 Bolton no stone.
NOTE: No record of his death in Army found; however, as Capt Houghton's company marched on 22 Jul 1776, and the term ended 1 Dec, it would seem that David's death on 19 Jan must have been directly related to the war.
REF: BVR; Berlin History, Rev W A Houghton 1895.

MAYNARD, Sgt Jotham Jr

SERVICE: S&S Vol 10 p 399; BHist Lex Alarm; BRR Resolve 1775 6 wks; BRR to Goose 1777 3 mos 14 ds £5; BRR 5 mos men 1775 £5-5.
BORN: 14 Mar 1741 Bolton s/o Jotham & Abiel.
MARRIED: 19 May 1763 Westborough, Dinah Powers (d 1822).
DIED: 1796 Berlin CRI no stone.
CHILDREN (b Bolton):
  Dinah - b 10 Apr 1764 m Joshua Wheeler
  Jotham - b 14 May 1766
  Hannah Allen - b 10 Apr 1768
  Persis - b 10 Feb 1771 d 1775
  Chloe - b 18 Sep 1773
  Antipass - b 27 Apr 1776
  Asa - b 6 Oct 1778
REF: BVR; Berlin History, Rev W A Houghton 1895; DARPI.

MERIAM, 2nd Lt Amos, Jr also Merriam & Miriam

SERVICE: S&S Vol 10 p 638, 656 & 823; BRR Money raised in Capt Nurse's Co for 3 yrs £10.
BORN: 24 Aug 1739 Lexington s/o Amos (d 1786 Berlin) & Hannah (Danforth) (d 1811 Berlin).
MARRIED: 15 Jul 1767 Bolton, Elizabeth

MERRIAM, 2nd Lt Amos, Jr (Cont)

Nurse (b 1747 d 1816) d/o Samuel.
DIED: 6 Mar 1818 Leominster.
CHILDREN (b Winchendon):
  Amos - b 2 Jun 1768 m Susy Knight
  Jonathan - b 24 Oct 1770
  Elizabeth - b 2 Nov 1772 d 28 Aug 1775
  Elizabeth - b 11 Nov 1776
  Luther - b 4 Jun 1779 m Clarissa Chase
NOTE: DARPI has wrong death date, that
of Amos Sr b 1715 d 1786.
REF: Lexington VR; BVR; Winchendon VR;
Leominster VR; DARPI.

MERRIAM, 2nd Lt Jonathan

SERVICE: S&S Vol 10 p 640; BHist Lex
Alarm; B Hist Siege of Boston; BRR
reinforce Northern Army Sep 1777 30 ds;
BRR Northern Army Oct 1777; BRR Winter
Campaign 1777 Ł3.
BORN: 16 Aug 1741 Bolton s/o Amos &
Hannah (Danforth).
MARRIED: unm.
DIED: 5 Jun 1823 Berlin Dea ae 81 GSB.
NOTE: Ł3 collected in Capt Nurse's Co
for 3 years.
REF: Berlin History, Rev W A Houghton
1895; BVR.

MERRIAM, Levi

SERVICE: S&S Vol 10 p 642; BHist Lex
Alarm; BHist Resolve 1776 NY 5 mos; BRR
5 mos Jul 1776 Capt D Nurse "a turn."
BORN: 23 Feb 1756 Bolton s/o Amos &
Hannah (Danforth).
MARRIED: 18 Jun 1778 Abigail Fife (d
1832 Berlin).
DIED: 17 mar 1812 "Esq" ae 56 GSB.
CHILDREN (b Berlin):
  Abigail - b 20 May 1779 m Sam'l Jones
    3rd
  Levi - b 8 Aug 1781 m Mary Stevens
  Sally - b 12 Jun 1783 m Wm Jones
  Hannah - b 17 Mar 1787 m Joseph Parks
  Jonathan Danforth - 8 Oct 1789 m Polly
    Goss
  Dilly - b 8 Oct 1793
  Merick - b 4 Aug 1796 d 1797
REF: BVR; Berlin History, Rev W A Hough-
ton 1895.

MERRIAM, Simon

SERVICE: S&S Vol 10 p 643.
BORN: 3 Jun 1749 Lexington s/o Nathaniel
& Esther.
MARRIED: 8 Apr 1779 Phebe Lock of Har-
vard (d 1815 in 62nd yr Bolton).
DIED: 1816 Bolton no stone.
CHILDREN (bpt Bolton):
  Azuba - bpt 1 Mar 1786

MERRIAM, Simon (Cont)

  Rebekah - bpt 1 Mar 1786 m Dr Cyrus
    Fay 1804
  Susannah - bpt 30 Apr 1786 m Nath'l
    Jones 1804
  Solomon - bpt 30 Sep 1787
  Abigail - bpt 19 Oct 1795
  Lydia - bpt 19 Oct 1795
  Oliver - bpt 19 Oct 1795
  Isabella - bpt 26 Mar 1797
REF: Lexington VR; BVR; DARPI.

MOOR, Abel, also Moore

SERVICE: S & S Vol 10 p 903 & 914; BHist
Lex Alarm; BHist Siege of Boston; Mill
Ann 10th Reg 1777.
BORN: 17 Feb 1742-3 Bolton s/o John &
Susannah (Willard).
MARRIED: 11 Jan 1764 Bolton Betty Whit-
comb d/o Dea David & Betty (White).
DIED: 1 Apr 1777 in 10th Reg.
CHILDREN (b Bolton):
  Abil - b 11 Jan 1768 m Lois Kathan in
    Putney VT
  Eunice - b 6 Apr 1772
  Stephen - b 11 Mar 1777
REF: BVR; Moore Genealogy, E S Bolton
1904; History of Captain John Kathan,
David L Mansfield 1902.

MOOR, Abijah, also Moore

SERVICE: S&S Vol 10 p 903 & 915.
BORN: 31 Aug 1724 Middletown CT s/o Dr
Abijah & Anna (Ward).
MARRIED: Eunice Gibbs (d 9 Jul 1813 ae
85 Putney VT.
DIED: 18 Apr 1792 Putney VT GS North Cem
Putney VT also SAR marker.
Children (b Princeton):
  William -
  Rufus - b 13 Oct 1750
  Bathsheba - m Josiah Sawyer 3rd 1770
    Bolton
  Tamar - m Elisha Hubbard 1773 Putney
    VT
  Abijah - b 1 Oct 1757
  Gideon - m Arvilla Hubbard 1782 Putney
    VT
  Eunice - d 19 Jul 1768 Bolton
    (b Bolton):
  Lois - b 12 Mar 1766
  Jephthah - b 11 May 1766
  Lucinday - b 8 May 1768
NOTE: In Capt Benj Hastings' Co at
Bunker Hill; lost cartridge box; Capt
Hastings requisitioned several to re-
place those lost.
REF: BVR; Princeton VR; DARPI; Brattle-
boro Chapter DAR.

MOOR, Abner, also Moore

SERVICE: S & S Vol 10 p 903 & 915; BHist Lex Alarm; BHist Siege of Boston; BHist 14th Reg.
BORN: 28 Sep 1736 Lancaster s/o John & Susannah (Willard).
MARRIED: 16 Nov 1769 Bolton, Elizabeth Hastings (b 1750 d/o Capt Benj & Abigail).
DIED: unk.
CHILDREN: unk.
NOTE: Paid Meeting House Tax in Bolton 1794; lived Chesterfield, NH; black-smith.
REF: LVR; BVR; Tolman Collection, N E Hist Gen Society.

MOOR, Dr Abraham

SERVICE: Not in S&S; no records of service.
BORN: 6 Mar 1747-8 Bolton s/o Abraham & Silence.
MARRIED: 1) 7 Dec 1769 Bolton, Sarah Johnson (d 1798 ae 54 Bolton GS1); 2) 24 Jan 1803 Bolton, Betsy Wales of Boston (m2 Noah Cook of Keene NH).
DIED: 7 Mar 1803 Bolton ae 55 GS1.
CHILDREN:
   Abraham – b 5 Jan 1785 m Eliza Bruce of Harvard
NOTE: Abraham 3rd was attending Harvard College at the time his father died. Dr Moor's will provides money for Abraham to continue his studies. No record of any other children. Although we have found no record of Dr Moor being in the Revolution there is every reason to believe he was.
REF: BVR; Moore Genealogy, Ethel S Bolton 1904; DARPI; Centennial Address, R S Edes, Bolton 1876; Worc Co Probate Records.

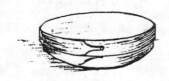

Eighteenth Century Pill Box
and Tooth Extractor

MOOR, Capt David, also Moore, More

SERVICE: S&S Vol 10 p 904, 917 & Vol 11 p 4; BHist Lex Alarm; BHist Siege of Boston; BRR 3 mos to NY 1776 ₤10; DNR Sgt 1776-7 Winter Campaign; BRR in Col John Jacobs Reg 1777; BRR 2 mos RI 1779 ₤5-11-1 or ₤5-6-8; BRR to RI 1781; BRR 2 mos Providence at ₤10 per mo; BRR 3 mos 14 ds to Goose, a turn.
BORN: 19 Nov 1742 Bolton s/o Abraham & Silence.
MARRIED: 11 Aug 1763 Lancaster, Elesebeth Whitcomb.
DIED: 27 Dec 1815 on passage from New Orleans.
CHILDREN (b Bolton):
   Sewell – b 18 Aug 1764 m Mehitable Dodge d 1836 ae 72
   Rachel – b 8 May 1768 m Rufus Moore 1785
   David – b 23 Jul 1770
   Betsy – b 27 Jul 1777
   Thomas – b 24 May 1780 m Eunice Houghton
   Naham – b 7 Aug 1782 d young
   Ezra – b 25 Aug 1783
NOTE: Rec'd ₤3-9-4 for the last campaign in Jersey Apr 1777; also rec'd the wages of Joseph Keys for sd Keys service in Jersey.
REF: LVR; BVR; Moore Genealogy, E S Bolton 1904; Tolman Collection, N E Hist Gen Society.

MOOR, Gardner, also Moore

SERVICE: S&S Vol 10 p 905 & 920; MilAnn Lex Alarm; MilAnn Coat Rolls 1776; MilAnn Dorchester Hgts 8 mos 1776.
BORN: 20 Apr 1757 Bolton s/o Joshua & Elizabeth (Sawyer).
MARRIED: 23 Jul 1778 Abigail Whitcomb (b 1756 d/o Israel & Azuba).
DIED: 5 Apr 1813 ae 57 of exposure Putney VT.
CHILDREN:
   ?Gardner? – d Putney VT ae 33 1809 relationship not proven
REF: BVR; VT censuses 1790 & 1800; VT VR at Montpelier.

MOOR, Corp Isaac, Jr, also Moore, More

SERVICE: S&S Vol 10 p 906 & 938 Vol 11 p 99; BRR 3 mos NY 1776 ₤10; BRR York Jul 1776 ₤5-3-4; DNR Winter Campaign 1776-7; BRR 3 mos 14 ds to Goose a half turn.
BORN: 8 Sep 1748 Bolton s/o Isaac & Mary.
MARRIED: 24 Jun 1768 Shrewsbury, Mary Bigelow of Shrewsbury (d 1825 ae 78).
DIED: 5 Jan 1825 ae 76 Berlin GSB.
CHILDREN (b Bolton):

MOOR, Corp Isaac, Jr (Cont)

Anna – b 16 Apr 1769 m1 Wm Stoddard m2 Elijah Ball
Asenah – b 3 May 1770 m David Barnes
Isaac – b 12 Jan 1772 m Patty Knowlton of Ipswich
Mary – b 8 Feb 1774
Olive – b 9 Jan 1776
Solomon – b 8 Aug 1777 m Hannah Fife
Abigail – b 13 Aug 1781 m Isaac Stone (b Berlin)
Sarah – b 1 Mar 1784 m Isaac Stone
Nancy – b 11 Oct 1786
Joseph – b 14 Aug 1787 m1 Sarah Pollard m2 Betsy Warner m3 Adeline Stone
Warren – b 7 Feb 1793 m1 Hannah Carter m2 Mrs Susan Keyes
NOTE: also served for Stow.
REF: BVR; Shrewsbury VR; DARPI; Berlin VR; Tolman Collection, N E Hist Gen Society; Moore Genealogy, E S Bolton 1904.

MOOR, Sgt Jacob also Moore

SERVICE: S & S Vol 10 p 906 & 922; BHist Lex Alarm; BRR 5 mos men 1775 £5-5; BRR Resolve 1775 10 wks; BRR Northern Army 1777; BRR Bennington Aug 1777; B Hist Sgt in Capt Hez Whitney's Co 1778.
BORN: 16 Nov 1745 Bolton s/o Isaac & Mary.
MARRIED: 30 Nov 1769 Bolton, Elizabeth Bailey (d 1828 ae 83 Princeton).
DIED: 14 Apr 1820 ae 75 Princeton "Capt" on GS.
CHILDREN:
Bailey – b 5 Dec 1773 Bolton
Lydia – m ___ King
Polly – m ___ Beals
NOTE: Elected constable in Princeton 1796; State Archives call him Capt.
REF: BVR; Prineton VR; Moore Genealogy, E S Bolton 1904; Tolman Collection, N E Hist Gen Society.

MOOR, John, Sr, also Moore

SERVICE: S&S Vol 10 p 907 & 924; MilAnn Northern Army 1776.
BORN: 3 Jan 1730-1 Lancaster s/o John & Susannah (Willard).
MARRIED: 30 Aug 1757 Lunenburg, Unity Willard of Lunenburg d/o Jona & Keziah.
DIED: 6 Jan 1811 Dummerston VT.
CHILDREN (b Bolton):
Willard – b 22 Apr 1759
John – b 17 Dec 1760
Jonathan – b 5 Jul 1764 physician m Rebecca Stevens 1799 Putney
Caleb – b 10 Dec 1765 m Achsah Whitney 1796 Bolton

MOOR, John, Sr (Cont)

Susannah – b 5 May 1767 m Jeremiah Priest 1787 Bolton
Berzaili – b 16 Dec 1768 d 1771 Putney
Charlotte – b 8 Jan 1772
Barzilla – b 26 Mar 1775
Unity – b 12 Sep 1776 m Prentice Kathan d Westmoreland NH
Abel – b 2 Sep 1779
REF: LVR; BVR; Hist of Capt John Kathan, David L Mansfield 1902.

MOOR, John, Jr, also Moore, Moores

SERVICE: S&S Vol 10 p 907, 925, 941; BRR Bennington Sep 1777; BHist Col J Jacobs' Reg 1777; BRR 3 mos to northward 1777; BRR 8 mos service May 1778 £100; BRR 2 mos RI 1779 £5-11-1; BRR RI Sep 1779 £50 per mo; BRR 8 mos Cont Army 1781; BRR L pd by J Temple for R Ruggles (receipt); BHist enlisted 3 yrs 1781.
BORN: 17 Dec 1760 Bolton s/o John & Eunity (Willard).
MARRIED: 31 Jul 1785 Putney VT, Susanna Underwood d/o Timothy & Rachel (Russell).
DIED: 17 Aug 1834 Woodstock VT.
CHILDREN:
John – went west
James – went west
Polly – d unm
NOTE: "Acc't dated Bolton, 25 June 1781. Bounties paid sd Moore & others to serve in Cont. Army for term of 3 years. Sd Moore rec'd £100 silver money" Mil. Ann.
REF: BVR; Hist of Capt John Kathan, David L Mansfield 1902; Underwood Family in America, Lucien M Underwood 1913.

MOOR, Jonathan, Jr, also Moore

SERVICE: S&S Vol 10 p 908 & 926; BRR Guard 6 mos 1779 £6-16s; BRR 9 mos York £2; BRR money raised in Capt Nurse's Co for 3 yrs £8; BRR Rutland 6 mos £25 per mo including all other wages.
BORN: 7 Mar 1743-4 Bolton s/o Abraham & Silence.
MARRIED: 28 Jul 1768 Bolton, Desiah Bailey.
DIED: Estate Adm 1793 Worc Co Probate.
CHILDREN (b Bolton):
Flavel – b 3 May 1769
Ebenezer – b 1 Nov 1770 m Rebecca Newman
Peter – b 21 Sep 1772 m Achsah Whitcomb 1797
Cephas – b 30 Mar 1773 m Anna Crouch in Stow
Arathusa – b 22 Feb 1774
Abraham – b 31 Dec 1775
Jonadab – b 15 Aug 1777 m Thankful

MOOR, Jonathan, Jr (Cont)

    Sawyer
  Silence - b 24 Oct 1779 d 1803 unm
  Jonathan - b 1781 m Lucy Worcester
    1804
  Thomas - b 28 Feb 1784 d 1858 unm
  Luther - b 1785 m Ruth Bride 1810
  Becca - b 9 Jan 1787 twin
  Hannah - b 9 Jan 1787 twin
  Benjamin - b 17 Mar 1789
  Otis - b 15 Aug 1792
NOTE: also served for Stow.
REF: BVR; Tolman Collection, N E Hist
Gen Society; Worc Co Probate Records.

MOOR, Phineas, also Moore

SERVICE: S & S Vol 10 p 910 & 931; BHist
Lex Alarm.
BORN: 6 Feb 1748-9 Bolton s/o Joshua &
Elizabeth (Sawyer).
MARRIED: 1) 27 Nov 1770 Bolton, Sarah
Nurse (d 1826 d/o Sam'l & Eliz); 2) 27
Oct 1833 Mrs. Ruth Ballard (d 1849 ae
87).
DIED: 15 Dec 1839 ae 88 Bolton GS1.
CHILDREN (b Bolton):
  Sarah - b 15 Apr 1771 d young
  Calvin - b 20 Mar 1773
  Levi - b 18 Feb 1777 m Betsy Greenleaf
  Betsy - b 12 Mar 1779
  Sarah - b 3 Jun 1781
  Benjamin - b 17 Jun 1784
  Stephen - b 23 Apr 1786 m Eunice Moore
  Nabby - b 12 June 1789 m Samuel Nurse
    II
REF: BVR; DARPI; Tolman Collection, N E
Hist Gen Society; History of Captain
John Kathan, David L Mansfield 1902.

MOOR, Reuben, also Moore, More

SERVICE: S&S Vol 10 p 910 & 931, Vol 11
p 7; BHist Siege of Boston; MilAnn 13th
Reg.
BORN: 21 Nov 1762 Sudbury s/o David &
Hannah (Parker).
MARRIED: 13 Dec 1781 Lancaster (also
recorded Berlin), Esther Russell of
Lancaster.
NOTE: 1790 census of Sudbury 1-0-1.
REF: Sudbury VR; LVR; Berlin VR; N E
Hist Gen Register Vol 57 p 58.

MOOR, Rufus, also Moore

SERVICE: S & S Vol 10 p 911 & 933; BHist
Guard 3 mos 1779 Ŀ4-6-1; BRR reinforce
Cont Army 9 mos 1779 Ŀ37-16-0; BRR rein-
force Cont Army 1780 3 mos; BRR rein-
force Cont Army RI 3 mos Jun 1780 Ŀ12; B
Hist West Point Exped 1781; BRR gunsmith
Ŀ2 per mo & bounty Ŀ7-10.

MOOR, Rufus (Cont)

BORN: 28 Aug 1761 Bolton s/o Samuel &
Zerish (Houghton).
MARRIED: 24 Mar 1785 Lancaster, his
cousin Rachel Moore (d Dummerston VT
1855).
DIED: 5 Dec 1836 Dummerston VT, govt GS
with Rev marker & flag, Dummerston Hill
Cemetery.
CHILDREN (b Bolton):
  Sophia - b 22 Apr 1786
  Sidney - b 16 Mar 1788
  Rufus - b 8 Oct 1790 d 1791
  Rachel - b 4 Apr 1792 d 1795
    Dummerston VT
  Rufus - b 10 Mar 1795
    (b Dummerston):
  Ira - b 8 Mar 1797 d 1821 Ohio
  Emory - b 6 Apr 1799 m Nancy Eastman,
    Newfane VT
  Rachel - b 7 Jan 1802 d 1803
  Martin - b 11 Feb 1804 m Dolly Marden
    1827
  Abel - b 24 Jan 1806 m Ruby Griffith
    1831
  Emily - b 26 Jan 1808 m James Nichols
    1829
NOTE: Descriptive List 1779 - age 19,
height 5'10", light complexion, gun-
smith, Cont Service; bounty set on In-
dian corn at 3d per bu, rye at 4s "Sd
Rufus Relinquishing all wages to the
Town."
REF: BVR; DARPI; Brattleboro Chapter
DAR; Tolman Collection, N E Hist Gen
Society; History of Captain John Kathan,
David L Mansfield 1902.

MOOR, Samuel, also More

SERVICE: S&S Vol 10 p 911 Vol 11 p 8;
BRR & BHist Cont Army 9 mos 1778 bounty
Ŀ37-10; BRR reinforce Cont Army 9 mos
1779 bounty Ŀ37-16; BRR Fishkill 9 mos
1778.
BORN: 12 Mar 1751-2 Worcester s/o Samuel
& Comfort (Mowers).
MARRIED: 1) Submit Taylor; 2) 6 Jan 1776
Abigail Hastings d/o Capt Benj.
DIED: 1787 Winchester NH.
CHILDREN:
  Charlotte - b 9 May 1775 m Joseph
    Thomsan (Mowers, int)
  Achsah - b 9 Feb 1780 Springfield
  Samuel - b 7 Sep 1781 Springfield
NOTE: Mass Archives 1778 decriptive list
gives age 25 height 6'2" complexion
sandy res Bolton; pensioned.
REF: LVR; Springfield VR; Tolman Collec-
tion, N E Hist Gen Society; Worcester
VR.

MOOR, Willard

SERVICE: S&S Vol 10 p 913; BRR 5 mos Boston 1776; BRR reinforcements RI 1778; BRR RI 6 wks Jul 1778.
BORN: 22 Apr 1759 Bolton s/o John & Unity (Willard).
NOTE: "A resident of Putney before 1790" per History of Captain John Kathan; 1790 census Putney VT 2-0-3.
REF: BVR; History of Captain John Kathan, David L Mansfield 1902.

MOOR, William, also Moore

SERVICE: S&S Vol 10 p 913 & 938 Vol 11 p 9.
BORN: 5 Dec 1755 Bolton s/o Abraham & Silence.
MARRIED: Anna ___.
DIED: Probably Putney VT.
CHILDREN (b Bolton):
  Abraham - b 27 Dec 1780
  Sally - b 25 Feb 1782
  Anna - b 29 Jun 1783
  Eunice - b 28 Mar 1785 m Stephen Moore
  William - b 14 Aug 1786
  James - b 14 Nov 1788
  Lucy - b 8 Mar 1791
  Navy - b 7 Mar 1793
  Thomas - b 29 May 1795
  Silence - b 9 Nov 1797
  Charles - b 16 Jun 1800 twin
  Charlotte - b 16 Jun 1800 twin
NOTE: Also enlisted as from Putney VT. "Wm Moore was in the party which arrested Noah Sabin, Tory, in 1776. Sabin was denied communion, reinstated later, and confined to his house."
REF: BVR; Putney 200 Years, Fortnightly Club 1953.

MOORE, Josiah

SERVICE: S&S Vol 10 p 927; BHist Lex Alarm; BRR 30 ds reinforce Northern Army.
BORN: 25 Mar 1739 Bolton s/o John & Susannah (Willard).
MARRIED: 10 May 1759 Bolton, Abigail Richardson d/o Caleb & Elizabeth.
DIED: 1812 Bolton no stone.
CHILDREN (b Bolton):
  Elizabeth - b 17 Jul 1761
  Abegill - 16 Dec 1763 m Nath'l Southwick
  Josiah - b 25 Apr 1766
  Caleb - b 1 Aug 1768 m Achsah Whitney
  Henry - b 23 Aug 1772 m1 Hannah Nurse 1797 m2 Polly Cook 1800
  Achsah - b 24 Jul 1774 m Stephen P Gardner 1798
  James - b 7 Jan 1777 m Hannah Peters 1800

MOORE, Josiah (Cont)

NOTE: Josiah Moore warned by Capt Jona Houghton to present himself equipt with arms & ammo & be in Boston 2 April or find an able bodied sub or pay fine of £10 within 24 hours or consider himself a soldier.
REF: BVR; DARPI; Richardson Memorial, John A Vinton 1876.

MOORE, Sewall

SERVICE: S&S Vol 10 p 933 & 934; BRR 2 mos RI 1779 £5-11-1 or £5-6-8.
BORN: 18 Aug 1764 Bolton s/o Capt David & Betty (Betsy) (Whitcomb).
MARRIED: 9 Nov 1787 Putney VT, Mehitable Dodge.
DIED: 19 Dec 1836 ae 72 Bolton no stone.
CHILDREN:
  Willard - b 15 Nov 1788 Chesterfield NH
  Betsy - b 26 Feb 1791 Boston or Bolton
  Ezra - b 30 Jun 1793 Boylston twin
  Sally - b 30 Jun 1793 Boylston twin
  Charles - b 5 Apr 1796 Worcester
  Mary - b 7 Apr 1799 Worcester
  Harriet - b 24 Oct 1801 Worcester
  John Dodge - b 26 Feb 1804 Worcester
  Tyler Dodge - b 4 Oct 1806
NOTE: Selectmen's Order Book, Bolton, "9 Feb. 1807, Paid Caleb Moore for money advanced to pay board of Sewell Moore & wife while in the House of Correction." Worc Co Probate records case 41578A, "Guardianship of Sewell Moore, Spendthrift" 16 Jan 1834.
REF: BVR; Worcester VR; Worc Co Probate Records; Pension Records; Bolton Selectmen's Order Book.

MOORE, Corp Uriah

SERVICE: S&S Vol 10 p 937; BRR Resolve 1775 6 wks; BRR to York 1776 2 mos £5-3-4; BRR Northern Army 1775; BRR reinforce Northern Army 30 ds 1777; BHist Capt Hez Whitney's Co 1777; BRR Bennington Aug 1777.
BORN: 14 Jul 1752 Bolton s/o Isaac & Mary.
MARRIED: 13 Dec 1781 Abigail Merriam "both of Bolton" (d 1835 Princeton).
DIED: 26 May 1820 ae 66 Princeton GS Old Cemetery.
CHILDREN (b Princeton):
  Hannah - b 7 Dec 1782 m Wm Babcock Jr
  Luther - b 20 sep 1784 d 1804
  Abigail - b 17 Dec 1787 d 1803
  Sally Meriam - b 4 Jun 1790 m Jotham Keys
  Lovice - b 28 Oct 1792 d Berlin 1853
  Mary - b 11 Sep 1795 m Capt Josiah

MOORE, Corp Uriah (Cont)

Cutting
Oliver - b 6 Jun 1798 d Hubbardston
        unm
NOTE: "Uriah Moore was in Shays' Rebel-
lion, was pardoned and took Oath of
Alliegence before Asa Whitcomb Esq." per
Hist Princeton.
REF: BVR; Princeton VR; History of
Princeton, F S Blake 1915; Moore Genea-
logy, E S Bolton 1904.

MORSE, Benjamin

SERVICE: S&S Vol 11 p 82 & 83.
BORN: 10 Mar 1763 bpt 16 Aug 1772 Sutton
s/o Benjamin & Mary (Barnard).
MARRIED: Susannah ___ (d 1835 ae 72
GS3).
DIED: 22 Feb 1844 Bolton GS3.
CHILDREN:
  Sally -
NOTE: Property sold at public vendue for
$900 by Caleb Wheeler, adm, to Sally
Morse, dau, 1844. 1870 map calls her
"Misses Moss."
REF: BVR; Morse Genealogy, J Howard
Morse 1903; Worc Co Probate Records,
Sutton VR.

MOSMAN, Joshua

SERVICE: S&S Vol 11 p 163; BHist Lex
Alarm; MilAnn in the Jerseys 1776, 1777.
BORN: 16 Jan 1738-9 Sudbury s/o Timothy
& Mercy (Whitney).
MARRIED: 19 Feb 1767 (int) Lancaster,
Ann Joyner.
DIED: after 1798 Salisbury VT, bur West
Salisbury VT no stone.
CHILDREN:
  Mark - d West Salisbury VT a vet of
        War of 1812 m Lois ___
NOTE: Joined church Salisbury VT 1798.
REF: Sudbury VR; LVR; Salisbury-Lei-
cester, VT Hist Soc; Soldiers of the Rev
War Buried in VT, Walter H Crockett.

MOSMAN, Ens Oliver

SERVICE: S & S Vol 11 p 163; MilAnn
Service in Jersey 1777; DNR Dec 1776.
BORN: 19 Jan 1760 Princeton s/o Timothy
& Mercy (or Martha) (Whitney).
MARRIED: 1) 1783 Dolly Trowbridge d/o
James D of Chesterfield NH (d 1791); 2)
after 1791 Delaware Co NY, wid Lucy ___.
DIED: 30 Apr 1835 ae 75 "at 11 AM"
Henderson, Jefferson Co NY.
CHILDREN (b Stratton VT):
  Mary - b 1784 m Lemuel Cobleigh
  Martin Trowbridge - b 1785 m Abigail
        Philips

MOSMAN, Ens Oliver (Cont)

Moses Jenry - m Polly French
NOTE: Was in Chesterfield NH in 1790
census.
REF: Princeton VR; Princeton History,
Vol 1, F E Blake 1915; DARPI.

MOSMAN, Lt Timothy

SERVICE: S&S Vol 11 p 164; BHist Lex
Alarm; BHist Siege of Boston.
BORN: 26 Feb 1744-5 Sudbury s/o Timothy
& Mercy (or Martha) (Whitney).
MARRIED: 10 Oct 1772 (int) Lancaster,
Lucy Bond of Weston.
DIED: Jul 1826.
NOTE: 1790 census Westminster VT shows
Timo Mossman 1-0-1.
REF: Sudbury VR; LVR; Princeton History,
Vol 1, F E Blake 1915; DARPI.

MUNGER, Sgt Jonathan

SERVICE: S * S Vol 11 p 202; BHist
Enlisted 3 yrs 1781.
BORN: 5 Sep 1741 Brimfield s/o Nathaniel
& Elizabeth (Bullen).
MARRIED: 1) Jan 1770 Rachel Moulton (d
1790 d/o Jona & Anna); 2) 1 Dec 1791
Elizabeth Paul d/o Robert.
DIED: 7 Apr 1808 Fenner NY.
CHILDREN (b West Parish, Brimfield, now
Wales MA):
  James - b 18 Oct 1770
  Elial - b 7 Jun 1775
  Zerah - b 26 Jan 1779 d 1794
        (b Union CT):
  Horace - b 24 Oct 1792
  Palace - b 23 Dec 1794
  Rachel -
        (b Fenner NY):
  Chauncey - b 11 Jul 1802
NOTE: Jonathan listed as "Sailor" before
enlistment for Bolton.
REF: DARPI; The Munger Book, J B Munger
1915.

MUZZEY, Benjamin

SERVICE: S&S Vol 11 p 256; BHist Lex
Alarm.
BORN: 15 Aug 1753 (bpt) Shrewsbury s/o
Benjamin & Hannah (Dicom).
MARRIED: Sara ___ (b 1756).
DIED: 1829 Chester VT.
CHILDREN:
  Benjamin - b 1783
  son - b 1784
  Asa - b 1799 Grafton VT
  dau - b between 1794-1799
REF: Worc. Co Probate Records; Shrews-
bury VR; The Mussey Family, Joanne Muzzy
Belsey, Eagle River AK 1975.

NEWMAN, Sgt John

SERVICE: S&S Vol 11 p 373; BHist 16th Reg; MilAnn Regt to Newport 1778.
BORN: 26 Oct 1763 Newbury s/o John 3rd & Abigail (Noyes).
MARRIED: 1) 21 May 1785 Newburyport, Jane Knap (d 14 Mar 1788 ae 24); 2) 15 Oct 1805 Newburyport, Sally Strong.
CHILDREN (b Newburyport):
  Sally – b 10 Aug 1810
  John – b 11 Jun 1812
  Mary – b 6 Apr 1819
NOTES: Descriptive List 1781 – fifer, 9th MA Reg, 18 yrs, 5´3" high, light complexion, light hair, res Lancaster.
REF: Newbury VR; Newburyport VR.

NORCROSS, Jacob

SERVICE: Drummer; S & S Vol 11 p 506; MilAnn Service in Jersey 1777.
BORN: 19 Oct 1751 s/o Joseph & Hannah (Sheppard).
MARRIED: 1 Mar 1781 Princeton, Elizabeth (Isabel) Bannar (1761-1807).
DIED: 25 Nov 1805 Princeton ae 54.
CHILDREN (b Princeton):
  Nancy – b 15 Aug 1781 m Timothy Rice
  Polly – b 16 Nov 1782 d young
  Lucinda – b 1784 m Silas Parmenter
  Jacob – d 5 Feb 1789
  Isabel – b 19 Jan 1787 publ Peter
    Stewart 1808
  David – b 10 Aug 1788 d 1792
  Betsy – b 8 Mar 1791 m Thomas Phelps
    1808
  Miriam – b 31 Jan 1804 m David Cheever
REF: Princeton VR; DARPI.

NURSE, Asa, also Nurss

SERVICE: S&S Vol 11 p 569; MilAnn Lex Alarm; BRR 3 mos Boston 1776; BRR money raised Capt Nurse´s Co for 3 yrs Ŀ5.
BORN: 17 Mar 1753 Bolton s/o Samuel & 2nd wife Abigail (Barnard).
MARRIED: 1) Sibyl Bailey; 2) Olive ___.
DIED: after 1791 DARPI.
CHILDREN (b Bolton):
  Daniel – b 1777 d 1803 ae 26
  Asa – bpt 21 May 1786
REF: BVR; DARPI.

NURSE, Dr Benjamin

SERVICE: S&S Vol 11 p 569; BHist Lex Alarm; BRR Resolve of 1775 6 wks; BRR winter campaign 1777 Ŀ9.
BORN: 16 Jan 1755 Bolton s/o Samuel & 2nd wife Abigail (Barnard).
MARRIED: 1) 6 Nov 1777 Sibella Bailey (d 1799 d/o Benjamin); 2) 2 Feb 1799 Kate Bailey (d 1819 d/o Benjamin).

NURSE, Dr Benjamin (Cont)

DIED: 24 Feb 1804 ae 49 Berlin GSB.
CHILDREN (b Berlin):
  Sibella – m Nathan Egery 1797
  Nabby – m Amasa Holt 1799
  Theophilus – b 9 Apr 1787 m 1815 Lois
    Brigham
  Theodore – b 25 Oct 1801 m Rebecca
    Goddard 1822
REF: BVR; Berlin History, Rev W A Houghton 1895; Berlin Grave List.

NURSE, Capt David, also Nurs, Nurss

SERVICE: S&S Vol 11 p 564, 566 & 569; BHist Lex Alarm; BRR NY 3 mos 1776; BRR to Goose 3 mos 14 ds "a turn;" BRR 5 mos men Ŀ6.
BORN: 19 Jan 1741-42 Bolton s/o Samuel & 1st wife Elizabeth (Kellog).
MARRIED: 3 Jun 1762 Rebecca Barrett (d 1825 ae 84 d/o Oliver.
DIED: 26 Dec 1825 DAR; 3 Sep 1827 ae 86 "Deacon" GS3.
CHILDREN (b Bolton):
  David – b 1 Oct 1762
  Stephen – b 10 Apr 1764 m Betsy
    Englund
  Oliver – b 25 Apr 1766 m Polly
    Houghton
  Rebekah – b 10 Jan 1768
  Elizabeth – b 6 Jan 1770 d 1849 unm
  Hannah – b 28 Mar 1772 m Jonathan
    Nurse
  Abigail – b 28 Apr 1774 m John Holman
  Sarah – b 13 Aug 1776 m Oliver Holman
  Catherine – b 30 Nov 1778 m Oliver
    Holman
REF: BVR; Barrett Bible, entries by Capt David Nurse; DARPI.

NURSE, John

SERVICE: S & S not listed; MilAnn p 150; BRR 5 mos Capt Nurse 1775 bounty Ŀ2-18-6; BRR money raised in Capt Nurse´s Co Ŀ7-7-6.
BORN: 17 Nov 1740 Bolton s/o Samuel & Elizabeth (Kellogg).
MARRIED: 1) 20 May 1766 Marlborough, Hezediah Hapgood (d 9 Jan 1785 Bolton); 2) 24 Oct 1786 Bolton, Sarah Sawyer (d 1834 Waterford, ME).
DIED: 4 Mar 1819 Waterford, ME "Deacon."
CHILDREN (b Bolton):
  Samuel – b 16 Sep 1766 m Rebecca Moore
  Mary – b 6 Oct 1768 m Jonas Holman
  John – b 15 Nov 1770 m Hannah Whitcomb
  Francis – b 1 Dec 1772 m Abigail
    Puffer
  Moses – b 31 Jan 1775 m Mercy Hapgood
  Daniel – b 20 May 1777
  Judith – b 22 Apr 1779

Home of Captain David Nurse on Nourse Road. Burned in the Early 1900's.

NURSE, John (Cont)

Lovina - b 4 Oct 1781 m Jona Whitcomb
Unice - b 30 Aug 1787
Sally - b 15 Jul 1789
NOTE: Went to Waterford, ME c1790 & became prominent in town & church, a deacon. The following is taken from the "Military Annuals of Lancaseter, Mass." by H S Nourse, 1889: "Occasionally a learned medical authority was invoked to aid some citizen in escaping from military duty: this may Sartify the Gentelmen whom it may Concarn that Mr John Nurse has a wickness in his Eye and is Lame and by Reson of them things in my Judgement is not fitt to Do Duity as a Solger in the malishea" - Stow 21 Aug 1776 - signed by Charles Whitman "Phasihion." But John paid a substitute and got this receipt: "This may certify that I Solomon Jones Received two pounds twelve shillings and six Pence of John Nurse for doing a quarter of a turn in the Continental Service to be done at New York" signd Solomon Jones.
REF: BVR; MVR; History of Waterford, ME, Warren & Warren 1879.

NURSE, 2nd Lt Jonathan also Nurss

SERVICE: S & S Vol 11 p 568-9; BHist Lex Alarm; BRR 3 mos Boston 1776; BRR 5 mos Capt D Nurse's Co £3; BRR money raised in Capt Nurse's Co for 3 yrs £7.
BORN: 1749 Bolton s/o Samuel & 1st wife Elizabeth (Kellogg).
MARRIED: 30 Oct 1772 Ruth Barrett (d 1841 ae 92 d/o Oliver & Hannah).
DIED: 24 Jul 1827 ae 78 "Deacon" GS2 Rev Marker.
CHILDREN (b Bolton):
Peter - b 10 Oct 1774 d 1840 ae 66 ME, minister
Jonathan - b 10 Mar 1776 m Hannah Nurse
Hannah - b 29 Jan 1778 m Henry Moore
Calvin - b 9 Mar 1779 m Mary Loring
Luther - b 8 Feb 1781 d 1801 ae 20
Eunice - b 26 Feb 1784 d 1787 ae 3
Silas - b 21 Sep 1786 m Sarah Fletcher
Samuel - b 25 Jun 1789 m Sarah Whitcomb
Sophia - b 30 Jan 1793 d 1795
Amos - b 17 Dec 1794 d 1808 "child of Jonathan"
REF: BVR; DARPI

NURSE, Samuel

SERVICE: S & S not listed; BRR Capt D Nurse's Co 5 mos 1775 £8-12-6; BRR to Goose 3 mos 14 ds £10.
BORN: 25 Apr 1715 Salem s/o Samuel & Dorothy (Faulkner).
MARRIED: 1) Elizabeth Kellogg (b c1721 d 1751 in 31st yr); 2) Abigail Barnard (d 1820 widow ae 86).
DIED: 8 May 1790 ae 75y 4m 2d (Barrett Bible); town records say 8 May 1775 in error.
CHILDREN (b Bolton to Elizabeth):
  John - b 17 Nov 1740 m1 Hezediah Hapgood m2 Sarah Sawyer
  David - b 19 Jan 1741-2 Capt m Rebecca Barrett
  Elizabeth - b 22 Jan 1743-4 d 1745
  son - b 4 Feb 1745-6 d 1745-6
  Elizabeth - b 4 Jan 1746-7 m Amos Merriam
  Jonas - b 18 Dec 1748
  Jonathan - b 1749 d 1827 m Ruth Barrett
  Sarah - b 8 Jan 1750 m Phineas Moor
    (b Bolton to Abigail):
  Asa b 17 Mar 1753 town record says son of Elizabeth in error
  Benjamin - b 16 Jan 1755 doctor m Sibella Bailey
  Abigail - b 7 Jan 1757 d 1764
  Eunis - b 5 Jul 1760
  Phebe - b 9 May 1762
  Abigail - b 18 Jun 1765 m Abraham Holman Jr
  Lucy - b 28 Jun 1769 m Ephraim Fairbank
  Barnard - b 10 Jun 1771 m Hannah Barrett
NOTE: A descendant of Rebecca Nurse who was executed in Salem for supposed witchcraft. Fought in F & I War.
REF: Salem VR; BVR; Barrett Bible; DARPI.

OAK, Beriah also Oakes, Oaks

SERVICE: S&S Vol 11 p 597, 600 & 604; BHist Lex Alarm.
BORN: 22 Nov 1743 Westborough s/o Nathaniel & Keziah (Maynard).
MARRIED: 31 Dec 1767 Bolton, Tabitha Foskett (Fosgate) (d 16 Sep 1820).
DIED: 1780 Bolton, probate Feb 1781.
CHILDREN (b Bolton):
  John - b 30 Mar 1768 m Mary Eaton of Sudbury
  Elizabeth - b 6 Feb 1770 m Abijah Woodward
  James - b 30 Oct 1771 m Sarah Walker of Sudbury
  Abraham - b 29 Mar 1773 m Joanna Walker of Rindge, NH

OAK, Beriah (Cont)

  Asa - b 6 Dec 1774 m Patty Robins
  Daniel - b 17 Jun 1776 m Hephsabah Bachelder
  Eunice - b 14 Mar 1778 m Ebenezer Randall of Stow
  Phebe - b 23 Dec 1779 m Samuel Danforth Jr
  Beriah - b 19 Aug 1781 m Eunice Ames
REF: BVR; Westborough VR; DARPI; Worc Co Probate Records.

OAK, Nathaniel, Jr, also Oakes, Oaks

SERVICE: S&S Vol 11 p 598, 600 & 604; BHist Lex Alarm; BHist 6 mos men 1780; MilAnn Cont Army.
BORN: 12 Jan 1742 Westborough s/o Nathaniel & Keziah (Maynard).
MARRIED: 1) 2 Jun 1773 Bolton, Susannah Hastings (b 1748-9 d/o Capt Benjamin); 2) ___ Gates.
DIED: 25 Mar 1830 Windham, VT.
CHILDREN:
  Seth -
  Calvin ? -
  Natahaniel III ? -
NOTE: Descriptive List 1780 - age 18 (error), height 5'7". Letter from Willard Oak, S Rutland, Jefferson Co, NY reads: "Seth Oak, my grandfather, and 3 of his brothers moved to Athens, Windsor Co., Vt. My father's name was Nathan."
REF: Westborough VR; BVR; National Archives Pension Records; DARPI; Soldiers of the Revolutionary War Buried in Vermont, Walter H Crockett.

OSBORNE, James

SERVICE: S&S Vol 11 p 687; BRR service in Boston with Gen Heath 1778.
BORN: 7 Jan 1762 Bolton s/o Thomas & Mary (Whitcomb).
MARRIED: 1) 13 Feb 1783 Lancaster, Rebecca Whitney of Bolton (d 19 Mar 1800 Stow); 2) 6 Sep 1801 (int) Stow, Lydia Gates (she m 2nd Ephraim Stone 1822, d 1839 ae 52).
DIED: before 1822 in Stow, no record.
CHILDREN:
  Rebecca - b 23 Jun 1783 Bolton
  Asa - b 29 Dec 1788 Stow
  John - b 1785 bpt 2 Mar 1788 (error)
  Sally - b 8 Mar 1791 Stow
  Polly - bpt 23 Nov 1794 Stow
  James - b 17 Mar 1798 Stow d 1842 ae 44
  Dolly - b 28 Feb 1800 d 18 Mar 1800
REF: BVR; LVR; SVR.

OSBORNE, Lt Thomas

SERVICE: S&S Vol 11 p 689; BHist Lex Alarm; BRR to Boston with Gen Heath 1778.
BORN: 1735.
MARRIED: 1) 26 Apr 1759 Bolton, Mary Whitcomb d/o Gen John & Mary; 2) 10 Mar 1772 Bolton, Sarah Whitcomb (d 1786 d/o Dea David & Betty); 3) 4 Jun 1791 Worcester, Mrs. Abigail Brown of Worcester.
DIED: 13 Sep 1810 ae 75 GS1.
CHILDREN (b Bolton):
  John - b 29 Apr 1760 d young
  James - b 7 Jan 1762 m Rebecca Whitney
  Molly - b 23 Feb 1764
  Nabby - b 10 Jul 1766 m Silas Coolidge
  John - b 3 Oct 1768 d 1843
  Ephraim - b 22 Jul 1773 m Dolly Whitcomb
  Becca - b 17 Nov 1781 m Asa Rice
  Marcy - b 5 Jun 1783 m Dr Elijah Flagg
  Betsy - b 5 Jun 1785 m John Wyman
  Lucy - b 22 Oct 1794
REF: BVR; Worc Co Probate Records, will of Dea David Whitcomb.

OSGOOD, Amos

SERVICE: S&S Vol 11 p 697; MilAnn Lex Alarm p 116.

PARK, James Russell

SERVICE: S&S Vol 11 p 824.
BORN: 1761 Holliston s/o James.
MARRIED: 1786 Anna Leland (d 1838 ae 80 Berlin).
DIED: 13 Jul 1813 ae 52 Berlin GSB.
CHILDREN:
  Joseph - b 11 Nov 1787
  Anna - b 13 Oct 1790 m Edw Johnson
  Charlotta - b 1794 d 1796
  Pamelia - b 3 Oct 1797 m Dea John Powers
REF: Holliston VR; Berlin History, Rev W A Houghton 1895; Berl VR.

PARKER, Moses

SERVICE: S&S Vol 11 p 889.
NOTE: Receipt dated Springfield 27 May 1782 for bounty paid sd Parker by Capt William Sawyer, Chairman of Class #4 of the Town of Bolton, to serve in the Continental Army for the term of three years.

PIERCE, John

SERVICE: S&S Vol 12 p 84; BHist Lex Alarm.
BORN: 22 May 1759 Bolton s/o John & Hannah (Stone).

PIERCE, John (Cont)

MARRIED: 16 May 1799 Dinah Sawyer of Harvard (d 1825 ae 52).
DIED: 12 Sep 1828 Harvard ae 69 GS Old Cem Harvard.
CHILDREN (b Harvard):
  Eliza - b 17 Apr 1800 d 16 Jun 1818
  John - b 13 Oct 1803
  Stillman - b 23 Apr 1809
NOTE: Also served for Groton.
REF: BVR; HVR; Groton During the Revolution, Samuel Abbott Green 1900.

PIPER, Sgt Abel

SERVICE: S S Vol 12 p 430; BHist Lex Alarm; MilAnn Dorchester Hgts with Capt Manassah Sawyer.
BORN: 1740 Bolton s/o John & Ruth.
MARRIED: 19 Jan 1769 Sybil Sawyer.
DIED: 7 Jun 1830 Phillipston.
CHILDREN (bpt Templeton):
  Abel - bpt 29 mar 1770
  Betty - b 17 Mar 1772 (Bolton) bpt Templeton
  Artemas - bpt 1 Aug 1784
  Sylvanus - bpt 2 Oct 1786
NOTE: In 1790 census Abel Piper is listed in Gerry 3-4-4.
REF: BVR; Templeton VR; Phillipston VR; DARPI; LDS Records.

PLATO, (Negro)

SERVICE: S & S Vol 12 p 461; MilAnn enlisted 1781 16th Reg 3 yrs.
NOTE: Descriptive List 1781 - Capt Moore's Co, Col Whitney's Reg - ae 19 yrs, height 5'7", complexion black, occupation farmer, engaged for Bolton 4 Jun 1781 for 3 yrs. Mass Archives. From Ipswich Vital Records - Plato Whipple formerly servant to Dea Whipple, and Phillis Choat, alias Cogswell, formerly servant to Jonathan Cogswell. Intentions 18 Aug 1785. 1790 census of Ipswich, MA, lists Plato Whipple under "other free persons" 7.
REF: Ipswich VR.

POLLARD, John

SERVICE: S&S Vol 12 p 504; BRR 5 mos with Capt Nurse 1775 L2-10.
BORN: 20 Apr 1729 Lancaster s/o William & Experience (Wheeler).
MARRIED: Elizabeth Williams of Groton (d 1816 ae 78).
DIED: 10 May 1814 Lancaster ae 85.
CHILDREN (b Bolton):
  John - b 15 Sep 1758 d young
  William - b 24 may 1761
  Walter - b 21 Oct 1761

POLLARD, John (Cont)

    Betsy - b 6 Mar 1763
    Abner - b 20 Sep 1764
    Amos - b 19 Jul 1766
    John - b 25 Jan 1768
    Moses - b 18 Jun 1770
    Aaron - b 14 Jul 1772
    Gardner - b 3 May 1774
    Mary - b 15 Mar 1776
    Susannah - b 25 Jun 1778
REF: LVR; BVR; Berlin History, Rev W A
Houghton 1895; DARPI.

POLLARD, Levi

SERVICE: Not listed in S&S; BRR 5 mos
1775 Ł2-10.

POLLARD, Thaddeus, also Polard, Pollord

SERVICE: S&S Vol 12 p 496, 506 & 510; B
Hist Lex Alarm; B Hist Capt Hez Whit-
ney´s Co.
BORN: 7 Aug 1746 Billerica s/o John &
Alice (Stearns).
MARRIED: 1) 24 Mar 1767 Shrewsbury,
Submit Maynard (d 1790); 2) 26 Dec 1790
Bolton, Mrs. Elizabeth (Sawyer) Atherton
(d 1831), wid of Eliakim.
DIED: 3 Sep 1803 ae 57 Harvard, GS Old
Cem Harvard.
CHILDREN (b Harvard):
    Zilpah - b 11 Apr 1767
    Eusebia - b 8 Dec 1768 d 1790
    Amory - b 8 Sep 1770
    Thaddeus - b 3 Jun 1772 m Achsah
        Atherton
    Luke - b 19 Feb 1774
    Abner - b 1 Jun 1776
    Sarah - b 20 Apr 1778
    Luther - b 25 Mar 1780
    Nathan - b 16 Mar 1782 d 1786
    Milley - b 11 Apr 1784
    Abel - b 27 Feb 1786
    Nabbie - b 29 Jul 1788 d 1790
    Nathan - b 19 Apr 1793
REF: Billerica VR; HVR; BVR; Shrewsbury
VR.

POLLARD, Thomas

SERVICE: S&S Vol 12 p 506; BRR resolve
1776 2 mos; BRR to Boston 1776 3 mos;
BRR money raised in Capt Nurse´s Co 3
yrs Ł10.
BORN: 1 Aug 1744 Bolton s/o William &
Experience (Wheeler).
MARRIED: 16 Dec 1773 Bolton, Deborah
Wood (d 1827 ae 87).
DIED: 7 Oct 1827 ae 84 Berlin GSB.
CHILDREN (b Bolton):
    Calvin - b 17 Sep 1774 d young
    Stephen - b 29 Jul 1776

POLLARD, Thomas (Cont)

    Luther - bpt 18 Dec 1782
REF: BVR; Berlin History, Rev W A Houghton 1895.

POLLARD, Walter

SERVICE: S & S Vol 12 p 506; BRR rein-
force Cont army RI 3 mos 1778 Ł12; BRR
guard Rutland 3 mos 1779 Ł4-6-1; BRR
Cont Army 1780 Ł12; BRR Cont Army 3 mos
1780; BRR service Rutland 3 mos 1779 Ł17
per mo including wages.
BORN: 21 Oct 1761 Bolton s/o John &
Elizabeth (Williams).
MARRIED: unm.
DIED: Lived Berlin, prob buried Old
Cemetery, but no stone.
REF: BVR; Berlin History, Rev W A Hough-
ton 1895.

POLLARD, Lt William, also Pollord

SERVICE: S&S Vol 12 p 506, 507 & 510; B
Hist Lex Alarm; BRR 3 mos Northward
1777; BRR Bennington Sep 1777; BRR
Winter Campaign 1777 Ł3; BRR Northern
Army 1777; BRR RI 6 wks 1778; BRR rein-
force army RI 1778; BRR Tower to Provi-
dence.
BORN: 19 Jun 1731 Lancaster s/o William
& Experience (Wheeler).
MARRIED: 7 Oct 1762 Bolton, Hannah
Whitcomb.
DIED: 16 Jun 1830 Berlin, no stone.
CHILDREN (b Bolton):
    Sara - b 25 May 1763
    Silas - b 17 Sep 1766
    Jonas - b 7 Mar 1768 d 1771
    Hannah - b 29 Oct 1769
REF: LVR; BVR; Berlin History, Rev W A
Houghton 1895.

POWERS, Sgt Henry

SERVICE: S&S Vol 12 p 651; BRR resolve
1776 2 mos; BRR Bennington Sep 1777; BRR
3 mos to Northward 1777; BRR Northern
Army; BRR to Goose 3 mos 14ds Ł5; BRR
money dep in Capt Nurse´s hands Ł0-18-0.
BORN: 13 Apr 1753 Harvard s/o Robert &
Anna (Wetherbee).
MARRIED: 1) 2 Jan 1774 Harvard, Hannah
Moore (d 1812 Berlin); 2) 8 Dec 1814
Berlin, Wid Eunice Spafford (d 1825
Berlin GSB).
DIED: 1825 Berlin, no stone.
CHILDREN (b Bolton):
    Anna - b 28 Jul 1774 m Silas Jones
    Hannah - b 14 Jul 1776 m Cornelius
        Moore
    Edward -
    Henry - b 17 May 1778

POWERS, Sgt Henry (Cont)

Robert – b 3 Aug 1780
Polly – b 13 Nov 1782 d young
    (b Berlin):
Polly – bpt 30 May 1784 m ___ Roberts
Moors – bpt 17 Sep 1786
Rebecca – bpt 7 Dec 1788 d young
Betsy – bpt 3 Jul 1791 d young
Prudy – bpt 22 Dec 1793
Betsy – b 22 May 1796 m Joel Dakin
Abijah – b 24 Nov 1798
John – b 31 Oct 1800 m Pamelia Park
Rebecca – b 10 Sep 1808 m Amos Proctor
REF: HVR; BVR; Berlin History, Rev W A Houghton 1895; DARPI.

POWERS, John

SERVICE: S&S Vol 12 p 653; BRR money raised in Capt Nurse's Co for 3 yrs Ь6; BRR 5 mos Boston 1776; BRR 5 mos Dorchester Jul 1776.
BORN: 10 Jan 1755 Harvard s/o Robert & Anna (Wetherbee).
MARRIED: 1) 30 May 1774 Lancaster, Mrs Ruth Fletcher of Littleton (John Powers of Shutesbury; 2) Anna Stacy (b Sturbridge d 1846 Rutland ae 88 yrs).
DIED: 24 Jun 1842 ae 87 Rutland.
CHILDREN (b Shutesbury, ch of John & "Hannah"):
Joanna – b 13 Jun 1797
Susanna – b 13 Jan 1800
prob sons as 1790 census lists 2-1-1
REF: HVR; LVR; Littleton VR; Rutland VR; Shutesbury Town Records.

PRATT, Abijah

SERVICE: Not listed in S&S; BRR money raised in Capt Nurse's Co for 3 yrs Ь8.
BORN: 28 Feb 1726-7 Lancaster s/o Josiah & Sarah (Wilson).
MARRIED: Mary Smith of Stow.
DIED: Prob d 3 Sep 1831 Rutland, VT; buried West Street Cem.
CHILDREN (b Bolton):
Elizabeth – b 28 Jun 1747 m Thaddeus Russell 1764
Jeremiah – b 26 Jun 1751
Bulah – b 6 Jul 1754
Stephen – b 25 May 1759 m Eunice Barnard
Deborah – b 4 Jun 1762
Abigail – b 16 Feb 1765 m Amasa Fuller 1784
NOTE: In 1790 census men of this name found in Taunton, Middleborough, Foxboro, Boylston, Mass.; Clarendon, VT.
REF: LVR; BVR; Berlin History, Rev W A Houghton 1895.

PRATT, Joseph

SERVICE: S&S Vol 12 p 697; BHist Lex Alarm; BHist Siege of Boston; BHist 14th Reg.
BORN: 13 Jul 1757 Bolton s/o Joseph & Katherine.
MARRIED: 6 Jun 1786 Elizabeth Sawyer of Harvard.
DIED: Buried Union Street Cem, South Weymouth.
CHILDREN (b Harvard):
Joseph – b 21 Mar 1784 m Mary Coolidge, went to Waterford, ME.
John – b 9 Jun 1786 d Harvard 22 Oct 1803 ae 17
REF: BVR; HVR; DAR 53rd Report to Smithsonian p 167; History of Waterford ME, Warren & Warren 1879.

PRATT, Stephen

SERVICE: S&S Vol 12 p 720; BRR resolve of Dec 1775 6 wks; BRR 5 mos men "a turn;" BRR 5 mos NY Jul 1776; BRR Bennington Sep 1777; BRR 3 mos to Northward 1777; BRR Northern Army 3 mos.
BORN: 25 May 1759 Bolton s/o Abijah & Mary (Smith).
MARRIED: 24 Mar 1778 Bolton, Eunice Barnard.
DIED: Prob d 20 Dec 1835 Bennington, VT, bur Village Cem.
CHILDREN (b Berlin):
Stephen – bpt 13 Apr 1783
Eunice – bpt 23 Nov 1783
Sally – bpt 13 Nov 1785
Infant – d 29 Apr 1778 Lancaster
Infant – d 5 Oct Lancaster
NOTE: Men of this name appear in 1790 census in Shutesbury, Cummington, Weymouth, & Lancaster, MA; Bennington & Pownal, VT; and Cornish, NH.
REF: BVR; LVR; Berl VR.

PRIEST, Abel

SERVICE: S&S Vol 12 p 777; MilAnn 8 mos Dorchester Hts 1776; BRR 3 mos NY 1776 Ь10; MilAnn with Capt Nurse in Jersey 1777; MilAnn 6 mos RI 1778 Ь12-10; BRR reinforce Cont Army 1779 Ь2-9-3; MilAnn 9 mos Claverack 1779; BHist 6 mos men 1780; BHist Cont Army 3 yrs 1781.
BORN: 26 Mar 1760 Harvard s/o John & Mary (Whitney).
MARRIED: 7 Mar 1785 Harvard, Zerviah Whitcomb (b 1767 d/o Gen John & Becca).
DIED: 21 Nov 1827
CHILDREN (b Harvard):
___ – d Mar 1787
John – b 10 Jan 1788
Abel – b 4 Apr 1792
Asa – b 16 Mar 1795

PRIEST, Abel (Cont)

Arad – b 21 Feb 1797
Jasper – b 17 Jun 1805
NOTE: Descriptive List 1780 – age 20
years, 5´8" high.
REF: HVR; DARPI.

PRIEST, Gabriel, Sr

SERVICE: S&S Vol 12 p 779.
BORN: 17 Jun 1720 Lancaster s/o Joseph &
Hannah.
MARRIED: 12 Feb 1742-3 (int) Harvard,
Sarah Sawyer.
DIED: 20 Mar 1781 Bolton.
CHILDREN (b Harvard):
Jonathan – b 7 Jul 1743 d young
      (b Bolton):
Sarah – b 25 Mar 1751 d 1756
Jonathan – b 7 Jul 1754 m Ann
   Sanderson
Olive – b 8 May 1755 d 1757
Gabriel – b 24 Jan 1757 m Hannah
   Hazeltine
Holman – b 3 Oct 1758 m Prudence
   Sawyer 1774
NOTE: The birth date of Holman is defi-
nitely wrong. He m Prudence in 1774 --
only 16! He died 1831 ae 85. His birth
probably occurred in 1746 between Jona-
than and Sarah.
REF: LVR; HVR; BVR; DAR Linage Book 59 p
327.

PRIEST, Corp Gabriel, Jr

SERVICE: S & S Vol 12 p 779; BHist Siege
of Boston; MilAnn Capt Hastings Co 1776;
MilAnn Bennington Alarm 1777; BHist Capt
H Whitney´s Co 1778.
BORN: 24 Jan 1757 Bolton s/o Gabriel &
Sarah (Sawyer).
MARRIED: 8 Mar 1781 Hannah Hazeltine of
Harvard (d 1810).
DIED: Between 1790 census and 1793 when
estate was appraised.
CHILDREN (bpt Bolton):
Gabriel – bpt 29 Sep 1793 s/o wid
   Hannah
Sally – bpt 29 Sep 1793 d/o wid Hannah
REF: BVR; HVR; Worc Co Probate Records.

PRIEST, Holman

SERVICE: S & S Vol 12 p 779; BRR Ben-
nington Sep 1777; BRR Northern Army; BRR
3 mos to Northward 1777.
BORN: 3 Oct 1745(?) Bolton s/o Gabriel &
Sarah (Sawyer).
MARRIED: 28 Apr 1774 Bolton, Prudence
Sawyer (d 1817 ae 76).
DIED: 22 Jan 1831 ae 85 Berlin GSB.
CHILDREN (b Bolton):

PRIEST, Holman (Cont)

Silas – b 6 Aug 1774 m Peris Barnes
Prudence – b 10 Oct 1783 m John Bruce
   Jr
REF: BVR; Berlin History, Rev W A Hough-
ton 1895.

PRIEST, James

SERVICE: S&S Vol 12 p 780; BRR 2 mos 10
ds York Sep 1776 "Half a turn;" BRR
Bennington Sep 1777; BRR 3 mos to North-
ward 1777; BRR Northern Army 1777; BRR
to York 2 mos pd by Cyrus Gates ₤2.
BORN: 1715 Boston s/o Joseph & Margaret
(Childs).
MARRIED: 8 Sep 1750 (int) Woburn, Hannah
Lawrence d/o Jonathan & Joanna.
DIED: Plymouth, VT date unknown.
CHILDREN (b Bolton):
Hannah – b 1750 m John Coolidge
Nathaniel – b 4 Sep 1759
Moses – b 8 Oct 1762 d 30 May 1858
   Plymouth VT
NOTE: Bolton Rev Records BRR call him
Jr.
REF: BVR; Genealogical Records of the
Founders & Early Settlers of Plymouth,
VT, Blanche B Bryant & Gertrude E Baker
1967.

PRIEST, Jeremiah, Jr

SERVICE: S&S Vol 12 p 780; BHist Lex
Alarm.
BORN: 10 Jan 1746 Harvard s/o Jeremiah &
Mary (Whitney).
MARRIED: 1) 14 Mar 1771 Bolton by Rev
Thos Goss, Rebecca Houghton (d 1785
Bolton); 2) 7 Oct 1787 (int) Susannah
Moore.
DIED: After 1826 Harvard.
CHILDREN (b Bolton):
Rebecca – b 24 Mar 1772 m Abel Davis
Leafe – b 11 Apr 1777
Hepzibah – b 28 Nov 1778 m Aaron Davis
REF: HVR; BVR; DARPI.

PRIEST, Job

SERVICE: S&S Vol 12 p 780; BHist 15th
Reg.
BORN: 27 Mar 1756 Harvard s/o Jeremiah &
Mary (Whitney).
MARRIED: 3 Jan 1774 "Job of Harvard"
Bolton, Martha Butler (b 1757 Bolton d
1790 Harvard, d/o Ephraim & Comfort
(Fay)).
DIED: 12 Aug 1820.
CHILDREN:
Daniel – b 2 Jan 1778 Harvard m
   Lucretia Sizer
Seth – bpt 21 Oct 1787 Stow

PRIEST, Job (Cont)

NOTE: Pensioned; list of 1813, Ensign $40, roll #141.
REF: HVR; BVR; SVR; DARPI; Lineage Book 89 p 270.

PRIEST, John

SERVICE: S&S Vol 12 p 781; BRR raised money for 3 yrs Capt Nurse's Co Ł4.
BORN: 22 Aug 1750 Harvard s/o John & Mary (Whitney).
MARRIED: 14 Jun 1775 Anna Houghton d/o John & Hepzibah (Priest).
DIED: 1 Nov 1815 ae 62 Harvard, GS Harvard Old Cemetery.
CHILDREN (b Harvard):
  Sarah - b 18 Jul 1776
  Eunice - b 4 Mar 1779
NOTE: Warned out of Bolton 1790.
REF: HVR.

PRIEST, Jonathan

SERVICE: S&S Vol 12 p 782; BHist Lex Alarm; drummer.
BORN: 7 Jul 1754 Bolton s/o Gabriel & Sarah (Sawyer).
MARRIED: 16 Dec 1774 Sudbury, Ann Sanderson of Sudbury.
DIED: unk.
CHILDREN (b Bolton):
  Ruth - b 4 Dec 1775
NOTE: A Jonathan Priest was in Jaffrey, NH in 1790 census 1-2-2.
REF: BVR; Sudbury VR.

PRIEST, Joseph, Jr

SERVICE: S S Vol 12 p 782; BRR 5 mos Capt D Nurse bounty Ł3; BRR 3 mos 14 ds to Goose 1777 bounty Ł10; BRR Capt Nurse's Co Ł4.
BORN: 28 Nov 1732 Lancaster s/o Joseph & Hannah.
MARRIED: unm.
DIED: 31 Jul 1817 Berlin GSB.
NOTE: Left residue of estate to town of Berlin to be used for "literary purposes" 1817.
REF: LVR; Berlin History, Rev W A Houghton 1895.

RAY, David

SERVICE: S&S Vol 12 p 994.
BORN: c1760 prob in Stow.
MARRIED: 6 Jul 1786 Stow, Mary Stow (b 1768 d/o Stephen).
DIED: 4 Aug 1794 ae 33y 8m 12ds GS1.
CHILDREN (b Stow):
  Ephraim - b 8 Feb 1787
  Abraham - b before 1790

RAY, David (Cont)

NOTE: Warned out of Bolton 1790, David Ray cordwainer of Stow with wife Mary and children Ephraim and Abraham. Elected to Overseers of Poor 1792.
REF: Stow VR; BVR.

REED, John

SERVICE: S&S Vol 13 p 76; BRR 10 Feb 1778 rec'd of Rich Townsend town money Ł14-10 1778; BRR rec'd of Col Whitcomb upon my acc't Ł10-7-5 1778.
BORN: 9 Jun 1758 Bedford s/o John & Ruhamah.
MARRIED: 1) 1 Dec 1785 Hannah Merriam; 2) 13 Nov 1801 (int) Bolton, Lucy Houghton d/o Capt Jonas & Lucy; 3) Rachel Clark (d 10 Apr 1844 or 1845 ae 96y 9m per GS or ae 84y 8m 18d per town records).
DIED: 9 Feb 1835 ae 80 Bolton GS3.
CHILDREN (b Bedford):
  Anna - b 2 Jul 1787 d 1807 consumption
  Otis - b 27 Mar 1791
  Hannah - b 6 Sep 1795 d 1819 m Joseph Colburn
  John - b 10 Apr 1798
    (b Bolton):
  Warren - bpt 31 Oct 1803
NOTE: Credited to Bedford.
REF: Bedford VR; BVR.

RICE, Sgt David

SERVICE: S&S Vol 13 p 149; BHist Lex Alarm; BRR Resolve 1775 6 wks; BRR 2 mos 10 ds York 1776 "a turn;" BRR reinforce Northern Army 30 ds 1777; BRR money raised Capt Nurse's Co 3 yrs Ł10.
BORN: 18 Feb 1757 Rutland s/o David & Love (Moore).
MARRIED: 8 Jun 1785 Rutland, wid Abigail Reed (d 1850 Princeton GS Princeton).
DIED: 2 Sep 1825 ae 68 Princeton.
CHILDREN (b Princeton):
  Hannah - b 13 May 1787 m Preston Pond
  John - b 21 Sep 1788 m Nancy Gibbs 1817
  David - b 24 Oct 1791 m Nancy Davis 1822, Capt
  Aaron - b 30 Jul 1793 m Susan Davis
  Betsy - b 20 Oct 1796 d 1799
  Reuben Walker - b 7 Mar 1798 m Mary Gibbs
  Nathan - b 3 Oct 1800 m Cynthia Derby
REF: Rutland VR; Princeton VR.

RICE, Eliakim

SERVICE: S&S Vol 13 p 152; BRR 5 mos NY Jul 1776 Ł10; MilAnn Capt Jonathan Houghton's Co 1776; BRR service RI 1780.

RICE, Eliakim (Cont)

BORN: 1 Apr 1756 Lancaster s/o Zebulon & Susannah.
MARRIED: 5 Nov 1778 Hannah Kendall "both of Winchendon."
DIED: 4 Aug 1834 Hartland, VT.
CHILDREN (b Ashburnham):
   John - bpt 23 Jul 1780
   Sarah - bpt 9 Jun 1782 d 1837 m Cary Allen
   Stephen - b 1792 d 1871 m Phebe Burbank 1814
NOTE: Other children, perhaps b Hartland, VT.
REF: LVR; Ashburnham VR; DARPI; DAR Lineage Book 107 p 207; DAR Lineage Book 130 p 16; Pension Application.

RICE, Harry (Henry)

SERVICE: Not in S&S; MilAnn service in RI 1781.
BORN: 14 Apr 1746 Sudbury s/o Isreal & Sarah (Rose).
MARRIED: 1) 25 Nov 1778 (int) Lancaster, Loas Holt of Lancaster; 2) 23 May in Barre Lucinda Brooks (d Mar 1804 d/o Dr Ephraim).
DIED: unkn.
CHILDREN: None known.
NOTE: Innkeeper in Barre 1806, removed soon after per Rice Genealogy.
REF: Sudbury VR; Lancaster VR; Genealogical History of the Rice Family, Andrew Ward 1858.

RICE, Samuel

SERVICE: S&S Vol 13 p 180-1; BRR money raised in Capt Nurse's Co 3 yrs Ł5-2; BRR money raised in Capt Nurse's Co Ł0-13-0.
BORN: 10 Aug 1720 Sudbury s/o Moses & Sarah (King).
MARRIED: 20 Jul 1741 Worcester, Dorothy Martin of Rutland (d 1790 Charlemont).
DIED: 20 Sep 1793 Charlemont.
CHILDREN (b Rutland):
   Moses - b 5 Apr 1742 m Ruth Pierce
   Asa - b 1747 m Lucy Smith
   Martin - b 1749 m Lucy Rice
   Samuel - m Dorothy Houghton
   Artemas - b 5 Apr 1758 m Asenath Adams
   Rachel - b 7 Oct 1762 m Thomas Tolman
   Lucy - d 15 Oct 1795
REF: Sudbury VR; Genealogical History of the Rice Family, Andrew Ward 1858.

RICE, Samuel

SERVICE: S&S Vol 13 p 180-1; BRR money raised in Capt Nurse's Co 3 yrs Ł5-2; BRR money raised in Capt Nurse's Co Ł0-

RICE, Samuel (Cont)

13-0; BRR money dep in Capt Nurse's hands Ł0-13-0.
BORN: 11 Apr 1762 Northboro s/o Seth & Rachel (Coolidge).
MARRIED: 1) 17 Oct 1784 Rispah Wilson (d Oct 1806); 2) 6 Oct 1813 Azuba Cobb (d Princeton 1836).
DIED: 14 Jan 1832 Princeton.
CHILDREN (b Northboro):
   Relief - b 1785
   Benjamin - b 1787
   Barnabus - b 1789
   Rachel - b 1792
   Seth - b 1794
   Persis - b 1796
   Samuel - b 1798
   Rispah - b 1801
   Jas A Bayard - b 1802
   Lucy - b 1814
REF: Northborough VR; Princeton History, F B Blake 1915.

RICHARDSON, Maj James

SERVICE: S&S Vol 13 p 243.
BORN: 1723 Roxbury s/o John Esq & Abigail.
MARRIED: Lydia ____ (d 1796 ae 69 GS1).
DIED: 21 Nov 1799 ae 76 Bolton GS1.
NOTE: Deputy Assistant Commissary General of Issues & later Assistant Commissary General of Issues; wages $90 per mo, $10 for rations plus 1 daily ration. See History of Rutland for description of trouble at Rutland Barracks which had to be settled by him.
REF: Roxbury VR; BVR; Worc Co Probate Records; History of the Town of Rutland, T C Murphy 1928.

RICHARDSON, Joshua

SERVICE: S&S Vol 13 p 253.
BORN: 1712 Roxbury s/o John Esq & Abigail.
MARRIED: unm.
DIED: 21 May 1793 Bolton ae 81 GS1.
NOTE: Patriotic service between 19 Apr 1775 and 13 Apr 1778.
REF: Roxbury VR; BVR; Worcester Co Probate Records.

ROBBINS, Jonathan, also Robins

SERVICE: S&S Vol 13 p 382, 426-7; BHist Lex Alarm.
BORN: 1 Aug 1742 Bolton s/o Jonathan & Elizabeth.
MARRIED: Sarah ____ (Lunah in DARPI).
DIED: 30 Jul 1794 Plymouth, Grafton Co, NH.
CHILDREN (b Bolton):

Built in 1738 by Josiah Richardson and used as an inn for several years, this was the home of Major James Richardson until his death in 1799. It was owned by S. V. S. Wilder from 1814 until 1845 and has been know as the Wilder Mansion since that time. The building was still standing as of 1983.

ROBBINS, Jonathan (Cont)

Jonathan - b 3 Mar 1767
Sarey - b 19 Apr 1769
Rachel - b 9 Jul 1771
Edward - b 29 Aug 1773
NOTE: Pension S377353; also served for Stow.
REF: BVR; DARPI; Pension Records.

ROSE, John also Ross

SERVICE: S & S Vol 13 p 570 & 587; BHist Lex Alarm.
BORN: 22 Mar 1732-3 Sudbury s/o John & Submit (Hoar).
MARRIED: 4 Nov 1762 Billerica, Mary Dunklee.
DIED: After 1784.
CHILDREN (b Billerica):
Mary - b 4 Aug 1763
Sarah - b 31 Jan 1765 bpt 9 Feb 1766
NOTE: DARPI gives birth of John as 2 Apr 1733; possibly date of bpt?
REF: Sudbury VR; Billerica VR; DARPI.

ROSS, William

SERVICE: S&S Vol 13 p 594; BHist Lex Alarm; BHist Siege of Boston; BHist Resolve Jun 1776; BRR 3 mos in NY 1776 Ł10; BRR 5 mos in NY Jul 1776 Ł12 paid by Nathan Ball, Abijah Pollard; DNR carpenter in Winter Campaign 1776-7; BHist 6 mos men 1780.
BORN: 17 Aug 1746 Sudbury s/o John & Submit (Hoar).
MARRIED: 19 Jan 1781 Concord, Abigail Dudley II (d 1824 ae 70 GS3).
DIED: ae 88 Bolton, GS3 Rev marker.
CHILDREN (b Bolton):
David - b 4 Feb 1781 m Rebecca Sawyer 1807
Elizabeth - b 18 Mar 1784
William - b 18 Dec 1786 m Deborah ___ d 1829 GS3
Abraham - b 10 Dec 1792
Polly - b 25 Mar 1794
Dorcas - b 27 Sep 1796 d young
Dorcas - b 2 Jun 1803
NOTE: Descriptive List 1780 - William

BOLTON SOLDIERS AND SAILORS IN THE AMERICAN REVOLUTION

ROSS, William (Cont)

Ross, ae 33, stature 5´9".
REF: Sudbury VR; BVR; Concord VR.

RUGG, Joseph

SERVICE: S & S Vol 13 p 649; MilAnn Capt
Jona Houghton's Co.
BORN: Possibly Jaffrey, NH.
MARRIED: 29 Nov 1792 Mary Hazen "both of
Lancaster."
DIED: 8 Jul 1844 Westminster.
CHILDREN (b Lancaster):
　Mary - b 9 Jun 1793 bpt 18 Oct 1795
　Joseph - b 21 Nov 1794 bpt 18 Oct 1795
　Sarah Harriman - bpt 28 Oct 1796
　Edward - bpt 29 May 1798 d 1822
　Nancy - bpt 7 Sep 1800
　Grenville - bpt 6 Jun 1802
　Elijah - bpt 3 Jun 1804
　Lucy - bpt 16 Feb 1806
　William - bpt 5 Jun 1808
　Christopher - bpt 29 Apr 1810 twin
　Augustus - bpt 29 Apr 1810 twin d 1812
　Julia - bpt 27 Jun 1813
　Harriet - bpt 4 Jun 1815
　Benj Hazen - bpt 25 May 1817
NOTE: LVR 1795 Joseph Rugg joined church
in Lancaster by cert from Jaffrey, NH;
LVR 22 Sep 1833 "Joseph & Mary Rugg
recommended to the church at Westminster
under the pastoral charge of Rev. Mr.
Hudson."
REF: LVR; Westminster VR.

RUGGLES, Robert

SERVICE: Not in S&S.
BORN: 11 Feb 1746 Boston s/o Samuel &
Hannah.
MARRIED: 1) 21 Dec 1769 Boston, Elizabeth Swett (d 15 May 1784 Bolton GS1);
2) 24 Nov 1784 Boston, Mary Swett; 3) 11
Mar 1802 Boston, Ruth Torrey.
DIED: unk.
CHILDREN:
　Betsy - d 12 Jun 1849 Bolton
NOTE: Robert Ruggles lived in Bolton but
was a merchant in Boston. It appears
that he was never personally in the war,
but paid for several others who were
soldiers. Boston Committee of Corres-
pondence requested Ruggles to explain
his absence on Muster Day. He said his
absence was occasioned by his being
obliged to go to Portsmouth to lay in
his claim to part of the goods on board
a prize sent in by Capt Manly 2 Aug
1776. NEHGSR XXXI p 292.
REF: Boston Births 1700-1800; BVR.

RUGGLES, York, also Rugles

SERVICE: S&S Vol 16 p 656-7; MilAnn Ƚ30
for Ruggles service 1777; MilAnn First
Reg 1779.
BORN: c1750 Africa.
NOTE: MilAnn res Cambridge & Boston "a
slave hired;" Descriptive List 1781 -
"age 31, stature 5´6", complexion black,
hair wool, birthplace Africa, res Cambridge." In list dated 18 Jan 1802
"rec. gratuity for actually serving 3
years under Resolve of 4 Mar. 1801 & 19
June 1801;" 1790 census Boston, he is
listed with 7 other free persons.

RUSSEL, Thaddeus

SERVICE: S&S Vol 13 p 682; BRR money
raised 3 years Capt Nurse's Co Ƚ6.
BORN: 27 Jan 1741 Cambridge s/o Eliezer
& Tabitha (Prentice).
MARRIED: 18 Jun 1764 Bolton, Elizabeth
Pratt d/o Abijah & Mary.
DIED: After 1790
CHILDREN (b Bolton):
　Lavina - b 24 Jun 1766 m Eleazer
　　　Jones, Wardsboro, VT
　Eleazer - b 5 Aug 1768 m Relief
　　　Sawyer, Boxboro
　Caleb - b 26 Jul 1770 m Sally Gould
　Eli - b 1773
　Oliver - b 10 May 1775 m Betsy
　　　Wheeler, Concord
　Elizabeth - b 21 Jan 1778
　Thaddeus - b 16 Feb 1780
　John - b 27 May 1782 d 1782
　Sally - b 15 Jun 1785 m John McBride
　Jonah - d 7 Jan 1786
REF: BVR; Genealogical Records of Rus-
sell Families, L H Russell 1898.

SALT, Joseph

SERVICE: S & S Vol 13 p 750; MilAnn Cont
Army 1st Reg.
NOTE: Reported a stroller; a Joseph Salt
of Scarborough also listed; may be the
same man; dates of service do not con-
flict.

SAWYER, Benjamin

SERVICE: S & S Vol 13 p 860; BHist Siege
of Boston; BRR 2 mos NY 1776 bounty Ƚ6;
DNR 1776-7 Winter Campaign; BRR 8 mos
Cont Army 1778 bounty Ƚ25; BRR reinforce
Cont Army Ƚ25; BRR reinforce Cont army
RI 3 mos Jun 1780 Ƚ12; BRR Cont Army 3
mos 1780; BRR 8 mos service 1778 Ƚ100.
BORN: 10 Sep 1758 Bolton s/o William &
Sarah (Sawtelle).
MARRIED: 6 Dec 1781 Rebecca Houghton (d
22 Dec 1832 ae 72).

65

SAWYER, Benjamin (Cont)

DIED: 30 Mar 1844 ae 85 Bolton, no stone.
CHILDREN (b Bolton):
  Rebecca - b 16 Mar 1782 m David Ross of Boston 1807
  Levi - b 1 Oct 1783 physician m Hannah Nurse 1818
  Benjamin - b 19 Feb 1785
  Betsy - b 27 Apr 1786 d young
  Jonah - b 31 Aug 1787 d 1817
  Salley - b 27 Oct 1788 d 3 Mar 1790
  William - b 30 Apr 1792 d 1819
  John - b 17 Feb 1794 m Abagail Moore 1821
  Lucy - b 3 Oct 1795 m Holloway Bailey 1825
  Betsy - b 6 Sep 1797 m Samuel Spafford 1820
  Cephas - b 20 Aug 1800
  Sally - b 3 Jul 1804 d 1804
REF: BVR.

SAWYER, Barnabas

SERVICE: S&S Vol 13 p 859; BRR 3 mos NY 1776 ₤10; BRR 5 mos to York 1776; DNR Dec 1776 fifer, Winter Campaign; BRR Boston Feb 1778 with Gen Heath; BRR Boston Sep 1778 3 mos ₤11-7-4; BRR 2 mos RI 1779 ₤5-11-1; BRR 3 1/2 mos 1778 this state or elsewhere ₤20 per mo inc all other wages.
BORN: 1 Apr 1761 Bolton s/o William & Sarah (Sawtelle).
MARRIED: 1) 14 Dec 1778 Bolton, Unity Houghton d/o Jonathan; 2) 19 Jun 1783 Bolton, Lydia Whitcomb d/o Paul & Rebecca.
DIED: Before 1791 when Lydia is called widow in Bolton tax lists.
REF: BVR.

SAWYER, Sgt George

SERVICE: S&S Vol 13 p 869; BHist Lex Alarm; BHist Siege of Boston; BHist Resolve Jun 1776 to York ₤10; BRR to Boston 3 mos 1776; BRR 5 mos NY Jul 1776 ₤10; DNR Winter Campaign 1776-7; BRR Bennington Sep 1777; BRR 3 mos to Northward 1777; BRR Service in Boston 1778.

SAWYER, Sgt George

BORN: 25 Nov 1757 in Bolton s/o Aholiab & Betty.
MARRIED: 3 Jul 1786 (int) Templeton, Lucy Merritt.
DIED: 30 Apr 1842 ae 84 at Mercer, Somerset Co, ME.
NOTE: George Sawyer rec'd ₤5 from Henry Powers for his engaging to do 1/2 a 3

SAWYER, Sgt George (Cont)

mos turn in Cont Army.
REF: BVR; Templeton VR; DARPI, US Pension Record S30087; Rev War records copied into Town Clerk's book by Town Clerk Richard S Edes.

SAWYER, Corp Isreal

SERVICE: S&S Vol 13 p 870; BHist Lex Alarm; BHist Siege of Boston; Pension Appl, Bunker Hill; Pension Appl, Surrender of Cornwallis at Yorktown.
BORN: 9 Sep 1751 Bolton s/o Aholiab & Betty.
MARRIED: 1) 25 Nov 1773 Bolton; Beulah Wilson (b 1756 Bolton d/o Nath'l & Eunice); 2) ___; 3) Catherine ___; 4) Anna Thompson (was in Allegany Co, NY in 1845).
DIED: 18 Jan 1832 Swanzey, NH.
CHILDREN:
  Gardner - b 19 Apr 1774 Bolton
  Elijah - b 1784, ae 61 in 1845
  Josiah - living in 1845
REF: BVR; DARPI; Pension Record S29427.

SAWYER, John

SERVICE: S&S Vol 13 p 874; BRR 2 mos NY 1776.
BORN: 31 Mar 1748 Bolton s/o Jonathan & Elizabeth (Whitney).
MARRIED: 29 Nov 1770 Bolton, Mary Moor III (d 8 Nov 1795 ae 45).
DIED: 30 May 1812 ae 64 "Deacon" GS1.
CHILDREN (b Bolton):
  Mary - b 23 Sep 1774 m Silas Reed 1792
  Betty - b 8 Feb 1777
  John - b 20 Jan 1779 m Ruth Carter 1802
  Lucy - b 24 Nov 1780
  Nabby - 25 Jan 1783 m Simeon Stone 1802
  Peter - b 21 May 1785
  Sophia - b 19 Oct 1788
REF: BVR.

SAWYER, Jonathan

SERVICE: S&S Vol 13 p 875; MilAnn Lex Alarm; BRR 2 mos NY 1777; BRR 2 mos RI 1777; BRR reinforce Army RI 1778 ₤4-8-6; BRR 6 wks RI Jul 1778.
BORN: bpt 24 Jun 1716 Lancaster s/o Jonathan.
MARRIED: 30 Sep 1740 Harvard, wid Elizabeth Whitney (d 1815 Bolton ae 105 GS1).
DIED: 21 Feb 1805 ae 90 Bolton GS1.
CHILDREN (b Harvard):
  Lois - bpt 26 Jul 1741 d 1746
  Peter - b 27 Nov 1743 d 1746
  Jonathan - b 24 Nov 1745 d 1746

SAWYER, Jonathan (Cont)

(b Bolton):
John - b 31 Mar 1748 m Mary Moor III
Adington - b 14 Oct 1752
Sara - b 26 Jun 1728 (error, possibly 1758) m John Nurse as his 2nd wife in 1786
NOTE: Also served for Lancaster.
REF: LVR; BVR; HVR.

SAWYER, Joseph

SERVICE: S&S Vol 13 p 878; BHist Lex Alarm; BRR 3 mos NY 1776 Ł15; BRR 5 mos Boston 1776-7 Ł3; BRR Bennington Sep 1777.
BORN: 8 Mar 1756 Bolton s/o William & Sarah (Sawtelle).
MARRIED: 31 Jul 1782 Bolton, Ruth Walcott (d 10 Jun 1830 ae 67 Bolton).
DIED: 12 Mar 1828 ae 72 yrs 4 d GS2 Rev Marker.
CHILDREN (b Bolton):
Eunice - b 10 Apr 1783 m Nathan Corey
Achsah - b 4 Feb 1785 m William Munroe
Joseph - b 15 Mar 1787 m Abigail Bender
Ruth - b 15 Jun 1789 m Dea Robert Peckham
Asenath - b 4 Apr 1791 m Joel B Fuller of Worcester 1834
Zilpah - b 29 May 1795 m Capt Oliver Adams
Sarah - b 20 Jan 1797
George - b 23 Jan 1800 m Abigail Shedd
Joel - b 24 Jul 1805 m Sarah Barrett
Nathan - b 18 May 1807 m Lucinda Pollard
NOTE: Mass Archives Descriptive List - Col Whitney's Reg, Capt Houghton's, Capt Nurse's Co, Jos Sawyer, about 20, 5'11" high, light complexion, light hair.
REF: BVR; DARPI.

SAWYER, Dea Josiah

SERVICE: S&S Vol 13 p 879; BHist Lex Alarm; BRR to Goose 3 mos 14 ds Ł5; BRR money raised Capt Nurse's Co 3 yrs Ł5.
BORN: bpt 24 Oct 1714 Lancaster s/o William & Hannah (Houghton).
MARRIED: 1) 28 Jul 1738 (int), Sarah Fairbank (d 1762 d/o Jabez); 2) 14 Jan 1764 Lancaster, Mary Tooker (d 1799).
DIED: 3 Jul 1805 ae 91 GSB.
CHILDREN (b Bolton):
Josiah - b 24 Nov 1738 d young
William - b 5 Mar 1740 m Hannah Barrett
Hannah - b 25 Jun 1743 m ___ Curtis
Rebecca - b 15 Feb 1745 m ___ Wilder
Sarah - b 6 Feb 1747 m Wm Wilder
Aholiab - 1749

SAWYER, Dea Josiah (Cont)

Josiah - b 8 Nov 1752 m1 Bathsheba Moor m2 Persis Baker m3 Wid Prudence Johnson
Levi - b 10 Nov 1764 d young
Silas - b 5 Jul 1766 m Sarah Howe
Thomas - b 9 Mar 1770 d 1771
REF: LVR; BVR; Berlin History, Rev W A Houghton 1895.

SAWYER, Josiah, Jr (3rd), also Sayer

SERVICE: S&S Vol 13 p 879 & 893; BRR Resolve 1775 6 wks; BRR 1 yr to York 1776; BRR 2 mos York 1776 Ł4; BHist Col Stearns Reg 1777; BHist reinforcement 1778; BRR Cont Army 9 mos 1778 Ł37-10; BRR Fishkill 9 mos 1778.
BORN: 8 Nov 1752 Bolton s/o Dea Josiah & Sarah (Fairbank).
MARRIED: 1) 6 Aug 1770 Putney, VT, Bathsheba Moore of Putney (d 1778); 2) 10 Feb 1779 Berlin, Persis Baker (d 1785); 3) 4 Jan 1786 Lancaster, Wid Prudence Johnson.
DIED: 1808 ae 56 Berlin GSB.
CHILDREN (b Bolton):
Alvan - b 30 Oct 1770
Eunice - b 10 Nov 1774 m Ephraim Babcock
Bathsheba - b 9 Mar 1778 d young
Susannah - b 19 Nov 1781 m Caleb Houghton
Bathsheba - b 1784 d young
(b Berlin):
Ira - b 31 Oct 1787
Lucinda - b 20 Apr 1789 m1 Amory Carter m2 Cummings Moore
Rufus - b 22 Sep 1790
George - b 6 Feb 1793
Asa - b 3 Sep 1795
Persis - b 18 Jun 1796 d young
Persis - b 18 Jun 1798 m Loring How
Sarah - b 12 Jul 1800 m Lewis Carter
NOTE: Descriptive List 1778 - ae 26, stature 5'11".
REF: BVR; Berlin History, Rev W A Houghton 1895.

SAWYER, Thomas

SERVICE: S&S Vol 13 p 886; MilAnn Lex Alarm; MilAnn Dorchester Hghts.
BORN: 1710 bpt 1716 Lancaster s/o Nathaneal.
MARRIED: 1) 21 Oct 1736 Lancaster, Elizabeth Osgood (d 28 May 1761 ae 52); 2) 25 Mar 1762 Bolton, Mary Houghton (d 3 Oct 1800 in 81st yr).
DIED: 31 Mar 1797 in 87th yr GS1.
CHILDREN (b Bolton):
Abraham - b 19 Sep 1737
Thomas - b 6 Feb 1739-40 m Prudence

SAWYER, Thomas (Cont)

Carter
Abner - b 9 May 1742 m Hannah Piper
Hooker - b 3 Nov 1744 d 1772
Elizabeth - b 12 Jun 1747 m Eliakim Atherton
Joseph - b 7 Jul 1750 d 1750
NOTE: Credited to Lancaster.
REF: LVR; BVR.

SAWYER, William

SERVICE: S&S Vol 13 p 887; BHist Lex Alarm; BHist Siege of Boston; BRR Capt D Nurse Co 5 mos 1775 Ł10; BRR Resolve 1776 5 mos NY; BRR 9 mos Cont Army 1778 Ł37-10.
BORN: 5 Mar 1740-1 Bolton s/o Josiah & Sarah (Fairbank).
MARRIED: 18 Jan 1764 Bolton, Hannah Barrett (d 1830 ae 88 d/o Oliver & Hannah).
DIED: 28 Feb 1822 ae 80 y 11 m GSB.
CHILDREN (b Bolton):
Abigail - b 5 May 1765 m Cotton Newton
William - b 6 Feb 1767
Amos - b 17 Mar 1769 m Persis Howe
Mary - b 8 Feb 1771 m Rufus Howe
Oliver - b 17 Apr 1774 ml Lucy Fairbank m2 Sapphira Rice m3 Eunice Bruce d/o Daniel, d 1845 Brimfield
Asa - b 2 Aug 1775 removed to Jaffrey, NH
Uriah - b 24 May 1778 m Sally Spofford
Polly - b 1780 m Rufus Howe
Hannah - b 6 Jan 1781 m Robert Fosgate Jr
Levi - b 1784 d young
REF: BVR; Berlin History, Rev W A Houghton 1895.

SAWYER, Lt William, Jr (3rd)

SERVICE: S&S Vol 13 p 887-8; BRR 5 mos Jul 1776 NY Ł12; BHist reinforcements 1778; BRR 9 mos Cont Army 1778 Ł37-10; BRR 5 mos men 1775 Ł10; BRR Fishkill 9 mos 1778.
BORN: 26 Sep 1749 Bolton s/o William & Sarah (Sawtelle).
MARRIED: 22 Dec 1769 Keziah Moor (d 1824 d/o Samuel & Zerish).
DIED: 1819 Bolton, no stone.
CHILDREN (b Bolton):
Levi - b 14 May 1769 d 1771
Zerish - b 17 Nov 1770
Abigail - b 30 Jan 1773
Keziah - b 20 Jun 1775
Polly - b 1 Nov 1777
Charity - b 24 Dec 1779
William - b 28 Mar 1782
Samuel - b 5 Jun 1784

SAWYER, Lt William, Jr (3rd) (Cont)

Josiah - b 30 Mar 1786
Phineas - bpt 15 Mar 1789
Sarah - bpt 15 Mar 1789
NOTE: Descriptive List, Col Whitney's Reg, Capt Houghton's & Capt Nurse's Co, 1778 - Wm Sawyer ye 3rd, about 28 years, about 5'9" high, fair complexion, brown hair. Mass Archives.
REF: BVR; DARPI.

SKINER, Robert, also Skinner

SERVICE: S&S Vol 14 p 275 & 281.
BORN: 15 Sep 1762 Mansfield s/o Solomon Jr & Sarah (Britnell).
MARRIED: unk.
DIED: 14 Apr 1779.
NOTE: Killed or died in war.
REF: Mansfield VR.

SMITH, Ens Ephraim

SERVICE: S&S Vol 14 p 396-7; MilAnn Lancaster Reg p 121.
BORN: 1744
MARRIED: Thankful Goodman (d 1837).
DIED: 30 Jun 1827 South Hadley.
CHILDREN: UNK.
REF: DARPI; History of Hadley, Sylvester Judd 1905.

SNOW, James, Jr

SERVICE: S&S Vol 14 p 609-10; MilAnn RI Alarm 1779; BHist 14th Reg.
BORN: 18 Nov 1756 Bolton s/o James & Deliverance (Davenport).
MARRIED: 2 Jan 1783 Leicester, Lidea Moor of Worcester.
DIED: 1811 GS Elliot Hill Cem Leicester.
NOTE: Pension #54909; Worcester Co Probate Records, will Case A 54910
REF: BVR; Leicester VR; Worc Co Probate Records.

SNOW, Samuel

SERVICE: S&S Vol 14 p 622-3; MilAnn Bennington 1777; MilAnn to Boston 1778; MilAnn Desc List 1780; MilAnn to West Point 1781.
BORN: 18 Sep 1763 Lancaster s/o Samuel.
MARRIED: 1 Apr 1784 Lancaster, Dorothy Richardson (both of Sterling).
DIED: unk.
NOTE: Descriptive List 1780 - ae 17 yr, 5'5" high.
REF: LVR; Sterling VR.

SOUTHGATE, Amos

SERVICE: S&S Vol 14 p 656; BHist Siege

SOUTHGATE, Amos (Cont)

of Boston.
BORN: 31 Dec 1751 Leicester s/o Steward & Elizabeth.
MARRIED: Abigail ___.
DIED: 21 Sep 1775 in siege of Boston.
CHILDREN (b Bolton):
  Eliz abeth - b 7 (or 4) Dec 1775 post-
     humous
NOTE: Died in war. Widow Southgate in 1790 census of Bolton. In Bolton tax list 1790 Widow Southgate is assessed for a mill.
REF: LEICESTER VR; BVR.

SPAFFORD, Job

SERVICE: S&S Vol 14 p 671; BerlHist Battle of Bunker Hill.
BORN: 1753 Boylston s/o Samuel.
MARRIED: 21 Nov 1776 Berlin, Esther Taylor d/o David & Esther (Jones).
DIED: 5 Apr 1840 ae 87 "Deacon" Berlin GSB.
CHILDREN (b Bolton):
  David - b 8 Aug 1777
  Betsy - b 12 Feb 1779
  Sally - b 30 Aug 1781
  Samuel - b 7 Aug 1783
     (b Berlin):
  Job - b 17 Oct 1785
  Benj Frnaklin - b 30 Jan 1787
  Esther - b 7 Jan 1793
REF: BVR; Berlin History, Rev W A Hough-ton 1895, BerlVR.

SPAFFORD, Samuel

SERVICE: S&S Vol 14 p 673.
BORN: 1763 Boylston s/o Samuel.
MARRIED: 20 Jan 1785 Berlin, Eunice Goddard.
DIED: 6 Nov 1809 ae 47 Berlin GSB.
CHILDREN (b Berlin):
  Sally - b 15 Mar 1786 bpt 21 Aug 1791
  James - b 2 Nov 1787 d 15 Apr 1790
  Eunice - b 18 July 1791
  Sally -
  Samuel - bpt 1 Dec 1793 m Betsy Sawyer
     1820
  Hannah - b 5 Oct 1795 d 15 Oct 1809
  Job - b 7 Jul 1798 d 9 Jul 1801 ae 3
  Betsy - b 26 Dec 1802
  Emerson - bpt 23 Dec 1808
  Jas Richardson - b 3 Aug 1808 d 8 Mar
     1815
NOTE: Served for Marlborough. Descriptive List 1780: ae 18 yrs, 5'8" high, complexion dark, hair brown, eyes brown, blacksmith.
REF: Boylston VR; Berl VR.

STANHOPE, Asa

SERVICE: Not in S&S; BRR Guard Stores 1776.
NOTE: Asa Stanhope may have been the son of Samuel and Elizabeth of Sudbury, and brother of Samuel Jr and Peter.

STANHOPE, Peter

SERVICE: S&S Vol 14 p 825; BRR 5 mos in Boston 1776; BRR 5 mos Dorchester Jul 1776.
BORN: 29 Nov 1759 Sudbury s/o Samuel & Elizabeth (Angier).
MARRIED: 30 Nov 1775 Bolton, Elizabeth Parmenter of Sudbury.
DIED: 1845 Robinston, ME.
CHILDREN:
  Elizabeth - b 1780 d 1879 m Sam'l
     Duncan 1813
REF: BVR; Sudbury VR; DARPI; DAR Lineage Book 122 p 125.

STANHOPE, Sanuel Jr

SERVICE: S&S Vol 14 p 824; BHist Lex Alarm; BRR siege of Boston 1775; BRR guard at Rutland 6 mos 1776; BRR RI 6 wks 1778; BRR money raised Capt Nurse's Co 3 yrs Ł8.
BORN: 15 Oct 1756 Sudbury s/o Samuel & Elizabeth (Angier).
MARRIED: 26 Feb 1778 Sudbury, Mary Good-now of Stow.
DIED: 27 Oct 1839 Attica, NY.
CHILDREN (B Bolton):
  Charlotte - b 27 Feb 1779
  Molly Anger - b 24 Sep 1780
  Levi - b 1738 (1783?) d 1861 m Lucinda
     Davis
REF: Sudbury VR; BVR; DARPI; DAR Lineage Book 69 p 158 & Book 96 p 20.

STEARNS, Jonathan

SERVICE: S&S Vol 14 p 880; BHist Capt Hez Whitney's Co 1778.
BORN: 26 Sep 1762 Harvard s/o Wiliam & Elizabeth (Bert).
MARRIED: 1) Hannah ___; 2) 1784 Molly Wright.
DIED: 20 Jul 1845.
CHILDREN (bpt Boxborough):
  Jonathan - bpt 4 Mar 1792
  Marcy - bpt 4 Mar 1792
  Salley - bpt 4 Mar 1792
NOTE: Pensioned.
REF: HVR; Boxborough VR; DARPI; DAR Lineage Book 137 p 92.

STILES, David

SERVICE: S&S Vol 15 p 17; BHist Lex

STILES, David (Cont)

Alarm.
BORN: bpt 2 Apr 1738 Boxford s/o Gideon & Sarah (Faulkner).
MARRIED: 1) 7 Aug 1760 Andover, Hannah Norton (d 30 Apr 1765 Bolton); 2) 11 Dec 1765 Bolton, Tabitha Oak (b 1737 Westboro d/o Nathaniel & Keziah).
DIED: 15 Apr 1811 ae 74 Westminster, VT, GS Bemis Hill Cem.
CHILDREN (b Bolton):
  Juda - b 12 May 1761 unm
  Hannah - b 19 Aug 1762 m Coffin Chapin
  Minde - b 20 Dec 1766 m Ephraim Smith
  Eunice - b 30 Jun 1769
  David - b 19 Aug 1771 m Mrs Elizabeth
    Wyman
  Gideon - b 29 Aug 1773 m Lydia Wyman
  Keziah - b 24 Jun 1775 m1 Wm Brooks m2
    David Bemis
  Nathaniel - b 22 Jun 1777 m1 Lucy
    Crosby m2 Mary Taft
REF: Boxford VR; BVR; Stiles Family of America, Leon Stiles, unpub mss.

STILES, Joshua

SERVICE: S&S Vol 15 p 21.
BORN: 6 Apr 1758.
MARRIED: 12 Mar 1781 Shrewsbury, Abigail Gale.
DIED: 14 May 1828 Boylston "Deacon."
CHILDREN (b Shrewsbury):
  Nabby - b 14 Feb 1782
  Percis - b 31 Jan 1784
REF: Shrewsbury VR; Boylston VR; Princeton History, F E Blake 1915; DARPI.

STRATTON, David, Jr

SERVICE: S&S Vol 15 p 168; BHist Lex Alarm.
BORN: 26 Dec 1742 Watertown s/o David & Hannah (Smith).
MARRIED: 5 Feb 1770 Dinah Wheeler (d 1837 ae 86 d/o Joseph & Deborah).
DIED: 13 Jun 1819 ae 76 GS1.
CHILDREN (b Stow):
  John - b 31 Oct 1770
  Lydia - b 25 Feb 1772 d unm
    (b Harvard):
  Lucy - b 5 Dec 1773 m Hooker Sawyer
    (b Bolton):
  Anna - b 12 Jan 1778 m Jesse Brown
  Susannah - b 8 Mar 1780 m Stephen Snow
  Isaac - b 2 May 1782 m Mary Goodale
  Betsy - b 27 Mar 1784 m Thomas Carr of
    Sudbury
  Achsah - b 26 Jul 1786 d 1849
  Mary (Polly) - b 15 Jul 1788 m Timothy
    Goodale
  Levinah - b 22 Sep 1790
  Dolly - bpt 26 May 1793 m Levi How Jr

STRATTON, David, Jr (Cont)

REF: BVR; HVR; SVR; A Book of Strattons, Harriet R Stratton 1918; Wheeler Family in America, Albert G Wheeler 1914.

SYMONDS, Jonathan

SERVICE: S&S Vol 15 p 338; MilAnn Lex Alarm; MilAnn Capt Nurse's Co the Jerseys 1777; MilAnn Bennington Alarm 1777; BHist Capt Hez Whitney's Co 1778.
BORN: 7 Aug 1755 Harvard s/o Jonathan & Judith (Cole).
MARRIED: 23 Jan 1778 Harvard, Hannah Clark of Harvard (d 1805).
DIED: 31 Oct 1830 ae 75 GS Old Cem Harvard.
CHILDREN (b Harvard):
  Silvester - b 12 May 1780 m Nabby
    Pollard
  Hannah - b 10 Jul 1788 m Geo Willard
  Jonathan Bowman - b 20 Mar 1791 m
    Sally Chaffin
NOTE: Also served for Harvard.
REF: HVR.

TAYLOR, David

SERVICE: S&S Vol 15 p 422.
BORN: 17 Sep 1723 Marlborough s/o Eleazer & Judith (Hapgood).
MARRIED: 1) 8 Apr 1746 Shrewsbury, Hazadiah Wheeler (d 1754 in 30th yr); 2) 17 Jul 1756 Shrewsbury, Esther Jones (d 1801 Berlin).
DIED: 30 Aug 1795 ae 72 Berlin GSB.
CHILDREN (b Bolton):
  Esther - b 28 Jan 1759 m Job Spafford
    1776
  Hannah - b 15 Sep 1760
  Lucy - b 9 Oct 1762
REF: Marlborough History, Charles Hudson 1862; Berlin History, Rev W A Houghton 1895; Shrewsbury VR; BVR.

TEVEN, Anthony (Antoine), also
Theven, Thevon, or Thurin

SERVICE: S&S Vol 15 p 498 571-2 & 711; MilAnn 16th Reg.
NOTE: Served for Bolton 1778. Belonged to France. Descriptive List 1781 - Frenchman, ae 35, 5'7" high, dark complexion, dark hair, hatter. Served continuously 10 Sep 1777 to 8 Jun 1783.

TOWNSEND, Abraham

SERVICE: S & S Vol 15 p 924; MilAnn reinforce Cont Army 1778; MilAnn Ticonderoga 1778.
BORN: 18 Nov 1751 (Townsing) Westborough s/o Joshua Jr & Mary.

TOWNSEND, Abraham (Cont)

MARRIED: 21 Jun 1781 Ashburnham, Molly
Gardner of Sherborn (d 1843 Berlin, VT).
DIED: 18 Apr 1834 Berlin, VT GS Wright
Cemetery.
CHILDREN (b Ashburnham):
  Molly – b 24 Apr 1783
  Priscilla – b 5 Apr 1785
  Naamah – b 17 May 1787
  Betcy – b 18 Jul 1790
  Abraham – b 25 Oct 1792 War of 1812 VT
  Benjamin – b 23 Jul 1799
NOTE: Widow rec'd pension.
REF: Ashburnham VR; Westborough VR;
Vermont Historical Gazetteer, Vol 4,
Abbie M Hemenway; Soldiers of the Revo-
lutionary War Buried in Vermont, Walter
H Crockett.

TOWNSEND, Corp James

SERVICE: S&S Vol 15 p 928; BHist Lex
Alarm; BRR 5 mos men 1775 £2; BRR rein-
force Northern Army 30 ds 1777; BRR
Northern Army Oct 1777; BRR to Goose 3
mos 14 ds 1777 £5.
BORN: 12 Aug 1733 Boston s/o Joshua &
Elizabeth (White).
MARRIED: 1) 29 May 1764 Bolton, Hannah
Merriam (d 1777 in 34th yr); 2) 8 Oct
1778 Lancaster, Olive Sawyer (d 1838 ae
89 Bolton).
DIED: 11 Jun 1801 in 68th yr Bolton GS1
Rev Marker.
CHILDREN (b Bolton):
  Hannah – b 9 Dec 1764
  James – b 26 Dec 1767 m Sarah Whitney
      1797
  Levi – b 6 May 1770
  Mary – b 2 Feb 1777 m Levi Prescott
      1797
  Nancy – b 29 Mar 1779 d unm GS3
  Elisha – b 21 Oct 1780 m Lucy Rand
      1807
  Able – b 12 Feb 1783
  Darius – b 30 Oct 1785
  William – b 4 Sep 1787 m Martha Wilder
      1813
  Deborah – b 20 Dec 1789
REF: Records of Town of Boston; BVR;
LVR.

TOWNSEND, Lt John

SERVICE: S&S Vol 15 p 929; BHist Lex
Alarm; BRR 3 mos NY 1776 £10; DNR Sgt
1776-7 Winter Campaign.
BORN: 16 May 1742 Bolton s/o Joshua &
Elizabeth (White).
MARRIED: 25 Jul 1770 Lancaster, Eunice
Fairbank of Lancaster.
DIED: 4 Apr 1827 ae 85 Putney, VT GS
West Hill Cem (no stone 1981).

TOWNSEND, Lt John (Cont)

CHILDREN (b Bolton):
  Eunice – b 9 Dec 1771 m Edwin Dunklee
  John – b 6 Sep 1774 m Abigail Whitney
  Martha (Patty) – b 18 Dec 1776 m Peter
      Benson
  Frances – b 18 Sep 1778
          (b Putney, VT):
  Nathan (or Nahum) – b 10 May 1782
  Nancy – b 12 Oct 1783 m Elias
      Greenleaf
  Abel – b 15 Sep 1785
  Betsy – b 1 Jan 1788
REF: BVR; LVR; Townsend Family Bible;
Putney 200 Years, Fortnightly Club 1953;
DARPI; Brattleboro Chapter DAR Grave
List.

TOWNSEND, Joshua

SERVICE: S&S Vol 15 p 931; MilAnn Lex
Alarm.
BORN: 14 Mar 1700 Boston s/o James &
Alice.
MARRIED: 11 Jan 1723 Boston by Dr Cotton
Mather, Elizabeth White (d 1779 in 76th
yr Lancaster).
DIED: 1790 Lancaster "in 90th yr of his
age...a native of Boston" GS Old Common
Cem Rev Marker.
CHILDREN (b Boston):
  Elizabeth – b 7 Oct 1724
  Ann – b 23 Oct 1726
  Mary – b 17 Jun 1728 d young
  Joshua – b 23 Jul 1731 moved to Boyls-
      ton & served in Rev for Boylston
      & Shrewsbury
  James – b 12 Aug 1733 in Rev
  Richard – b 4 Feb 1735 Lt in Rev
          (b Bolton):
  Mary – bpt 24 Feb 1739-40 Lancaster
  John – b 16 May 1742 Lt in Rev, re-
      moved to Putney, VT
  Ann – b 8 Jul 1745
REF: BVR; LVR; Records of Town of
Boston.

TOWNSEND, Lt Richard, also Townshend & Townsin

SERVICE: S&S Vol 15 p 932 & 935; MilAnn
Lex Alarm; BHist Col John Jacobs Reg
1777; BRR to Bennington 1777; BRR 3 mos
to Northward 1777 £10-6-8; BHist Capt
Hez Whitney's Co 1778; BRR 2 mos RI 1779
£5-11-1; BRR Northern Army; BRR 3 1/2
mos 1778 this state or elsewhere £20 per
mo inc all other wages.
BORN: 4 Feb 1735 Boston s/o Joshua &
Elizabeth (White).
MARRIED: 18 Oct 1757 Thankful Wilson (b
1740 d/o Nathaniel & Eunice).
DIED: 28 Nov 1814 ae 79 "at the house of

TOWNSEND, Lt Richard (Cont)

his son Robert, in Lancaster."
CHILDREN (b Bolton):
  Richard - b 2 Sep 1759 m Susannah
    Houghton
  Robart - b 14 Dec 1760 m Betsy Holman
  Eunice - b 22 Dec 1764
  Thankful - b 15 Jul 1767
  Nathaniel - b 27 Jul 1769
  Elizabeth - b 18 Jun 1771
  Ann - b 20 Apr 1773
REF: Records of Town of Boston; LVR;
BVR.

TOWNSEND, Richard, Jr, also Townsand
& Townshend

SERVICE: S&S Vol 15 p 923, 932 & 935;
MilAnn Bennington 1777; MilAnn Guard at
Boston 1778; BRR 3 mos Boston 1778 ₤11-
7-4; BRR 2 mos RI 1779 ₤5-6-8.
BORN: 2 Sep 1759 Bolton s/o Lt Richard &
Thankful (Wilson).
MARRIED: 2 Oct 1780 Bolton, Susannah
Houghton Jr (b 1761 d/o Jonathan &
Mary).
DIED: Perhaps before 1807 in Putney.
NOTE: Three generations of this family
in the Revolution : Joshua b 1700, Lt
Richard b 1735 & Richard Jr b 1759. In
Putney 1790 census 1-1-1. In Putney
1800 census M/0-0-1-0-1 F/0-0-1-0-1.
Susannah Townsend warned out of Rocking-
ham 1807. Later she m Ashbel Johnson of
Putney.
REF: BVR; Rockingham Warnings.

TOWNSEND, Robert

SERVICE: S & S Vol 15 p 935; MilAnn Camp
at Hull; MilAnn Capt Nurse's Co in the
Jerseys; MilAnn reinforce Cont Army
1778; BRR 3 mos NY 1776 ₤10; BRR 5 mos
men 1776; DNR Winter Campaign; BRR Ben-
nington Sep 1777; BRR Northern Army; BRR
3 mos to Northward 1777 ₤10-6-8; BRR 8
mos Cont Army 1778 ₤25; BRR 2 mos in RI
1779 ₤5-11-1 (₤5-6-8); BRR 8 mos service
1778 ₤100.
BORN: 14 Dec 1760 Bolton s/o Lt Richard
& Thankful (Wilson).
MARRIED: 13 May 1792 Bolton, Elizabeth
Holman d/o Abraham & Abigail (Atherton).
DIED: 2 Sep 1826 ae 66 GS Middle Cem
Lancaster.
CHILDREN (b Lancaster):
  Henry - b 10 Mar 1793 d 1822
  Abigail Holman - b 1 Apr 1795 m Abel
    Whitney
  Nancy Wilson - b 25 Sep 1797 m John
    Holman
  Warren - b 24 Nov 1800 m Almira
    Bennett

TOWNSEND, Robert (Cont)

NOTE: Copy of Robert Townsend's portrait
at Bolton Historical Society. Third
generation in Revolution: Joshua b 1700,
Richard b 1735, Robert b 1760.
REF: BVR; LVR.

VAUGHN, Robert, also Veaghn

SERVICE: S&S Vol 16 p 301-2; MilAnn Cont
Army 1777.
NOTE: Engaged for Bolton and claimed by
both Bolton and Westminster. Claimed
residence in both towns in separate
enlistments, but does not appear in the
vital records of either one. Deserted
10 Apr 1776. Described as 27 yrs old,
5´4" tall, dark complexion. Not found
in 1790 census of MA, NH or VT, although
there are many families with this sur-
name in Middleboro.

WALCOTT, Jesse, also Walcutt, Walkott &
Wolcutt

SERVICE: S S Vol 16 p 416-7, 489 & 707-
8; BHist Resolve 1776; BRR 5 mos NY Jul
1776; BHist reinforcements 1778; BRR 6
mos RI 1778; BRR Cont Army 9 mos 1778 L
33-6-8; BRR Fishkill 9 mos 1778.
BORN: 27 Feb 1734 Salem s/o Jabez &
Lydia (Flint).
MARRIED: 24 May 1755 (int) Stow, Rebekah
Conant of Stow.
DIED: After 1799 (d 4-1-1800 per DAR).
CHILDREN (b Marlborough):
  Jabez - b 17 Dec 1756 m Mary Baker
    1781
  Phebe - b 1 Dec 1758 m Ezra Smith 1779
  Esther - b 5 Mar 1761 m Jacob Whitney
    1779
  Ruth - b 2 Jun 1763 m Joseph Sawyer
    1782
    (b Bolton):
  Eunice - b 24 Feb 1766 m Reuben
    Chaffin 1788
  Rebecca - b 30 Apr 1769 d 1775
  Josiah - b 19 Feb 1773 d 1775
  Rebecca - b 10 Nov 1776 d 1778
  Achsah - b 23 Jun 1780 d 1785
NOTE: Descriptive List - ae 44, 5´9"
high, light complexion, light hair.
Sold his homestead 1799, no record of
death.
REF: MVR; BVR; SVR; The Walcott Book,
Arthur Stuart Walcott 1925; N E Hist Gen
Register Vol 57; DARPI.

WALKETT, Jabez, also Wolcutt

SERVICE: S & S Vol 16 p 488 & Vol 17 p
705; BHist Lex Alarm; BRR Bennington Sep
1777; BRR 3 mos to Northward 1777; BRR

WALKETT, Jabez (Cont)

Northern Army.
BORN: 17 Dec 1756 Marlborough s/o Jesse & Rebecca (Conant).
MARRIED: 27 Nov 1781 Bolton, Mary Baker d/o Judge Samuel.
DIED: About 1815 Bolton (Town Records), no stone.
CHILDREN (b Bolton):
  Polly (Mary) - b 26 Jun 1782
  Josiah - b 16 Feb 1784
  Betsy - b 14 Apr 1786
  Josiah - bpt 7 Jan 1787
  Polly - bpt 7 Jan 1787
  Sally - b 8 Jun 1788
  Jabez - b 15 Jul 1790
  Lydia - b 14 Nov 1792
  Jesse - b 7 Mar 1795 changed name to Samuel Baker Walcott
NOTE: A wheelwright per N E Hist Gen Soc; Walcott Book states Jabez left family and guardian appt 1796. Funeral expenses paid by Town of Bolton 1815 per Selectmen's Order Book. Walcott Book states Jabez d Livermore, ME 1825 (error).
REF: MVR; BVR; The Walcott Book, Arthur Stuart Walcott 1925; Bolton Selectmen's Order Book; DARPI.

WASSON, Thomas

SERVICE: S & S Vol 16 p 678-9; MilAnn enlisted Cont Army 3 yrs 1781.
BORN: 26 Dec 1748 Shirley.
MARRIED: Mary Boyd of Shirley (d 1832 ae 83 Hudson, NH).
DIED: 18 Nov 1832 Hudson, NH ae 84.
NOTE: Name "Wassel" in Military Annals appears to be an error. He is sometimes listed as a fifer, other times as a drummer. Credited to Worcester. Drummer Jan to Aug 1777 15th Reg; Fifer Nov 1777 to Mar 1778; Musician Mar to May 1778; Fifer Jan 1779 at Providence, RI; Musician Feb to May 1779; Drummer Jun 1779 Providence; Drummer Aug 1779 Salem; Fifer Jul 1780 Camp Ten Eyck; Fifer Major Aug to Nov 1781 Cont Army.
REF: DARPI; NH VR at Concord.

WELCH, John

SERVICE: S&S Vol 16 p 808; BHist Lex Alarm.
BORN: 10 Mar 1751 Bolton s/o Paul & Betty.
MARRIED: 23 Sep 1784 Harvard, Ruth Corley of Bolton.
DIED: "John Welch buried King's Cem, Ithaca, NY" per Cayuga Chapter DAR.
NOTE: Pension S41309.
REF: BVR; HVR.

WELCH, Jonas, also Welsh

SERVICE: S&S Vol 16 p 811 & 858; BHist Lex Alarm 1775; BHist Siege of Boston; BHist Col Wade's Reg 1777; BRR RI 6 mos 1778 ₤12-10; BRR Cont Army 1780 3 mos; BRR reinforce Cont Army 3 mos RI 1780 ₤12.
BORN: 1753 prob s/o Paul & Betty.
MARRIED: 6 Jun 1792 (int) Bolton, Betty Holman of Bolton (d 1867 GS1).
DIED: 30 Nov 1840 ae 87 GS1 marked "A Rev. Soldier" Rev Marker.
NOTE: He is listed in 1840 census of pensioners ae 87.
REF: BVR; Clinton Courant newspaper.

WELCH, Sgt Silas, also Welsh

SERVICE: S&S Vol 16 p 815 & 860; BHist Lex Alarm; BHist Siege of Boston.
BORN: 24 Nov 1744 Bolton s/o Paul & Betty.
MARRIED: 20 Feb 1766 Bolton, Mary Merriam (d 1814).
DIED: 8 Sep 1775 in Siege of Boston.
CHILDREN (bpt Bolton):
  Anna - bpt 29 May 1808
  Orringe - bpt 29 May 1808
  Silas - bpt 29 May 1808
  Sophia - bpt 29 May 1808
  Mary - bpt 29 May 1808
NOTE: Widow Mary m 2nd Jonathan Atherton 1784.
REF: BVR.

WETHERBEE, David

SERVICE: S & S Vol 16 p 923; BHist Turner's Reg Butts Hill 1781.
BORN: 12 Feb 1757 Lunenburg s/o Paul & Hannah (Pierce).
MARRIED: 23 Feb 1778 Eunice Kingman of Stoughton.
DIED: Before 17 Sep 1840 GS South Cem Lunenburg.
CHILDREN:
  Eunice - b 16 Jun 1779 m John Carter
  Susannah - b 15 Jun 1781 m a Mitchell
  Betsy - b 25 Apr 1783 unm
  David - b 31 Mar 1785 d young
  Mary - b 26 Dec 1787 unm
  Sally - b 29 Nov 1789 m John C Young
  Sophia - b 5 Jan 1792 m Jesse Baker
  Martha - b 16 May 1794 m Job Young
  John - b 20 Feb 1798 m1 Mary Ann Upton m2 Kate
  James - b 10 Jul 1802 unm
  David - b 5 Oct 1805
NOTE: Pensioned. Worc Co Probate Case A63047 17 Sep 1840. Children's births per a descendant. Also served for Stow.
REF: Lunenburg VR; Worc Co Probate Records.

WHEELER, Sgt Caleb

SERVICE: S&S Vol 16 p 964.
BORN: 17 Nov 1757 Sudbury s/o Elisha & Mary.
MARRIED: 1) 26 Nov 1778 Sudbury, Jerusha Dorr; 2) 23 Dec 1798 Sudbury, Mrs Rebecca Maynard.
DIED: 1824 Bolton.
CHILDREN (b Sudbury):
    Lucretia - b 7 Dec 1779 m Dexter Fairbanks
    Susanna - b 9 Aug 1781 m Obed Smith
    Edward - b 4 Jun 1783 m Lucretia Bent
    Abigail Gridley - b 3 July 1785 m Marcus Cutler
    Mary Loring - b 6 May 1787
    Jerusha - b 30 Apr 1789 m Joseph Goss
    Caleb - b 17 Jul 1791 m Dolly Willis
    Jonas - b 3 Nov 1793
    Maynard - b 15 Mar 1803
    Adeline - b 4 Apr 1805 m Wm Hunt III
NOTE: Served for Sudbury. Lived in Bolton after about 1802. Called Colonel in Bolton.
REF: Sudbury VR; BVR; Wheeler Family in America, Albert G wheeler 1914; DARPI.

WHEELER, Deliverance

SERVICE: S&S Vol16 p 966; BHist Resolve Jun 1776; BRR Capt D Nurse´s Co 5 mos £3; BHist to York Jul 1776 £12 (see note).
BORN: 23 Dec 1749 Stow s/o Thomas & Mary (Gates).
MARRIED: 5 Jun 1773 (int) Stow, Elizabeth Whitman of Marlborough.
DIED: 24 May 1814 ae 65 Whitingham, VT.
CHILDREN (b Stow):
    Deliverance - b 16 Mar 1775 m Phebe Salter
    Zacchariah - b 15 Nov 1777
    Sally - b 25 Nov 1781 m Rowell Pike
    Suzie - b 1782 m Robert Boyd
    Daniel - b 11 Dec 1783
         (b Ashburnham):
    Betsy - bpt 7 Aug _____ m Luther Boyd
    Polly - bpt 15 Jul _____ m Oris Pike
    Abigail - bpt 19 Jul 1789
    John - b 17 Nov 1794
NOTE: 5 mos to York paid by Capt David Nurse £6, Jonathan Nurse £3, D Wheeler £3.
REF: SVR; MVR; Wheeler Family of America, Albert G Wheeler 1914; Mr Arthur Deliverance Wheeler, Town Clerk, Whitingham, VT; History of Whitingham, Leonard Brown 1886; DARPI.

WHEELOCK, Sgt John, also Whelock

SERVICE: S&S Vol 16 p 1005-6 & 1029; MilAnn Siege of Boston, fifer; MilAnn

WHEELOCK, Sgt John (Cont)

Cont Army; MilAnn service in RI 1779; MilAnn service in RI 1781.
BORN: 1759 Charlton.
MARRIED: 1787 Lydia Davis (1767-1821).
DIED: 13 Jun 1816 Charlton.
CHILDREN:
    Sally - b 1791 m John Spurr 1810
REF: DARPI; DAR Lineage Book 141 p 169.

WHETCOMB, Abel, also Whitcomb

SERVICE: S&S Vol 16 p 1032 & 1036; MilAnn Capt Manassah Sawyer´s Co 1776.
BORN: 2 May 1759 Bolton s/o Dea David & Betty (White).
MARRIED: 8 May 1780 Elizabeth Townsend (d 1849 d/o Joshua Jr).
DIED: 16 Jun 1841 ae 82 GS2
CHILDREN (b Bolton):
    Abel - b 22 Nov 1781 m Sophia Holman
    Joshua Townsend - bpt 23 Aug 1789
    Jonathan Townsend - bpt 31 Jul 1791
    Susannah Townsend - bpt 9 Mar 1794 m Thomas Osborn
NOTE: Also claimed by Stow. By will of his father, Dea David, Abel inherited the homestead which was in th family ca 1730-1908, and is still standing.
REF: BVR; Whitcomb Genealogy, Charlotte Whitcomb 1904.

WHETCOMB, Asa

SERVICE: S&S Vol 16 p 1033; BRR Rutland Guard 1782 (Timothy Ruggles Co).
BORN: 26 Jan 1766 Bolton s/o Gen John & Becke.
MARRIED: 2 Feb 1786 Bolton, Sarah Whetcomb.
DIED: 13 Jan 1806 ae 40 GS1.
CHILDREN (b Bolton):
    Silas - b 22 Sep 1787 d 1795
    Betsy - b 18 Nov 1789 m Silas Reed
    Sarah - b 20 Aug 1792 m Samuel Nurse
    Asa - b 28 Feb 1795 d 1796
    Fanny - b 8 Aug 1797 m Gen Amory Holman
    Asa - b 4 Aug 1799
    Paul - b 28 Aug 1802
    Cephas - b 1 Sep 1804 name changed to James
NOTE: Widow Sarah m 2nd Stephen Brooks of Templeton. By will of his father, Gen John, Asa inherited the homestead and Gen John´s gun and sword.
REF: BVR; Whitcomb Genealogy, Charlotte Whitcomb 1904; Worc Co Probate Records.

WHETCOMB, Corp David, Jr, also Whitcomb

SERVICE: S&S Vol 16 p 1033; MilAnn Kips Bay 15 Aug 1778.

Home of David Whitcomb, still standing (1983) on Sugar Road.
He was killed in the Revolution.

WHETCOMB, Corp David, Jr (Cont)

BORN: 17 Feb 1749 Bolton s/o Dea David & Betty (White).
MARRIED: 28 May 1776 Sarah Whetcomb.
DIED: 2 Sep 1778 in the Army GS1.
CHILDREN (b Bolton):
  Sarah - b 26 Sep 1777
  David - b 19 Feb 1779
NOTE: Died in war, but date uncertain; DARPI says 30 Aug 1778; BVR, GS1 & S&S all say 2 Sep 1778; MilAnn says in Battle of Kips Bay (15 Aug). Widow Sarah m 2nd Peter Sawyer.
REF: BVR; Whitcomb Genealogy, Charlotte Whitcomb 1904; DARPI; Worc Co Probate Records.

WHETCOMBE, Richard

SERVICE: S&S Vol 16 p 1036; MilAnn Capt Manassah Sawyer's Co 1776.
BORN: 9 Nov 1756 Bolton s/o Jonas & Hannah (Sawtelle).
MARRIED: 1802 Sibbel Haskell of Harvard.
DIED: 9 Oct 1810 ae 54 GS1.
CHILDREN: none.
NOTE: Sibbel m 2nd Peter Tinney 11 Jun 1815.
REF: BVR; Whitcomb Genealogy, Charlotte Whitcomb 1904.

WHITCOM, Lt Paul

SERVICE: S&S Vol 17 p 26; BHist Lex Alarm.
BORN: 20 Dec 1732 Lancaster s/o Josiah & Loruhama (Whitney).
MARRIED: 19 Sep 1759 Rebecca Whitney of Harvard.
DIED: 15 Mar 1802 Bolton "Capt" GS1.
CHILDREN (b Bolton):
  Elizabeth - b 14 Aug 1760
  Silas - b 23 Oct 1761 m Lucy Eveleth
  Rebecca - b 17 Mar 1763
  Lydia - b 14 Feb 1766
  Mary - b 27 Nov 1767 twin
  Sarah - b 27 Nov 1767 twin

WHITCOMB, Lt Paul (Cont)

NOTE: Called "Capt," prob in militia?
REF: LVR; BVR; Whitcomb Genealogy, Charlotte Whitcomb 1904.

WHITCOMB, Elihu

SERVICE: S&S Vol 17 p 29; BHist Col Furness Reg 1777.
BORN: 1760 Bolton s/o Levi & Sarah (Gates).
MARRIED: 1800 Boston Elizabeth Ruggles.
DIED: 17 Mar 1825 Saco, ME per DARPI.
CHILDREN:
  Levi - b 1802
  Justin - b 1804 twin
  Increase - b 1804 twin
  Peregrin White - twin
  Felix Penn - twin
  Samuel -
  Albert -
NOTES: Attended Harvard College and became minister; was in Saco, ME 11 yrs. Burned to death in forest fire (Saco Hist Society).
REF: Whitcomb Genealogy, Charlotte Whitcomb 1904; Saco Historical Society; DARPI; BVR.

WHITCOMB, Ephraim, also Whetcomb

SERVICE: S&S Vol 17 p 927.
BORN: 22 Jul 1751 Bolton s/o Isreal & Azuba (Houghton).
MARRIED: 14 Jan 1777 Bolton, Sarah Longley d/o Nathaniel.
DIED: 1807 in Bolton GS1.
CHILDREN (b Bolton):
  Bulah - b 20 Oct 1778 m Jonathan Priest Houghton
  Lovisa - b 24 Mar 1780 m Abraham Gilbert
  Ephraim - b 23 Jan 1781 m Nancy Gilbert 1807
  Sarah - b 23 Aug 1782
  Lucretia - b 14 Apr 1784
  Molly - b 8 Apr 1788

WHITCOMB, Ephraim (Cont)

    Azuba - b 5 May 1790
    Isreal - b 11 May 1792 m Abigail
        Holman
    Nathaniel - b 18 Apr 1794
    Lucinda - b 5 May 1796
    Eleazar - b 29 Apr 1798
NOTE: Muster list for Sterling 1781.
DAR gives death as 1819.
REF: BVR; Whitcomb Genealogy, Charlotte
Whitcomb 1904.

WHITCOMB, Ezra, also Whetcomb, Whitcom

SERVICE: S&S Vol 16 p 1033 & Vol 17 p 26
& 29.
BORN: 27 Nov 1752 Bolton s/o Simon &
Thankful (Houghton).
MARRIED: 13 Jun 1774 (int) Templeton,
Joanna Bruce.
DIED: Killed or died in Army 1781.
CHILDREN (b Winchendon):
    Levinah - b 3 Sep 1775
    Simon - b 9 Feb 1777
            (b Templeton):
    Samuel - b 1 Mar 1779
NOTE: Died in the War.
REF: BVR; Whitcomb Genealogy, Charlotte
Whitcomb 1904; Templeton VR.

WHITCOMB, Brig Gen John, also Whetcomb

SERVICE: S&S Vol 16 p 1034 & Vol 17 p
31; BHist Lex Alarm; MilAnn Battle of
Bunker Hill; MilAnn Brig Gen Cont Army 5
Jun 1776.
BORN: 20 Feb 1712 Lancaster s/o John &
Rebecca (Wilder). Rebecca m 2nd Samuel
Chamberlain.
MARRIED: 1) 12 Jun 1735 Mary Carter (d
1744 ae 26); 2) 3 Feb 1745 Becca Whit-
comb (d 1804 ae 76).
DIED: 17 Nov 1785 ae 73 Bolton GS1.
CHILDREN (b Bolton):
    Abigail - b 13 Feb 1738-9 m Desire
        French
    Mary - b 20 Jan 1739-40 m Thomas
        Osborne
    Dorothy - b 13 Apr 1743 m Samuel Jones
        of Berlin as 2nd wife
    Becke - b 3 Dec 1745 m Calvin
        Greenleaf
    Rachel - b 14 Nov 1747 m Tille
        Whitcomb
    Jonathan - b 26 Jan 1749-50 m1 Achsah
        Fairbank m2 Mary Gardner
    Elizabeth - b 9 Nov 1752 m Rufus
        Houghton
    Sarah - b 1 Feb 1754 m Oliver Barrett
        Jr 1775
    John - b 12 May 1760 m Azuba Whitcomb
    Prudence - b 30 Jun 1762 m Stephen
        Brooks

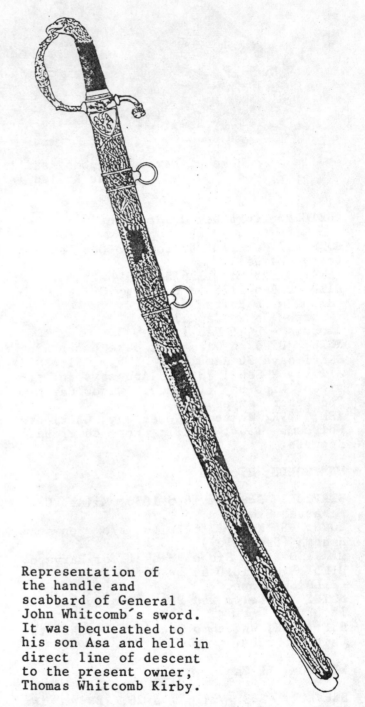

Representation of
the handle and
scabbard of General
John Whitcomb's sword.
It was bequeathed to
his son Asa and held in
direct line of descent
to the present owner,
Thomas Whitcomb Kirby.

WHITCOMB, Brig Gen John (Cont)

    Asa - b 26 Jan 1766 m Sarah Whitcomb
    Zevirah - b 11 Mar 1767 m Abel Priest
NOTE: Became a Colonel in F & I War. A
justice of the peace. Repr to Gen
Court. Provincial Congress 1775 elected
him "First Major General of Mass. Army."
Elected to Council 1776-80.
REF: BVR; LVR; Whitcomb Genealogy, Char-
lotte Whitcomb 1904; "A Forgotten
Patriot," H S Nourse, Am Antiquarian
Society, Worcester; DARPI.

Slate head stones of General John Whitcomb and his wives in the Old South Burial Ground in Bolton. Mary´s was carved by Jonathan Worcester, a stonecutter of Harvard. Note that Becke´s stone erroneously lists her husband´s name as Jonathan. Sketched by Phillis E. Veinot.

WHITCOMB, John, Jr, also Whetcomb, Witcum & Witcumb

SERVICE: S&S Vol 16 p 1034, Vol 17 p 32, 666 & 667; BRR 2 mos RI Apr 1777; BRR 3 mos to Northward 1777; BHist reinforcements 1778; BRR Cont Army 9 mos 1778 ₤ 37-10; BRR Fishkill 9 mos 1778.
BORN: 12 May 1760 Bolton s/o Gen John & Becca (Whitcomb).
MARRIED: 31 May 1780 Bolton, Azuba Whetcomb (d 1838 d/o Isreal & Azuba).
DIED: 3 Dec 1798 ae 38 Bolton GS1.
CHILDREN (b Bolton):
  Becke - b 28 Nov 1780
  Azuba - bpt 26 Feb 1786 ml Abraham
      Holman m2 Capt Oliver Sawyer
        (b Templeton):
  Nabby - bpt 10 Feb 1788
  Isreal - bpt 6 Sep 1789
        (b Bolton):
  Lucy - b 14 Mar 1797
NOTE: Descriptive List 1778 - ae 18 yrs 5´6" high, light complexion, light hair.
REF: BVR; Whitcomb Genealogy, Charlotte Whitcomb 1904; Templeton VR; DARPI.

WHITCOMB, Jonas

SERVICE: S&S Vol 17 p 24; BHist Lex Alarm.
BORN: 13 Feb 1723 Lancaster s/o Jonathan & Rachel (Woods).
MARRIED: 17 May 1753 (int) Bolton, Hannah Sawtelle of Stow (d 1796).

WHITCOMB, Jonathan Jr Esq (Cont)

DIED: 31 Dec 1792 ae 69 Bolton GS1.
CHILDREN (b Bolton):
  Sarah - b 4 Sep 1753 ml David Whitcomb
      Jr m2 Peter Sawyer 1786
  Richard - b 9 Nov 1756 m Sibyl Haskell
  Jonas - b 13 Feb 1764 m Lucy Walcott
  Joel - b 2 Jun 1767 m Nabby Walcott
REF: LVR; BVR; Whitcomb Genealogy, Charlotte Whitcomb 1904.

WHITCOMB, Jonathan, Jr Esq Also Whetcom, Whitcom

SERVICE: S&S Vol 16 p 1034, Vol 17 p 26 & 33; BHist Lex Alarm; BRR 3 mos NY Nov 1776; BHist Col John Jacob´s Reg 1777.
BORN: 26 Jan 1749-50 Bolton s/o Gen John & Becca (Whetcomb).
MARRIED: 1) 30 Mar 1771 Berlin, Achsah Fairbank (d 5 Jan 1796); 2) 18 Oct 1796 Leominster Mary Gardner d/o Rev Francis.
DIED: 14 Feb 1830 ae 80 Rev Marker "Esq" GS1.
CHILDREN (b Bolton):
  Ephraim - b 1 Jan 1774 twin
  John - b 1 Jan 1774 twin
  Achsah - b 27 Dec 1777
  Becke - b 26 Apr 1779
  Sarah - b 3 Apr 1781
  Jonathan - b 5 Apr 1783
  Molly - b 17 Dec 1785
  Abigail - b 13 Apr 1788
  Elizabeth - b 18 Jul 1790 d 1815

WHITCOMB, Jonathan, Jr Esq (Cont)

Luke - b 5 Nov 1792
Francis - b 18 Sep 1797 d 1827
Susannah - b 24 Jul 1799
Henry Gardner - b 7 Sep 1801 d 1806
Lucinda - b 5 Sep 1803
Sophia - b 18 Sep 1805
Edwin Asa - b 24 Jul 1807
Asa - bpt 27 Sep 1807 (same as previous ?)
REF: BVR; Whitcomb Genealogy, Charlotte Whitcomb 1904.

WHITCOMB, Jonathan, also Whetcomb & Whitcom

SERVICE: S&S Vol 16 p 1034, Vol 17 p 26 & 33; BHist Fifer Lex Alarm; BRR NY 5 mos 1776; DNR Winter Campaign 1776-7; BRR RI 2 mos 1777; BHist Col Jacob's Reg 1777.
BORN: 27 Apr 1749 Bolton s/o Isreal & Azuba (Houghton).
MARRIED: 1 Jun 1773 Releaf (Leaffe) Fife.
DIED: 1822 Florida, MA (moved before 1805).
CHILDREN:
Leaffe - b 4 Jan 1774
Jonathan - m a dau of Samuel Whitcomb
Patience - m Silas Osgood
Sally - m Jeremiah Slocum
Betsy - m Stephen Townsend
REF: BVR; Whitcomb Genealogy, Charlotte Whitcomb 1904.

WHITCOMB, Jotham

SERVICE: S&S Vol 17 p 34; DNR in the Jerseys 1776-7; MilAnn Capt Moore's Co to RI 1781.
BORN: 8 Aug 1737 Harvard s/o Jonathan & Deliverance (Nutting).
MARRIED: 14 May 1766 Deborah Robbins d/o James of Harvard.
DIED: 17 Feb 1821 Boxborough.
CHILDREN (b Harvard):
Tryphena - b 8 Jun 1767 m Jeremiah Richardson
Leonard - b 31 Mar 1769
Moses - b 5 Jul 1771
Betty Fletcher - bpt 3 Apr 1774 m a Wright
Abigail Leland - bpt 5 Oct 1777 m Joseph Tucker
Peter - bpt 25 Mar 1781 m Sarah Wyman
NOTE: Lived in section of Harvard which became Boxborough in 1783.
REF: HVR; Whitcomb Genealogy, Charlotte Whitcomb 1904; Boxborough VR.

WHITCOMB, Nathaniel, also Whetcomb & Whitum

SERVICE: S&S Vol 16 p 1035, Vol 17 p 35 & 286; BHist 6 mos men Cont Army 1780.
BORN: 17 Jun 1762 Bolton s/o Levi & Sarah (Gates).
NOTE: Descriptive List 1780 - ae 18, 5'3" tall, light complexion, engaged for Bolton; A Nathaniel Whitcomb was in Rockingham, VT in 1800.
REF: BVR; Whitcomb Genealogy, Charlotte Whitcomb 1904.

WHITCOMB, Silas, also Whetcomb

SERVICE: S&S Vol 16 p 1035, Vol 17 p 36; BRR Bennington Sep 1777; BRR 3 mos to Northward 1777; BHist Capt Hez Whitney's Co 1778; BRR reinforce Cont Army 3 mos 1779 Ł2-9-3.
BORN: 23 Oct 1761 Bolton s/o Lt Paul & Rebecca (Whitney).
MARRIED: 16 Jun 1793 (int) Lucy Eveleth of Stow.
DIED: 20 Dec 1809 Bolton in 49th yr GS1.
CHILDREN (b Bolton):
John - b 17 Oct 1793 d 1795
Lucy - b 28 Dec 1794 m Amory Holman of Berlin
Nabby - b 17 Mar 1796 d 1816 ae 20
Clarissa - b 7 Jun 1797 GS1
Rebecca - b 27 Nov 1799 d 1903 ae 104 GS1
Silas - b 17 Mar 1801 d 1803
Sally - b 13 Sep 1802 GS1
Silas - b 25 Jul 1804
Francis - b 11 Oct 1807
Elizabeth - b 20 Nov 1809 GS1
REF: Worc Co Probate Records; BVR; Whitcomb Genealogy, Charlotte Whitcomb 1904; Berlin History, Rev W A Houghton 1895.

WHITCOMB, Sgt William, also Whetcomb

SERVICE: S&S Vol 16 p 1036, Vol 17 p 37; MilAnn Lex Alarm; BHist Siege of Boston; BHist Resolve Jun 1776 Ł10; BRR 5 mos NY Jul 1776 Ł10; BHist Col Wade's Reg 1777; BRR RI 1779 6 mos Ł12-10.
BORN: 6 Sep 1741 Bolton s/o Isreal & Azuba (Houghton).
MARRIED: 1) 13 Dec 1768 Bolton, Lucy Merriam (d 1773); 2) 19 Jun 1777 Sarah Sawyer (d 1838).
DIED: Before 1814 when Sarah appears as a widow in town records.
CHILDREN:
Sarah - b 2 Oct 1769
Rufus - b 23 Apr 1770
Lucy - b 16 Mar 1772
Molly - b 31 May 1783
Sally Merriam - b 27 Jul 1784 d 1808
NOTE: D Forbush was paid $8.33 for house

WHITCOMB, Sgt William (Cont)

rent for the widow of William Whitcomb 10 mos per town records 1814.
REF: BVR; Bolton Selectmen's Order Book.

WHITE, Enoch

SERVICE: S&S Vol 17 p 69; MilAnn Bennington 1777; BHist Capt Hez Whitney's Co 1778.
BORN: 18 Dec 1757 Marlborough s/o Samuel & Sarah (Fosgate).
MARRIED: 1) 3 Mar 1801 Hannah Hale d/o of Ambrose of Stoddard, NH; 2) 26 Apr 1823 Widow Zerviah Converse of Marlborough, NH.
DIED: 16 Nov 1835 Marlborough, NH GS Center Cemetery.
CHILDREN (b Marlborough, NH):
  Lucy Hale – b 29 Jun 1802 m Charles McCollester
  Samuel – b 23 Dec 1803 m Harriet Wade
  Hannah – b 12 Feb 1810 m Willard Converse
  Ambrose C – b 4 Dec 1824 m Maria Fosgate
REF: MVR; History of Marlborough, NH, Charles A Bemis 1881; Ancestral Chronological Record of Wiliam White Family, Thomas & Samuel White 1895.

WHITE, Samuel

SERVICE: S&S Vol 17 p 122; BHist Lex Alarm; White Geneal Bennington 1777.
BORN: ca 1735 Scituate s/o Thomas & Rachel (Horten).
MARRIED: 1 Dec 1756 Marlborough, Sarah Fosgate ("Fosdick").
DIED: 12 Oct 1788 Bolton, no stone.
CHILDREN (b Marlborough):
  Enock – b 18 Dec 1757 m Hannah Hale
        (b Bolton:)
  Robert – b 11 Jan 1759 d 1815 unm
  Rachel – b 8 Mar 1761 m Phineas Sampson
  David – b 16 Sep 1763 twin d young
  Jonathan – b 16 Sep 1763 twin m & had son John
  Sarah – b 27 Nov 1768 d unm
  Benjamin – b 24 Jun 1770 m Roxanna Andrews
  Beulah – b 30 Apr 1773 m Royce McCollester
REF: BVR; MVR; Ancestral Chronological Record of William White Family, Thomas & Samuel White 1895.

WHITE, William

SERVICE: S&S Vol 17 p 141; BHist Lex Alarm; BRR Resolve 1776 5 mos NY.
BORN: 1736 Scituate s/o Thomas & Rachel

WHITE, William (Cont)

(Horten).
MARRIED: 1) 3 Jul 1766 Bolton, Lydia Goodell of Salem (b 1740); 2) 24 Mar 1777 Templeton, Elizabeth Ball of Templeton (d 1820 ae 84).
DIED: 17 Feb 1798 ae 53 GS Center Cem Templeton.
CHILDREN (b Bolton):
  Ledea – b 19 Jan 1767
  Marcy – b 26 Dec 1768
  Judith – b 11 Oct 1770
  William – b 27 Nov 1772
  Emma – b 16 Oct 1774
  Amy – b 14 Oct 1775
        (b Templeton):
  David – b 29 Mar 1777
  Rachel – b 11 Jun 1777 (error, 1779?)
  John – b 27 Mar 1783
  Thomas – b 20 Jan 1783-4
  Ruth – b 7 Oct 1786
REF: BVR; Templeton VR; Ancestral Chronological Record of the William White Family, Thomas & Samuel White 1895.

WHITNEY, Abraham

SERVICE: S&S Vol 17 p 206; BHist Lex Alarm.
BORN: 20 Dec 1748 Harvard s/o Abraham & Sarah (Whitney).
MARRIED: 28 Feb 1776 Concord, Rebecca Dudley of Acton (d 1838 ae 81).
DIED: 26 Aug 1833 ae 84 Harvard GS Old Cemetery Harvard.
CHILDREN (b Harvard):
  Abraham – b 3 Mar 1777 d 1778
  Abraham – b 29 Nov 1779 d 1808
  Josiah – b 18 Aug 1781
  John – b 31 Jul 1783
  Samuel – b 28 May 1785
  Simeon – b 20 Mar 1787
  Rebecca – b 13 Oct 1789
  Abel – bpt 8 Jul 1792 d 1799
  Joseph – bpt 9 Aug 1795 d 1799
  Sarah – b 11 Feb 1797
  Mary – b 17 Jan 1800
  Elizabeth – b 22 Sep 1802
REF: HVR; Concord VR; DARPI.

WHITNEY, David

SERVICE: S&S Vol 17 p 212; BHist Capt Hez Whitney's Co 1778.
BORN: 14 Aug 1761 Marlborough s/o Samuel & Abigail (Cutler).
MARRIED: 1 Jun 1786 Concord, Betsy Darby (d 4 Jan 1843 ae 77 GS3).
DIED: 17 Sep 1838 ae 77 GS3.
CHILDREN (b Rindge, NH):
  Samuel – b 17 Dec 1788
  Betsy – b 2 Jan 1792
  Nancy – b 20 Mar 1794

WHITNEY, David (Cont)

Sally - b 20 May 1796
David - b 14 Apr 1798 d 1816 Bolton
Lucy - b 6 Jun 1800
Joseph - b 12 Aug 1802 Major m Eliza Saunders
Nathan - b 30 Jul 1804
NOTE: The Bolton Public Library was given in 1903 by the Misses Anna & Emma Whitney in memory of their father, Major Joseph Whitney.
REF: MVR; Descendants of John Whitney, Frederick C Pierce 1895; BVR.

WHITNEY, Ephraim

SERVICE: S&S Vol 17 p 217; BHist Resolve Jun 1776 Ł10; BRR 5 mos to York Jul 1776 bounty Ł10.
BORN: 2 Apr 1754 Harvard s/o Jonas Jr & Zebudah.
MARRIED: 7 Dec 1780 Stow, Sarah Burges of Harvard.
DIED: 25 Mar 1824 ae 70 Royalston.
CHILDREN (b Royalston):
  Lucy - b 8 Apr 1792
  Ephraim - b 5 Aug 1793
  Hannah - b 31 Jan 1795
  Sarah - b 18 Aug 1798
REF: HVR; SVR; Royalston VR; Descendants of John Whitney, Frederick C Pierce 1895.

WHITNEY, John

SERVICE: S&S Vol 17 p 227 & 229; BHist enlisted 3 yrs 1781; DNR in the Jerseys Dec 1776.
BORN: 3 Oct 1746 Harvard s/o Abraham & Sarah (Whitney).
MARRIED: 9 Jan 1771 Bolton, Sarah Atherton (b 1751 d 1832 d/o Jonathan & Ruth).
DIED: 25 apr 1802 ae 55y 6m 22d GS1 Rev Marker.
CHILDREN (b Bolton):
  Isaiah - b 23 Oct 1773
  Achsah - b 20 Dec 1775 m Caleb Moore
  Milla - b 26 Dec 1777
  John - b 13 Apr 1780
  Heber - b 19 Jan 1782 d 1785 ae 3
  Asenah - b 23 Feb 1784 m Thomas Houghton
  Artemus - b 13 May 1786 m Rebecca Smith
  Sarah - bpt 5 Sep 1790
  Hannah bpt 6 Sep 1794
REF: BVR; HVR; Harvard History, Henry S Nourse 1894; DARPI.

WHITNEY, Josiah, Jr

SERVICE: S&S Vol 17 p 235; BHist Capt Hez Whitney´s Co 1778.

WHITNEY, Josiah, Jr (Cont)

BORN: 25 Feb 1753 Harvard s/o Gen Josiah & Sarah.
MARRIED: 10 Jan 1776 Harvard, Anna Scollay.
DIED: 2 Jun 1827 Nelson, NH.
CHILDREN:
  Nancy - b 12 Apr 1777 m Nathaniel Breed
  Sally - b 26 Jun 1778 m Capt P V Burnap
  Lois - b 15 Mar 1781 m Ezra Wardwell
  Steven - b 1 July 1784 m Mary Burgess
  Lucy - m Asa Lawrence 1811
  Josiah - b 24 Feb 1787 m Sarah Eames
  James - b 26 Dec 1789 m Anna Goss
  Lydia - b 6 Jul 1795 m Henry Melville
  Scollay - b 6 Oct 1798
  Betsy - b 4 Jun 1801 m Asa Spaulding
REF: HVR; Descendants of John Whitney, Frederick C Pierce 1895.

WHITNEY, Richard

SERVICE: S&S Vol 17 p 244; BHist Capt Hez Whitney´s Co 1778.
BORN: 2 Feb 1752 Harvard s/o Richard & Mary.
MARRIED: 15 Dec 1772 Harvard, Mercy Willard (b 1755 d 1836).
DIED: 28 Sep 1835 ae 82y 7m GS Harvard Center Cem "A Revolutionary Soldier."
CHILDREN (b Harvard):
  Betsy Willard - b 5 Jun 1774
  Polly - b 16 Mar 1777 d young
  Levi - b 26 Apr 1781
  Polly - b 15 Feb 1789
REF: HVR.

WHYBERT, William

SERVICE: S&S Vol 17 p 290; BHist Crane´s Artillery; MilAnn 16th Reg Cont Army.
NOTE: Matross (gunners assistant). Credited to Bolton. 1790 census Boston shows Mrs Vibert with 0-1-4-1 servant.

WILDER, Abel

SERVICE: S&S Vol 17 p 333; MilAnn Dorchester Heights; MilAnn RI 1778; BRR reinforcements RI 1778; MilAnn the Bolton-Princeton Co; BRR 3 mos Boston L 11-7-4; BRR 3 1/2 mos 1778 in this state or elsewhere Ł20 per mo inc all other wages.
BORN: 16 Jun 1760 Bolton s/o William & Sarah (Sawyer).
MARRIED: 28 Mar 1779 Bolton, Hannah Green.
DIED: 6 Jun 1806 ae 46 Dublin, NH.
CHILDREN (b Bolton):
  Abel - b 27 Mar 1779 d Peterborough,

WILDER, Abel (Cont)

    NH 1858
Betty - b 6 Dec 1780 d 1818
    (b Dublin, NH):
Daniel - b 15 Jun 1783
Hannah - b 4 May 1785 m L Stiles
Sally - b 19 Aug 1787 d 1822
Cyrus - b 13 May 1789 m N Irving
Dorcas - b 1 Jan 1792 m J Greenwood
Levi - b 18 Aug 1794 m Betsy Pope
Polly - b 11 Aug 1796 d 1818
James - b 24 Mar 1799 m Mary Crombie
John - b 18 Jan 1801 M Harriet Lakin
NOTE: Abel Wilder removed to Dublin, NH ca 1780 where he became Commander-in-Chief of the 20th Reg of NH Militia. He was buried with full military honors, and friends erected a large monument in his honor.
REF: BVR; DARPI; Book of the Wilders, Rev M H Wilder 1878; Peterborough Soldiers of the Rev, Hildreth Allison.

WILDER, Daniel

SERVICE: S&S Vol 17 p 336; BRR reinforce Cont Army RI 1780 ₤12; BRR reinforce Cont Army 1780 ₤19.
BORN: 21 Aug 1763 Bolton s/o William & Sarah (Sawyer).
MARRIED: Northern VT, Polly Gould.
DIED: Michigan.
CHILDREN (b Malone, NY):
  Abel - m Hannah Payne
  Orra -
  Joseph F -
  Alvin -
  Daniel -
  William O -
  Lucretia -
  Polly -
  Sarah Elizabeth -
  Melinda -
  Jerusha -
NOTE: Carpenter in northern VT; removed to Malone, NY; had 11 children; removed to Michigan where he died.
REF: BVR; Book of the Wilders, Rev M H Wilder 1878.

WILLARD, William, Jr

SERVICE: S&S Vol 17 p 396; BHist Capt Hez Whitney's Co 1778; BRR reinforcements RI.
BORN: 13 Feb 1754 Harvard s/o William & Elen.
MARRIED: 12 Jan 1781 (int) Harvard, Patience Haseltine (d 1844).
DIED: 5 Apr 1839 ae 85 Harvard.
CHILDREN (b Harvard):
  William - b 4 Jan 1782
  ____ - b 16 Mar 1784 twin

WILLARD, William, Jr (Cont)

  ____ - b 16 Mar 1784 twin
  John - b 29 Nov 1785
  Nathaniel - b 6 Oct 1788
  Artemas - b 6 Oct 1790
  Orsimus - b 7 Aug 1792
REF: HVR.

WILSON, Jeremiah

SERVICE: S&S Vol 17 p 567; BHist Lex Alarm.
BORN: 28 Dec 1746 Bolton s/o Nathaniel & Eunice (Davenport).
MARRIED: 1 Dec 1768 Leominster, Eunice Whitcomb of Leominster.
DIED: 8 Jun 1834 ae 87 Norwich, VT.
CHILDREN (b Bolton):
  Nathaniel - b 21 Dec 1769
  Benjamin - b 14 Dec 1771 m Sallie Hill
  Dorritha - b 27 Jul 1773
  Jeremiah - b 29 May 1775
  Peter - b 26 Jun 1777
  David - b 7 Feb 1780 m Polly Newton
    1809
  Eunice - b 30 Aug 1785 m Truman Newton
    1807
NOTE: Lineage Book says he was in Battle of Bunker Hill. Jeremiah Wilson was in Norwich, VT by 1807 when his dau Eunice m Truman Newton.
REF: BVR; DARPI; Whitcomb Genealogy, Charlotte Whitcomb 1904; Richard Newton of Sudbury MA, Rev William M Newton 1912.

WILSON, Sgt John

SERVICE: S&S Vol 17 p 567; BRR Lex Alarm; BRR 5 mos to York 1776 ₤10; BRR 3 mos to York 1776 ₤10; MilAnn Carpenter in Capt D Nurse's Co in the Jerseys 1776-7; BRR reinforce Cont Army 1778.
BORN: unk.
MARRIED: Hannah ____.
DIED: Possibly in Hinesburg, VT.
CHILDREN (b Petersham):
  John - b 16 Apr 1764
    (b Bolton):
  Sarah - b 4 Jan 1773
  Mary - b 24 Sep 1776
  Zerviah - b 13 Feb 1777
  Beulah - b 14 Oct 1778
NOTE: Removed to Fitzwilliam, NH in 1781; to Putney, VT ca 1788; to Hinesburg, VT ca 1791; still there in 1802. Was in Deerfield 1765, perhaps more children b there.
REF: BVR; Petersham VR; Pension Records of John Jr; History of Deerfield MA, George Sheldon 1896.

WILSON, John, Jr

SERVICE: S&S Vol 17 p 567; DNR Winter Campaign 1776-7; BRR reinforce Cont Army RI 3 mos Jun 1780 ₤12; BRR Cont Army 1780 3 mos ₤19; BRR Capt Moore's Co RI 1781 ₤10.
BORN: 16 Apr 1764 Petersham s/o John & Hannah.
MARRIED: Mary Wheeler.
DIED: 16 Oct 1847.
CHILDREN: unk.
NOTE: Pension application states he was b Petersham, removed to Deerfield 1765, to Bolton ca 1772-3, to Fitzwilliam, NH 1781, to Putney, VT 1788, to Hinesburg, VT 1791, to Louisville, St Lawrence Co, NY 1802. Pensioned 9 May 1833.
REF: Petersham VR; History of Deerfield MA, George Sheldon 1896; Statements in Pension Application; DARPI.

WILSON, Paul Also Willson

SERVICE: S&S Vol 17 p 547 & 577; MilAnn Dorchester Hghts 1776; BHist reinforce Cont Army 1779 ₤37-16; BRR 9 mos at ₤2 per mo & ₤7-10 bounty; With Capt Jason Duncan's Co Dummerston, VT.
BORN: 12 Jul 1758 Bolton s/o Nathaniel & Eunice (Davenport).
MARRIED: 19 May 1778 Lancaster, Ruth Burnham d/o Nathaniel of Lunenburg.
DIED: Probably in Dummerston, VT.
CHILDREN: unk.
NOTE: Descriptive List 1779 - "21 years; 5'8"; complexion light; engaged for Town of Bolton, marched 22 July 1779." "Bounty to be rated on Indian corn at 3s per bu., rye at 4s per bu. Sd Paul relinquishing all wages to the Town."
REF: BVR; LVR; Early Records of Lunenburg; VT Petitions for Land Grants.

WOOD, Corp Joseph, also Woods

SERVICE: S&S Vol 17 p 575 & 847; BHist Lex Alarm; Pension Record Bunker Hill; BHist Siege of Boston; DNR Winter Campaign 1776-7; BRR 5 mos NY 1776 ₤10; BHist 15th Reg; VT Rangers Sgt 1778.
BORN: 1755.
MARRIED: 11 Apr 1782 Bolton, Keziah Goddard of Marlborough.
DIED: 12 Oct 1807 Sudbury, Rutland Co, VT.
CHILDREN: Probably at least one daughter. Had grandson named Ira S Cornish.
NOTE: Widow applied for pension, 1839, at Saybrook, Ashtabula Co., OH. Lived Sudbury, VT after 1807. Affadavit of grandson, Ira S Cornish, says sd Ira accompanied grandmother to visit grand-

WOOD, Corp Joseph (Cont)

father's grave in Sudbury, VT.
REF: BVR; DARPI; GSA Pension Records.

WOODBURY, Isreal, also Woodbrry

SERVICE: S&S Vol 17 p 803 & 811.
BORN: 13 Apr 1756 Beverly s/o Samuel & Edith.
MARRIED: 4 Oct 1781 Beverly, Mrs Anna Morgan of Beverly (d 1844 ae 80 Bolton GS3).
DIED: 23 Aug 1847 ae 91y 4m 10d GS3 "A Soldier of the Revolution."
CHILDREN (b Bolton):
  Abigail - b 21 Jul 1782 m1 Daniel Howard m2 Silas Young
  Nancy - b 22 Feb 1784 d 1784
  Isreal - b 13 Nov 1785 m Olive Snow
  Nancy - b 24 Feb 1788 m Caleb Joy
  Aseneth - b 3 Oct 1790 m Thomas Davis 1819
  Luke - b 21 Sep 1792 m Sally Conant 1826
  Nathan - b 13 Aug 1794 m Clarinda Whitney 1819
  Malachi - b 10 Mar 1800
  Amory - b 23 May 1803 twin
  Emily - b 23 May 1803 twin m Thomas Davis 1828
  Lorenzo - b 16 May 1806 m Sara Tufts 1844
NOTE: Credited to Beverly. Came to Bolton ca 1781-2.
REF: Beverly VR; BVR; DARPI.

WOODBURY, Sgt Samuel

SERVICE: S&S Vol 17 p 818.
BORN: 17 May 1724 Beverly s/o Samuel & Hannah.
MARRIED: 6 Jan 1746 Beverly, Ede Wood (d 1797 Bolton).
DIED: 24 Jul 1814 ae 90 GS1.
CHILDREN (b Beverly):
  Samuel - b 10 Mar 1748
  Edith - b 4 Feb 1750 d 1808 Bolton
  Anna - b 2 Mar 1752
  Hannah - b 1 May 1754
  Isreal - b 13 Apr 1756
  Abigail - b 15 Oct 1758
  Betty - b 29 Mar 1761
  William - b 15 Aug 1763
  Thomas - bpt 20 Jul 1766 d 1820 Bolton
NOTE: Credited to Beverly.
REF: Beverly VR; BVR.

WOODBURY, William, also Woodbrry

SERVICE: S&S Vol 17 p 803 & 819.
BORN: 15 Aug 1763 Beverly s/o Samuel & Edith (Wood).
MARRIED: 1) 1 Apr 1791 Bolton, Eunice

WOODBURY, William (Cont)

Houghton (d 23 Oct 1817 ae 47 Bolton d/o
Timothy Houghton Esq of Nova Scotia; 2)
6 Dec 1818 Bolton, Mrs Susan Haven wid/o
Elijah.
DIED: unk.
CHILDREN (b Bolton):
  Joseph – b 25 Nov 1791
  Harriot – b 4 Oct 1793 m Wm B Chaplin
    1814
  Edith – b 15 Apr 1795 m James Ellis
    1816
  Almira – b 4 Jan 1797
  Maryann – b 8 Feb 1799 m George
    Cunningham
  Eunice – b 6 Dec 1800 m Joseph Sever
    of Northboro
  William – b 10 Jul 1802 m Harriet
    Holman 1827
  Charles Francis – b 29 Apr 1806 m
    Clymenia Woodbury
  Elizabeth Almira – b 11 Feb 1808 m
    Anson Peck 1829
  Mildred – b 24 Feb 1810
  Clymenia – b 26 Oct 1819
  Eleanor Jane – b 26 Oct 1821
  Elijah Haven – b 24 Jan 1824
NOTE: Credited to Beverly.
REF: Beverly VR; BVR.

WORCESTER, Ebenezer

SERVICE: S&S Vol 17 p 785; BHist Lex
Alarm; BRR Boston 1776 3 mos; BRR to
York Jul 1776 £2-15-4.
BORN: 5 Jul 1749 Harvard s/o Jonathan &
Rebekah.
MARRIED: 26 Sep 1770 Elizabeth Hale of
Stow.
DIED: After 1790, probably in Brandon,
VT.
CHILDREN (b Stow):
  Nabbe – b 31 Oct 1770
    (b Harvard):
  Rebecka – b 30 Dec 1772
  Bette – b 12 Sep 1774
    (b Bolton):
  Bezaleel Hale – b 5 Oct 1777
  Ebenezer – b Oct 1779
  Molly – b 5 Jun 1781
    (b Berlin):
  John – b 20 Mar 1783
NOTE: Berlin Church Record: "Ebenezer
Wooster and wife dismissed from Berlin
Church to Church in Brandon, VT" 1788.
BVR spells name Worster. In 1790 census
he is found in Brandon, VT.
REF: BVR; HVR; SVR; Berlin VR.

CROSS-INDEX

Since the genealogical sketches in this book are arranged alphabetically, a complete name index was not deemed necessary. This cross-index covers only the names that are buried in the text. Thus, to find a person named Jones first consult this cross-index for possible mention of the person in non-Jones genealogies, and then scan the Jones genealogies.

ABBOTT, Anna 34 Polly 34
ADAMS, Asenath 63 Eliza-
  beth 1 Lidia 30 Oliver 67
ALBERT, Daniel 17 Penina
  17
ALDEN, Sarah 7
ALDRICH, Saml 10
ALLEN, Cary 63 Shobal 10
ALLISON, Margaret 20
AMES, Eunice 57 Timothy 20
ANDREWS, Roxanna 79
ANGIER, Elizabeth 69
ATHERTON, Abigail 34 35 72
  Achsah 59 Benjamin 28 34
  Betsy 34 35 Eliakim 35 59
  Elizabeth 35 59 Ephraim
  68 Jonathan 73 80 Julia 2
  Ruth 80 Sarah 80 Silence
  27
ATWOOD, Philip 25
AUSTIN, Eunice 7 Sarah 20
  Timothy 13

BABCOCK, Abram 22 Betsy 9
  Ephraim 67 Jonas 40 Lucy
  20 Reuben 26 Wm 22 Wm Jr
  53
BACHELDER, Hephsabah 57
BACON, Daniel 13
BADCOCK, Persis 9 Wm 42
BAILEY, Benjamin 44 55
  Desiah 51 Elizabeth 51
  Holloway 66 Kate 55 Lucy
  21 Sibella 55 57 Sibyl 55
  Silas 21 Susannah 47
  Timothy (illus) 4
BAKER, Abel 39 Betsy 20
  Betty 21 Dinah 45 46
  Edward 20 Jesse 73 Jona
  12 Jonathan 45 Lydia 7
  Mary 9 72 73 Persis 67
  Polly 39 Rhoda 25 Samuel
  21 73
BALDWIN, Elizabeth 14
BALL, Elijah 51 Elizabeth
  79 Experience 31 Hannah 9
  41 42 Lucy 42 Lydia 26 27

Mary 41 42 Nathan 31 64
BALLARD, Ruth 52
BANCROFT, Rachel 32
BANNAR, Elizabeth 55 Isa-
  bel 55
BANNISTER, Jane 39
BARKER, Betsy 45 Susan 45
BARNARD, Abigail 55 57
  Ephraim 42 Eunice 60 Mar-
  tha 5 Mary 13 54
BARNES, Daniel 46 David 51
  F 42 Fortunatus 2 Jacob
  38 Lydia 2 Nancy 45 Peris
  61 Persis 44 Saml 11 Wm
  26
BARRETT, 31 Hannah 56 57
  67 68 Oliver 35 55 56 68
  Oliver Jr 76 Rebecca 55
  57 Ruth 56 57 Sarah 67
BARRON, Abigail 37
BARTLETT, Levina 3 Molly
  46
BAXTER, Mary 48
BEALS, 51
BEAMAN, Deborah 14 Hannah
  14
BECKWITH, Jared 11
BEMIS, David 70
BEMUS, Mehetabel 30
BENDER, Abigail 67
BENNETT, Abigail 39 Almira
  72 Eunice 13 Josiah 13
BENSON, Peter 71
BENT, Lucretia 74
BERRY, William 15
BERT, Elizabeth 69
BIGELOW, Jane 37 Mary 5 27
  50 Timo 15 Wm 37
BILLINGS, Josiah 22
  Sylvanus 23
BLODGETTE, Abigail 25
BLOOD, Joseph 13
BOND, Lucy 54
BOUTELL, Elizabeth 11
BOWKER, Bathsheba 12 13
BOWMAN, Simeon 2
BOYD, Luther 74 Mary 73

Robert 74
BOYLSTON, 46
BOYNTON, Esther 17 Jos 10
BREED, Nathanie 180
BREWER, John 13 Sarah 22
BRIDE, Asa 12 James 41
  Ruth 52
BRIGHAM, Anna 34 Barnabus
  22 Elizabeth Rice 3 Ju-
  dith 14 Lavinia 21 Lois
  55 Lucy 2 3 5 Luther 44
  Mary 36 Mehitable 43
  Moses 23 Persis 5 Ruth 38
  Saml Jr 38 Samuel 2 34
  Susanna 40 Susannah 34
  Thos 2
BRITAIN, James 22
BRITNELL, Sarah 68
BRITTEN, Stephen 38
BROOKS, Betsy 20 Betty 25
  Ephraim 63 Lucinda 63
  Stephen 74 76 Wm 70
BROWN, Abel 38 Abigail 58
  Caty 12 Deborah 48 Eliza-
  beth 15 Jesse 70 John Jr
  12 Mary 19 Mary H 10 Saml
  13 Winthrop 45
BRUCE, Anna 18 Benj 47
  Betty 10 Daniel 68 Eliza
  50 Eunice 68 James 23
  Joanna 76 John 23 John Jr
  61 Mary 12 43 44 Molly 44
  Otis 12 Ruth 25 Timothy
  12
BULLEN, Elizabeth 54
BURBANK, Phebe 63
BURGES, Sarah 80
BURGESS, Mary 80
BURGOYNE, 46
BURNAM, Roxanna 15 Sally
  12
BURNAP, P V 80
BURNHAM, Benj 47 Nathaniel
  82 Ruth 82
BURPEE, Jona 42
BURR, Alanson 7
BURRELL, Anna 28 Nancy 28

BUSH, Eunice 35 Hannah Jr 6 Hepsibah 2 22 Levi 9 Rebecca 17
BUSS, Dorothy 20
BUTLER, Comfort 61 Ephraim 61 Martha 61 Patience 22

CAHOON, Susan 21
CAMPBELL, James 30 Jane 30 Jennie 30
CAPEN, Hannah 39
CARR, Thomas 70
CARTER, Amory 67 Dolly 32 Dorothy 43 Hannah 51 John 73 Leonard 2 Lewis 67 Martha 14 Mary 9 76 Nancy 11 Prudence 67 68 Ruth 66 Zilpah 9
CEVER, Rebecca 47
CHACE, Alanson 30
CHAFFIN, Betsy 33 Reuben 72 Sally 70
CHAMBERLAIN, Rebecca 76 Samuel 76
CHAPIN, Coffin 70
CHAPLIN, Wm B 83
CHASE, Anna 8 25 Chas 20 Clarissa 49 Lois 19 Moses 32
CHEEVER, David 55
CHILDS, Margaret 61
CHOAT, Phillis 58
CLARK, Eunice H 11 Hannah 70 Joseph 48 Rachel 62
CLOYES, Keziah 26 27
CLURE, Henry 11
COATS, John 38
COBB, Azuba 63 Mary 10
COBLEIGH, Lemuel 54
COGSWELL, Jonathan 58 Phillis 58
COLBURN, Joseph 62 Thomas 15
COLE, Judith 70 Phineas 10
CONANT, Rebecca 73 Rebekah 72 Sally 82
CONVERSE, Willard 79 Zerviah 79
COOK, Daniel 45 Noah 50 Oliver 12 Polly 53
COOLIDGE, Isaiah 13 John 61 Josiah 24 Lydia 9 Mary 24 60 Rachel 63 Silas 58
COPELAND, Martha 7 Mary 7
COREY, Molly 35 Nathan 67
CORLEY, Ruth 73
CORNISH, Ira S 82
COTTING, Maverick 41
COWEN, Chas 8
CRANE, 80 Tabitha 24
CROCKER, Nathaniel 26
CROMBIE, Mary 81
CROSBY, Lucy 18 70 Sally 3 Samuel 3

CROSMAN, Sarah 10
CROSS, Eben 45 Peter 25
CROUCH, Anna 51
CUNNINGHAM, George 83
CURTIS, 67
CUTLER, Abigail 79 Marcus 74
CUTTER, Wm P 20
CUTTING, Josiah 53 54

DAGGETT, 5
DAILEY, Russell 8
DAKIN, Joel 60
DANFORTH, Hannah 48 49 Rebecca 19 Samuel Jr 57
DARBY, Betsy 79
DAVENPORT, Deliverance 68 Eunice 81 82
DAVIS, Aaron 61 Abel 61 Catherine 11 Eli 40 Ephraim 38 Jacob 1 Lucinda 69 Lydia 74 Nancy 62 Polly 33 Sarah 33 Susan 62 Thomas 82
DAWES, James 9
DAY, Daniel 13
DERBY, Cynthia 62
DEXTER, David 30
DICOM, Hannah 54
DILL, James 1
DIVOLL, Alice 44
DODGE, Mehitable 50 53
DORR, Jerusha 74
DOWSE, Benj 24
DRESSER, Elizabeth 24
DRURY, J 16
DUBOIS, Catherine 29
DUDLEY, Abigail II 64 Joseph 46 Rebecca 79
DUNCAN, Jason 15 82 Saml 69
DUNKLEE, Edwin 71 Mary 64
DUNLAP, Betsy 20
DUNTON, 19 Beckey 36 Becky 36 Rebecca 36
DUTTON, Abigail 1

EAMES, Anna 19 Sarah 80
EASTMAN, Nancy 52
EATON, Mary 57
EDDY, Amu 30 Olive 30
EDES, Richard S 66
EDWARDS, Mary 1
EGERY, Nathan 55
ELLIS, James 83
EMERSON, Lestina 31
EMERY, Hannah 20
ENGLUND, Betsy 55
EUSTIS, John 48 Sally 46
EVANS, Clarissa 5
EVELETH, John 35 Lucy 75 78

FAIRBANK, Achsah 76 77

Beulah 46 Caleb 26 Ephraim 2 57 Eunice 28 71 Hepzibah 5 Jabez 3 5 67 Jona 39 Keziah 27 47 Lucy 68 Sarah 67 68
FAIRBANKS, Dexter 74 Elizabeth 20 Silas 43
FALLASS, Betsy 7 William 7
FARMER, Sarah 40 41 Susan 40
FARNSWORTH, 34 Mercy 31
FARWELL, Mary 34
FAULKNER, Dorothy 57 Sarah 70
FAY, Comfort 16 61 Cyrus 49 Dinah 6 Joseph 19 Levi 40 Martha 43
FERGUSON, Betsy 20
FIFE, Abigail 49 Hannah 51 Hepsibah 2 Leaffe 78 Releaf 78 William 42
FISK, Lucinda 27
FISKE, Sarah 7 25
FITCH, Nathan 15
FLAGEL, 30
FLAGG, Abijah 46 Elijah 58
FLETCHER, Mary 1 Phineas 16 Polly 5 Ruth 60 Sarah 56
FLINT, Lydia 72
FORBES, Susannah 6
FORBUSH, D 78
FORSYTH, Abigail 29
FOSDICK, Sarah 79
FOSGATE, Ezekeel 27 Joel 42 Maria 79 Robert Jr 68 Sarah 79 Tabitha 57
FOSKETT, Lydia 19 Phebe 12 Tabitha 57
FOSTER, John 31 Mary 10 33 Nathan 18 Sally 48 Sarah 30
FRENCH, Desire 76 Martha 6 Polly 54
FROST, Hephsibah 33
FRYE, Hannah 10
FULHAM, Tabitha 18
FULLER, Amasa 60 Joel B 67

GALE, 5 Abigail 70
GARDNER, Francis 77 John 26 Mary 76 77 Molly 71 Stephen P 53
GARFIELD, Dorothy 40
GARY, Keziah 28
GATES, 57 Cyrus 12 61 Hannah 43 Lydia 57 Mary 74 Sarah 75 78
GIBBS, Eunice 49 Mary 62 Nancy 62
GIBSON, A 45 Lucy 40
GILBERT, Abraham 75 Nancy 75 Naoma 23
GILSON, Eunice 30

GLEASON, Eliz 34 Mary 37 Moses 37 Prudence 7
GODDARD, 6 Eunice 69 Hannah 8 Jacob 36 James 7 Keziah 82 Mary 20 Rachel 18 Rebecca 55
GOETH, Achsah 20 21
GOODALE, Mary 70 Timothy 70
GOODELL, Lydia 79
GOODFREY, Raache 12
GOODMAN, Thankful 68
GOODNOW, Elizabeth 32 Hannah 40 Mary 69
GOODWIN, Mercy 23
GOSS, Anna 80 Asa 22 Joseph 74 Luther 9 Martha 30 48 Mary 33 Polly 49 Saml 39 Thomas 33 Thos 61
GOTT, Anna 34
GOTTING, Myra 40
GOULD, Polly 81 Sally 65
GRAHAM, Deliverance 15
GRAVES, George 31 Mary 12
GREEN, Aaron 27 Hannah 80 Josiah 5 Sibbel 2
GREENLEAF, Betsy 52 Calvin 76 Daniel Jr (illus) 29 Elias 71
GREENWOOD, J 81
GREGG, Polly 26
GRIFFITH, Ruby 52
GROVE, Hannah 7
GWINN, Mary 32 Polly 32

HADLEY, Sarah 44
HAGER, Abigail 32
HALE, Elizabeth 83 Hannah 79 Mary 25 Sarah 31
HAPGOOD, Ephraim 6 Hezediah 55 57 Judith 70 Mercy 17 55
HARRINGTON, Eli 5 Grace Mahan 21 Hannah 18 23
HARRIS, Amory 45 Joel 10
HARWOOD, Sarah 17
HASELTINE, Patience 81 Richard 16
HASKELL, Sibbel 75 Sibyl 77
HASTINGS, Abigail 50 52 Benj 28 37 49 50 52 Benj Jr 6 Benjamin 57 Elizabeth 50 Susannah 57
HATCH, John 15
HATHAWAY, Silence 24
HAVEN, Elijah 83 Susan 83
HAYWARD, Matilda 30
HAZELTINE, Hannah 61
HAZEN, Mary 65
HEARD, Saml 26
HEATH, Gen 16 18 30 57 66 Timothy 25

HEYWOOD, Lucretia 10 Stevens 10
HIGHLANDS, Mart 25
HILDRETH, Richard 42
HILL, Jeremiah 21 Levi 29 Sallie 81
HILLS, Sylvester 7
HINDS, Benj 34
HOAR, Submit 64
HODGES, 25
HODGMAN, Mary 8
HOLDEN, Beulah 15
HOLDER, Phebe 18 Thomas 23
HOLMAN, Abigail 72 76 Abraham 72 77 Abraham Jr 57 Amory 74 78 Betsy 72 Betty 73 Elizabeth 72 Harriet 83 John 55 72 Jonas 55 Nathl 13 Oliver 55 Silas 1 Sophia 74
HOLT, Amasa 55 Jotham 9 Loas 63
HOPPIN, Elizabeth 36
HORTEN, Rachel 79
HOSMER, John 23 Persis 8
HOSMORE, Nathan 6
HOUGHTON, Abel 18 Abigail 35 Anna 62 Annis 29 Azuba 75 78 Becca 35 Betty 41 Caleb 67 Capt 3 14 67 68 Dorothy 63 Eunice 36 50 82 83 Hannah 67 Hepzibah 62 Jemima 17 John 62 Jona 48 53 65 Jona Jr 10 Jonas 42 62 Jonathan 42 62 66 72 Jonathan Priest 75 Levi 35 Lucy 62 Martin 3 Mary 36 39 67 72 Maverick 41 Miriam 36 Olive 32 Polly 55 Rebecca 12 61 65 Relief 21 Rufus 76 Susannah 72 Susannah Jr 72 Thankful 76 Thomas 80 Timothy 83 Unity 66 Zerish 52
HOW, Abigail 20 Deborah 9 Levi Jr 70 Loring 67 Lydia 11 Martha 9 Prudence 34 Sibbil 3 Sibella 2 Sibellah 9 Thaddeus 34
HOWARD, Daniel 82 Melly 39 Rebecca 30 Susannah 39
HOWE, Catherine 3 Damaris 44 Deborah 2 Elizabeth 3 38 Ephraim 8 Fortunatus 14 Hannah 26 Isabella 3 John 2 Josiah 23 Lemuel 43 Levi 12 Mary 5 23 Parker 9 Parna 20 21 Persis 68 Polly 5 Rufus 68 Sarah 23 67 Sibella 3 Thankful 34
HUBBARD, Arvilla 49 Elisha 49 Lucy 39

HUDSON, Lucretia 1 Robert 22
HUNNEWELL, Eleanor 5
HUNT, Hannah 8 Henry 23 Lois 23 Wm III 74
HUSTIN, Sally 1
HUSTON, Margaret 44

IRVING, N 81
IVORY, John 16 Martha 16 Sarah 16
JACOB, Col 78 John 77
JACOBS, J 51 John 37 50 71
JEWELL, Jona 47
JEWETT, John (illus) 41
JOHNSON, 6 Ashbel 72 E Jr 23 Edw 58 Hannah 40 Joshua 3 Lewis H 9 Lucy 36 Mary 29 Prudence 67 Sarah 50 Susannah 44
JONES, Anna N 29 Dolly 17 Eleazer 65 Esther 69 70 Lavania 18 Lavinia 18 Mary 18 Nathl 49 Pelatiah 8 Saml 3rd 49 Samuel 17 76 Samuel Jr 18 Silas 59 Solomon 44 56 Susannah 30 Wm 49
JORDAN, Mary 5
JOSLIN, Susannah 12 14
JOY, Caleb 82
JOYNER, Ann 54

KATHAN, John 53 Lois 49 Prentice 51
KAYE, Amanda 25
KELLOG, Elizabeth 55
KELLOGG, Elizabeth 55-57
KEMP, Lydia 22
KENDALL, Hannah 63
KEYES, David 13 Susan 51 Ziba 13
KEYS, Jotham 53 Thomas 1
KIDDER, Polly 30
KILBURN, Sally 30
KIMBALL, James 10
KIMMENS, John 36
KING, 51 Eliza 7 Isaac 6 Persis 7 Sarah 63
KINGMAN, Eunice 73
KIRBY, Thomas Whitcomb (illus) 76
KITTREDGE, Elizabeth 24
KNAP, Jane 55
KNIGHT, Amaziah 44 Elizabeth 34 35 Jonathan 34 35 Mary 37 Susy 49
KNIGHTS, Elizabeth 24
KNOWLTON, Hersey 7 Patty 51 Rebecca 8

LAKE, Allison 26
LAKEMAN, James 32
LAKIN, Harriet 81

LANE, Amasa 15
LARKIN, Peter 2
LAUGHTON, Hannah 8 Jeremiah 8 Rachel 8
LAWRENCE, 13 Asa 80 Hannah 61 Joanna 61 Jonathan 61
LEIGHTON, Lydia 25
LELAND, Anna 58
LEWIS, Rebecca 29
LINCOLN, Sophia 42
LOCK, Phebe 49
LONGLEY, Col 10 Deborah 16 John (illus) 46 Lucretia 17 N 44 Nathaniel 16 75 Natl 20 Robert 15 Sarah 45 46 75
LORING, Mary 56
LOWELL, Ruth 14
LULL, Abigail 1
LUNAH, Sarah 63
LYON, Mary 41 42

MacDONALD, John 31
McALLISTER, Elizabeth 34 39 40
McBRIDE, John 65 Nancy 12 Nanny 12 Sarah 41 Wm 47
McCOLLESTER, Charles 79 Royce 79
McWAIN, Laura 45

MANCHESTER, Sarah 11
MANLY, Capt 65
MANSFIELD, Susannah 11
MARDEN, Dolly 52
MARSH, Silence 28
MARTIN, Dorothy 63 Phebe 11
MASON, Martin 11
MATHER, Cotton 71
MAYNARD, Francis 13 Israel 22 Jas 23 Jotham 9 Keziah 57 Miriam 16 Rebecca 74 Submit 59
MEAD, John 45
MELLEN, Hannah 41 42
MELVILLE, Henry 80
MERRIAM, Abigail 53 Amos 57 Bilhah 8 Hannah 62 71 Mary 73
MERRICK, Henry 10
MERRIFIELD, Eunice 9
MERRITT, Lucy 66
MILLINGTON, Ann 29
MILLS, Prudence 34
MIRICK, Capt 12 Dorothy 40
MITCHELL, 73
MOODY, Commodore 46
MOOR, Abner 31 Abraham 39 Bathsheba 67 David 44 Hezediah 47 Keziah 68 Lidea 68 Mary III 66 67 Phineas 57 Samuel 31 68 Silence 39 Zerish 68

MOORE, Abigail 38 66 Asenath 8 Bathsheba 67 Caleb 53 80 Capt 58 78 82 Cornelius 59 Cummings 67 Eliz 32 Emily 36 Eunice 52 Hannah 59 Henry 56 Isaac 38 Jacob 2 9 20 John 20 Jonathan Jr 9 Levi 28 Love 62 Margaret Stuart 20 Martha 13 Olive 37 Rachel 52 Rebecca 55 Rufus 50 S 22 Sally 13 Stephen 53 Susannah 36 61 Thomas 36 Uriah 12
MOORES, Hannah 2
MORGAN, Anna 82
MORSE, Abigail 27 Anna 34 Joshua 34 Theodore 27
MOULTON, Anna 54 John B 23 Jona 54 Rachel 54
MOWERS, Comfort 52
MUNROE, William 67

NEAL, Mary 7
NEWMAN, Rebecca 51
NEWTON, Arad 2 Cotton 68 David 43 Eunice 34 Polly 81 Sarah 38 Silas 39 Truman 81
NICHOLS, James 52 Rebecca 36 Sarah 6 Silence 28
NICKLESS, Elizabeth 16 Hannah 16
NORCROSS, 21
NORTON, Hannah 70
NOURSE, Asa 23
NOYES, Abigail 55
NURSE, Abigail 34 35 Benj 9 Capt 3 5 7 12-14 16 20 26 39 42 43 48 51 58-60 62 63 65 67-70 72 Caty 35 D 3 22 23 49 62 68 74 81 David 3 5 8 18 19 35 74 David (illus) 56 Eliz 52 Elizabeth 48 49 Hannah 53 66 John 44 67 Jonathan 74 Phebe 1 Saml 44 52 Samuel 35 49 74 Samuel II 52 Sarah 35 52
NUTTING, Deliverance 78

OAK, Keziah 70 Nathaniel 70 Nathl Jr 31 Tabitha 70
OAKS, John 9
OGDEN, 37
OSBORN, Thomas 74
OSBORNE, Thomas 76
OSBURN, Nabby 18
OSGOOD, Abel 34 Elizabeth 67 Silas 78

PAIRCE, Hannah 15
PARK, Abigail 19 Pamelia 60

PARKER, Betsy 28 Hannah 52 Lucy 30 Susannah 35
PARKS, Joseph 10 49
PARMENTER, Elizabeth 69 Silas 55
PARMINTER, Mercy 43
PARTRIDGE, Ede 14 Harriet 6 Rhoda 14
PATCH, Eunice 40 Lydia 46
PAUL, Elizabeth 54 Robert 54
PECK, Anson 83
PECKHAM, Robert 67
PELTON, Jemima 1
PERRY, Anna 26 Betsy Dodd 14
PETERS, Hannah 53
PHELPS, Thomas 55
PHILIPS, Abigail 54
PHILLIPS, Patty 14
PHINNEY, Mary 2
PIERCE, Aretas 10 Calvin 12 Hannah 73 Patty 25 Ruth 63
PIKE, Oris 74 Rowell 74
PIPER, Hannah 68
POLLARD, Abijah 64 Amory 1 Curtis 22 Elizabeth 41 Experience 39 Lucinda 67 Nabby 70 Nancy 37 38 Oliver 45 Sarah 51 Thaddeus 1 Thaddeus Jr 1 William 3
POND, Preston 62
POPE, Betsy 81
PORTER, Lydia 23 Nancy 26 Sally 26
POWERS, Henry 66 John 58 60 Miriam 26
PRATT, Abijah 65 Elizabeth 26 65 Joel 9 Mary 6 65
PRENTICE, Tabitha 65
PRESCOTT, Levi 71
PRIDE, Josiah 21
PRIEST, Abel 76 Benj 14 Betsy 23 Daniel 23 Eunice 1 7 8 Gabriel Jr 33 Hannah 18 Hepzibah 36 62 James 18 Jeremiah 51 Luther 13 Prudence 13 Ruth 12 Sally 15 Sarah 15 Silas 8
PROCTOR, Amos 60
PUFFER, Abigail 55 Hannah 32 Sophia 9 Stephen 23

RAND, Lucy 71
RANDALL, Ebenezer 57 Josiah 34
RAYMOND, Ruth 27
READ, John 48
REED, Abigail 29 62 Eunice 41 42 Hannah 13 Mary 38 Samuel 42 Silas 66 74

RICE, Asa 58 Grace 38 Hannah 26 27 Josiah 48 Lucy 63 Mary 23 Peter 38 Sapphira 68 Simon 38 Sophia 26 Submit 34 Thomas 10 Timothy 55 James Jr 13
RICHARDS, Abigail 26 Mary 14
RICHARDSON, 2 Abigail 53 Caleb 53 Capt 28 Dorothy 68 Elizabeth 14 53 James (illus) 64 Jeremiah 78 Josiah (illus) 64 Peter 2 Sarah 31
RINDGE, Royal 7
RINE, Ruth 16
ROBBINS, 40 Deborah 78 Hannah 10 James 78 Jonathan 10 Martha 30
ROBERTS, 60
ROBINS, Patty 57
ROBINSON, Sarah 45 46
ROGERS, Jane 44
ROPER, Sarah 25
ROSE, Sarah 63
ROSS, David 66 John 36 Keziah 36 Lois 37 Molly 38 Submit 36
RUGG, Abel 43 Damaris 41 42 Nancy 16
RUGGLES, Elizabeth 75 Lucy 34 R 51 Timothy 74
RUSSELL, Ephraim 34 Esther 52 Ezekiel 31 Nancy 14 Rachel 51 Rhoda 34 Submit 31 32 Thaddeus 60

SABIN, Noah 53
SADEY, Mary 48
SALTER, Phebe 74
SAMPSON, Benj 1 Jonathan 26 Phineas 79
SANBORN, Mehitable 15 Stephen 45
SANDERSON, Ann 61 62
SARGENT, J 6
SAUNDERS, Eliza 80 John 31
SAWTEL, Abigail 31 32
SAWTELLE, Abigail 31 Hannah 75 77 Sarah 65-68
SAWYER, Alvin 26 Asa 3 13 Betsy 69 Caleb 35 Daniel 40 Darius 19 Dinah 58 Elizabeth 1 35 50 52 59 60 Esther 19 Eunice 37 Experience 28 Hannah 19 23 Hepsibah 20 Hooker 70 John 45 Jonas 3 Joseph 72 Josiah 3rd 49 Josiah Jr 5 Lucy 28 Luther 15 Manassah 58 74 Mary 10 Olive 71 Oliver 77 Peter 75 77 Prudence 61 Rebecca 64 Relief 65 Rufus 9 Sarah

55 57 61 62 78 80 81 Silas 39 Sybil 58 Thankful 51 52 William 58 Wm 12
SCOLLAY, Anna 80
SEAVER, Caroline 10 Rebecca 47
SERA, Sally 16
SEVER, Joseph 83 Sarah 16
SHAYS, 54
SHEDD, Abigail 67
SHEPPARD, Hannah 55
SHERMAN, Eliel 13
SHURTLEFF, Nancy 5
SIZER, Lucretia 61
SKIMMINGS, Phebe 19
SLEAD, Polly 41
SLOCUM, Jeremiah 78
SMITH, Calvin 27 Capt 28 Elizabeth 14 Ephraim 70 Ezra 72 Hannah 70 Jane 44 Jonas 13 Lucy 63 Martha 23 Mary 60 Obed 74 Rebecca 80 Ruth 15
SNOW, Keziah 41 Olive 82 Sarah 41 47 Stephen 70
SOUTHWICK, Nathl 53
SPAFFORD, Betsy 27 Eunice 59 Job 70 Samuel 66
SPAULDING, Asa 80
SPOFFORD, Sally 23 68 Saml 23 26
SPRING, Francis 15
SPURR, Abigail 45 John 74
STACY, Anna 60
STEARNS, Alice 59 Col 12 15 46 John 40 Martha 37
STEELE, Anna 1
STEPHENS, Elizabeth 2 Samuel 2 Susannah 19
STEVENS, Deborah 25 Martha 5 Mary 49 Mrs 5 Rebecca 51
STEWART, Peter 55
STILES, L 81
STOCKWELL, Betsy 36
STODDARD, Wm 51
STONE, Adeline 51 Ephraim 57 Hannah 58 Isaac 51 Jeduthan 38 Simeon 66
STOW, Aaron 43 Mary 62 Stephen 62
STRATTON, Geo 2
STRONG, Sally 55
STUART, Martha 20
SULLIVAN, Gen 19 46
SWETT, Elizabeth 65 Mary 65
SWITCHER, Timo 28
SYMONDS, Jonathan 18

TAFT, Mary 70
TAINTOR, Susannah 5 6
TAYLOR, David 69 Esther 69

Lucy 13 Phineas 33 Rufus 27 Submit 52
TEMPLE, J 51
TENNEY, Archie 43 Jonathan 43
THOMPSON, Anna 66 Sally 18
THOMSAN, Joseph 52
THURSTON, Capt 8 Rebeckah 1
TIBBETTS, Ruth 34
TILESTON, Thomas 38
TILTON, Anna 21
TINNEY, Peter 75
TOBIAS, 32
TOLMAN, Thomas 63
TOOKER, Mary 67
TORREY, Ruth 65
TOWER, Ruth 36
TOWNSEND, Abigail 28 Elizabeth 13 74 James 3 Joshua Jr 28 74 Robert 35 Sarah 28 Stephen 78
TROWBRIDGE, Dolly 54 James D 54 Lydia 33
TUCKER, Joseph 78
TUFTS, Sara 82
TUPPER, Benj 25
TURNER, Avery 6 Capt 25
TYLER, John 3

UNDERWOOD, Phebe 41 Rachel 51 Susanna 51 Timothy 51
UPTON, Mary Ann 73

VOSE, Col 7

WADE, 35 Col 6 32 73 78 Harriet 79
WAIT, Olive 44
WALCOTT, Jabez 5 Lucy 77 Nabby 77 Ruth 67 Samuel Baker 73
WALES, Betsy 50
WALKER, Dolly 30 Dorothy 30 James 45 Joanna 57 John 10 30 Molly 27 Sarah 57
WARD, Anna 49 Hollis 41
WARDWELL, Ezra 80
WARNER, Betsy 51 Phebe 8 Rebecca 10 Roxanny 15 Wm 11
WASHBURN, Seth 47
WEEKS, Betsy 11 Betty 11
WELCH, Mary 1
WELDER, James 41
WESTON, Ezekiel 30 Louisa 30
WETHERBEE, Almond 11 Anna 59 60 Betsy 18
WHEELER, 25 Abr 47 Anna 22 Azuba 45 46 Betsy 65 Caleb 54 D 74 Deborah 70 Dinah 70 Experience 58 59

WHEELER, (Continued)
Hazadiah 70 Joseph 70
Joshua 48 Levi 17 Mary 82
Matilda 14 Peregrin 17
Philadelphia 14
WHEELOCK, Abigail 30
WHETCOMB, Azuba 77 Becca
77 Isreal 77 Sarah 74 75
WHIPPLE, Dea 58 Plato 58
WHITCOMB, Abigail 50 Ach-
sah 51 Anna 45 46 Asa 54
Asa (illus) 76 Azuba 23
50 76 Becca 28 60 76 77
Becke 8 Becke (illus) 77
Becky 28 Betsy 53 Betty
23 49 53 58 Col 62 David
49 58 David (illus) 75
David Jr 77 Dolly 58
Dorothy 16 43 Elesebeth
50 Elizabeth 40 Eunice 81
Fanny 35 Hannah 55 59
Israel 23 50 John 8 28 58
60 John (illus) 76 77
Jona 56 Jonathan 20 22 35
Lucinda 35 Lydia 66 Mary
24 45 57 58 Mary (illus)
77 Patience 33 Paul 37 66
Rebecca 17 66 Rufus 47
Samuel 78 Sarah 8 56 58
Tille 76 Zerviah 60
WHITE, 6 Betty 49 74 75
Elizabeth 71 Leonard 15
Phineas Jr 30 Ruth 40

Saml 23 Susannah 24 Tabi-
tha 21
WHITING, Lemuel 32
WHITMAN, Charles 56 Elizabeth 10 45 74 Nathl 35
WHITNEY, Abel 72 Abigail
71 Achsah 51 53 Betsy 13
Betty 2 13 Capt 71 Clar-
inda 82 Col 3 8 9 14 58
67 68 Eliz 3 Elizabeth 66
H 61 Hez 19 22 37 48 51
53 59 70 78-81 Hezekiah
33 Isaiah 13 Jacob 72
John 1 Loruhama 75 Martha
54 Mary 60-62 Mercy 54
Moses 2 Prudence 29 Re-
becca 57 58 75 78 Sarah
71 79 80
WICKERS, Thomas 19
WIGGIN, Harriet 20
WIGGINS, Widow 20
WILDER, 17 Abigai 19 Abraham 36 Betsy 2 9 Deborah
40 Martha 71 Prudence 20
Rebecca 17 76 S V S (il-
lus) 64 Wm 67
WILKINS, Lois 12 Mary 44
WILLARD, Abijah 31 Eunity
51 Geo 70 Jona 51 Jos 10
Joseph 33 Keziah 51 Mary
2 Mercy 80 Orsamus 37
Sarah 30 Sibel 31 Susan-
nah 49-51 53 Unity 51 53

Wm Jr 33
WILLIAMS, Elizabeth 58 59
J 7 Rebecca 19
WILLIS, Dolly 74
WILSON, Beulah 66 Eunice
66 71 Josiah 23 Lydia 47
Nathaniel 71 Nathl 66
Rhoda 15 Rispah 63 Sarah
60 Thankful 71 72
WINN, Rebecca 13
WOOD, Abram 42 Beulah 41
43 Bowdoin 21 Deborah 59
Ede 82 Edith 82 Lidia 26
WOODBURY, Clymenia 83 John
1
WOODMAN, Artemas 5
WOODS, Bethia 40 Rachel 77
Saml 22 Sarah 41
WOODWARD, Abijah 57 Lucy 7
WORCESTER, Eben 42 Jona-
than 77 Lucy 52
WRIGHT, 78 Molly 69 Phebe
1 2
WYMAN, David 11 Elizabeth
70 John 58 Lucy 9 Lydia
70 Sarah 37 78

YOUNG, Jane 44 Job 73 John
C 73 Silas 82